Money

MARK F. DOBECK
AND EUEL ELLIOTT

GREENWOOD GUIDES TO BUSINESS AND ECONOMICS
Wesley B. Truitt, Series Editor

GREENWOOD PRESS
WESTPORT, CONNECTICUT • LONDON

Library of Congress Cataloging-in-Publication Data

Dobeck, Mark F.
 Money / Mark F. Dobeck and Euel Elliott.
  p. cm.—(Greenwood guides to business and economics, ISSN 1559–2367)
 Includes bibliographical references and index.
 ISBN 0–313–33852–3 (alk. paper)
 1. Money. I. Elliott, Euel. II. Title.
 HG221.D49   2007
 332.4—dc22   2006029476

British Library Cataloguing-in-Publication Data is available.

Library of Congress Catalog Card Number: 2006029476
ISBN-10: 0–313–33852–3
ISBN-13: 978–0–313–33852–6
ISSN: 1559–2367

First published in 2007

Greenwood Press, 88 Post Road West, Westport, CT 06881
An imprint of Greenwood Publishing Group, Inc.
www.greenwood.com

Printed in the United States of America

The paper used in this book complies with the
Permanent Paper Standard issued by the National
Information Standards Organization (Z39.48–1984).

10 9 8 7 6 5 4 3 2 1

Money

Contents

Illustrations

Series Foreword

Scanning the pages of the newspaper on any given day, you will find headlines like these:

- OPEC points to supply chains as cause of price hikes
- Business groups warn of danger of takeover proposals
- U.S. durable goods orders jump 3.3 percent
- Dollar hits two-year-high versus yen
- Credibility of WTO at stake in trade talks
- U.S. GDP growth slows while Fed fears inflation growth

If this seems gibberish to you, then you are in good company. To most people, the language of economics is mysterious, intimidating, impenetrable. But with economic forces profoundly influencing our daily lives, being familiar with the ideas and principles of business and economics is vital to our welfare. From fluctuating interest rates to rising gasoline prices to corporate misconduct to the vicissitudes of the stock market to the rippling effects of protests and strikes overseas or natural disasters closer to home, "the economy" is not an abstraction. As Robert Duvall, president and CEO of the National Council on Economic Education, has forcefully argued, "Young people in our country need to know that economic education is not an option. Economic literacy is a vital skill, just as vital as reading literacy."[1]

Understanding economics is a skill that will help you interpret current events, playing out on a global scale or in your checkbook, ultimately helping you make wiser choices about how you manage your financial resources—today and tomorrow.

It is the goal of this series, Greenwood Guides to Business and Economics, to promote economic literacy and improve economic decision making. All seven books in the series are written for the general reader, high school and college student, or the business manager, entrepreneur, or graduate student in business and economics looking for a handy refresher. They have been written by experts in their respective fields for nonexpert readers. The approach throughout is at a basic level to maximize understanding and to demystify how our business-driven economy really works.

Each book in the series is an essential guide to the topic of that volume, providing an introduction to its respective subject area. The series as a whole constitutes a library of information, providing up-to-date data, definitions of terms, and resources covering all aspects of economic activity. Volumes feature such elements as timelines, glossaries, and examples and illustrations that bring the concepts to life and present them in historical and cultural contexts.

The selection of the seven titles and their authors has been the work of an Editorial Advisory Board, whose members are the following: Alan Carsrud, Florida International University; Alan Reynolds, Cato Institute; Wesley Truitt, UCLA; Walter E. Williams, George Mason University; and Charles Wolf, Jr., RAND Corporation.

As series editor I served as chairman of the Editorial Advisory Board and want to express my appreciation to each of these distinguished individuals for their dedicated service in helping bring this important series to reality.

The seven volumes in the series are as follows:

- *The Corporation* by Wesley B. Truitt, UCLA
- *Entrepreneurship* by Alan L. Carsrud, Florida International University, and Malin Brännback, Åbo Akademi University
- *Globalization* by Donald J. Boudreaux, George Mason University
- *Income and Wealth* by Alan Reynolds, The Cato Institute
- *Money* by Mark F. Dobeck and Euel Elliott, University of Texas at Dallas
- *The National Economy* by Bradley A. Hansen, University of Mary Washington
- *The Stock Market* by Rik W. Hafer, Southern Illinois University-Edwardsville, and Scott E. Hein, Texas Tech University

Special thanks to our senior editor at Greenwood, Nick Philipson, for conceiving the idea of the series and for sponsoring it within Greenwood Press.

The overriding purpose of each of these books and the series as a whole is, as Walter Williams so aptly put it, to "push back the frontiers of ignorance."

Wesley B. Truitt, Series Editor

NOTE

1. Quoted in Gary H. Stern, "Do We Know Enough about Economics?" *The Region*, Federal Reserve Bank of Minneapolis, December 1998.

Preface

We want to reassure the reader that *Money* is not about yet more investment advice; nor do we try to offer predictions about what the financial markets will be doing next week, next month, or ten years from now. We are not trying to make any of our readers either a small or large fortune. This is, however, a book about money; it is also about financial markets and those innovations in the financial world that are shaping our future.

This is very much meant to be an optimistic book. At a time when many Americans have become deeply concerned about financial markets, following the economic travails of 2001–2002 and various corporate and financial market scandals (some of which we discuss in this book), we seek to take a longer-term perspective. We provide a historical context for understanding contemporary money matters and financial markets, and also to better understand the future and what we might expect as we look forward to the decades ahead.

There are a plethora of books about money, finance, and financial markets. Probably the great majority of these books are concerned with investment strategies, how to beat the market, planning for retirement, and the like. There are a few other works that provide a very intelligent discussion of the historical development of money, and some that explore the modern innovation in money and financial systems. However, few if any other works have really systematically attempted to (1) provide an integrated discussion of both historical development and contemporary realities, and (2) discuss the historical, philosophical, and political-economic aspects of money, financial systems, and globalization.

Money seeks to take a few steps back and try to put the enormous changes in a broader perspective. What do all the changes that have occurred really entail? What are the major elements of these changes? Essentially, what we seek to do is address the underlying mechanisms of the financial markets. Today's economy is increasingly global, fueled by the nearly instantaneous flow of information and the corresponding ability of individuals and financial institutions to move money from one point of the globe to another in a matter of seconds. With its almost literal flood of daily financial activity, money is no longer something tangible, such as the paper money in one's pocket (or the gold and silver coins of a century ago), or even the computer-generated bank statement, or the debit card many of us possess.

The traditional constraints of money, bounded by national boundaries and flowing within clearly delineated monetary channels as dictated by central banks and international conventions at the international level, and by strict regulatory regimes and stable, consistent ways of doing business at the national level, no longer exist. Increasingly, every financial institution and indirectly every individual become to some degree interconnected. The performance of a stock pension fund can be profoundly affected by a currency crisis in Thailand, a bank failure in London, or a debt default in Argentina.[1]

In order to better put these amazing facts in perspective, *Money* is organized into ten chapters. Chapter One begins with a discussion of the "old" world of money and illustrates the enormous changes that have taken place in what constitutes money, and the role that it plays in today's world. Traditional forms of money, such as barter, and money in colonial America are discussed. This chapter helps to illustrate the point that the concept of money has mutated or evolved over time. The creation of coins, the development of banks in the Middle Ages, and the creation of complex financial derivatives in the late twentieth century have all been extraordinarily important innovations that have to be understood in their historical context. This chapter discusses the social and psychological context of money.

Chapters Two and Three offer important discussions of monetary policy and banking institutions. Chapter Two examines the institutions that conduct monetary policy. Modern nations have central bank authorities, and these entities have special responsibilities in the conduct of monetary policy, which can have a profound influence on inflation, unemployment, trade, and a host of critical economic variables. The interest rates established by the U.S. Federal Reserve, bank reserve requirements, and the different ways of measuring money supply are discussed. The gold standard and the development of the post–World War II financial system are also elaborated upon.

Chapter Three begins with a historical overview of the U.S. banking system, the evolution of the U.S. currency, and the role of the Bank of the United States. Other important landmarks in banking-related legislation include the critical New Deal legislation that ushered in sweeping regulatory changes. Chapter Three is also critical in that it helps the reader better understand the structure of the banking system, with discussion of the types of commercial banks, savings and loans (and the savings and loan crisis of the 1980s), credit unions, and other entities.

Chapter Four covers an array of important topics ranging from the collapse of the post–World War II international order known as Bretton Woods and the fixed exchange rate system based on the dollar and convertibility to gold, to a discussion of exchange rate systems including fixed exchange rate and alternative floating exchange rate systems. The role of the Russian ruble and the euro, as well as the impact of the World Trade Organization on national currency systems are discussed, along with the role of the World Bank, the International Monetary Fund, and the Bank for International Settlements. The thrust of the chapter is to point out the extraordinarily important role that international organizations play in the modern financial order.

Chapter Five discusses the functions of formal, regulated financial markets and the role that the ongoing evolution of globalization trends and technological advances in information and communications technology are having upon financial markets. Important milestones in the development of financial markets, including the establishment of the Chicago Board Options Exchange, are discussed. Importantly, the trend away from auction to automated exchange and the role of computers in facilitating these changes are discussed in detail. In short, Chapter Five demonstrates how the new world of globalization and technology is creating both opportunities and challenges for the financial markets, investors, and the average citizen.

Chapter Six is primarily concerned with the complex, multifaceted bond market. The bond market is a crucial mechanism for firms, governments, or even individuals to raise money for various purposes. They also serve as an important investment vehicle for many institutions and individuals. There are many different types of corporate and government bonds, and the roles of these financial instruments are explored. One particular bond-like instrument, known as securitized assets, is enormously important in today's financial world. Securitized assets include mortgage-based and student-financial-aid-based instruments that allow people to buy homes, go to college, and the like.

Chapter Seven examines important issues relating to the role of short-term debt instruments for both government and private entities. Much of the discussion focuses on the foreign exchange market, which handles trillions of dollars in transactions on a daily basis. This chapter explores in detail the major actors, the strategies, and the kinds of issues that confront those who are engaged in this enormously powerful market.

Chapter Eight explores the important role of derivatives and how they have transformed finance. We discuss different types of derivatives, currency, equities, and credit derivatives, for example, and why they are so important in understanding modern finance. The theoretical basis of the modern derivatives market, the Black-Scholes equation for evaluating a fair price for a simple option, is also discussed. Most important, we discuss derivatives and related instruments in the context of risk as they are essentially a means of reducing the riskiness of a particular investment. No discussion of derivatives would be complete, however, without an analysis of the difficulties that occurred in the 1990s with Orange County, which defaulted due to bad derivatives-based investments, and the collapse of Long Term Capital Management in 1998.

The book concludes with chapters on risk and an informative exploration of new technological innovations for money and payment systems. Chapter Nine deals with the ways financial markets seek to assess risk. For example, an investor needs to assess the risk of purchasing stock A (the risk being that stock A will decline) versus putting money in a relatively risk-free investment such as government bonds (but which provides lower rates of interest). While the potential returns on the riskier investment may be much greater, so are the penalties for being wrong. Risk assessment and analysis is an activity engaged in by individuals, investment banks, national governments including central banking authorities. This chapter describes the different types of risks, ranging from system-level risk to country risk, political risk, foreign exchange risk, and others. Institutional innovations to manage risk, such as the Basel Accords, are also discussed.

Given the enormous geopolitical changes that have occurred over the past three decades or so, intelligent risk assessment is more and more critical. What has the fall of Communism in the Soviet Union and the transition to a market economy meant for financial markets? What does the new financial system in Russia look like? These matters are covered in this chapter.

The final chapter traces the development of credit cards and alternative means to access capital. The physical nature of money and issues related to transportation, security, and storage are important but often overlooked variables. Advances in technology have enabled money to become dematerialized. Examples of innovative new developments are introduced. While speculative, this chapter offers insights into future developments that may drastically affect individuals and institutions.

This book is designed to be accessible to high school and college students, as well as a more general adult audience. The technical aspects of the discussion, such as the chapters on money and capital markets, and derivatives, have been kept to a minimum. Moreover, while the early chapter provides an important historical context, so that Chapters One and Two should be read together, the later chapters can stand on their own. We, the authors, sincerely hope that readers will take away from this effort important insights and new understandings as to how a very important part of the modern world, the world of money, functions.

NOTE

1. Euel Elliott would like to thank Mark Frost, a former graduate student and later colleague, for making this point time and again.

Chronology

Before 3000 BCE	Early forms of money: Natives in parts of India used almonds, Guatemalans used corn, the ancient Assyrians used barley, natives of the Nicobar Islands used coconuts, Mongolians used bricks of tea, peoples of Southeast Asia used rice, Native American tribes used string beads (wampum).
3000 BCE	Mesopotamia establishes itself as a center of trade; commodities such as barley and silver are used as standard methods of payment.
2000–1000 BCE	Pieces of copper used in Italy; clay tables used for recording exchanges in Babylonia.
1000 BCE	Coins are first used in Lydia.
6th–4th centuries BCE	Ancient Greek financial system evolves; silver coins first used.
200 BCE	Romans begin to mint silver coins; Romans establish banks and a system of loans.
2nd century AD	The first paper money appears in China.
1171	The Bank of Venice is established; by 1500, some 4,000 Venetian citizens have bank accounts.
1266	The sterling system is established in England, under the rule of King Henry III, linking weights to coinage; under the traditional British system 12 pennies equaled a shilling, 20 shillings equaled a pound, and 21 shillings equaled a guinea; the smallest currency unit was the farthing, which was valued at one-fourth of a penny.

15th century	The Medici bank is established in Florence.
17th century	The term *dollar* is used to describe the Spanish pieces of eight. Amsterdam emerges as a financial trade center; the Amsterdam Stock Exchange is founded in 1602; the "Tulipmania" craze, 1636–1637.
1668	Bank of Sweden founded (officially designated as a central bank in 1897).
1694	The Bank of England established as the Governor and Company of the Bank of England.
1775	The Office of the Treasurer established in the American colonies; American paper money first issued (the new currency was quickly devalued and the U.S. government ceased printing money from 1780 to 1861).
1781	The first modern, private commercial bank in America is chartered in Philadelphia.
1789	The U.S. Department of Treasury is established by Congress.
1791	U.S. Congress grants a charter for the First Bank of the United States (in 1811, Congress voted against renewing the charter).
1792	The Coinage Act establishes the U.S. Mint in Philadelphia, then the seat of the federal government (the Mint became an independent agency in 1799 and, with the Coinage Act of 1873, was moved to the Treasury Department); the mint began producing copper coins in 1793 (one cent and one-half cent pieces), silver coins in 1794, and gold coins in 1795; in 1793, Congress also allowed all foreign coins in the United States to be accepted as legal tender.
1816	A second Bank of the United States is chartered; in 1832, President Andrew Jackson vetoed a congressional act for a charter renewal; the charter expired in 1836 and the bank was closed.
1838	The Free Banking Act authorizes state-chartered banks; the period from 1837 to 1862 is known as the Free Banking Era.
1851	Western Union established; its last telegram was transmitted in January 2006.
1852	Wells Fargo founded, opening in San Francisco as a bank, to capitalize on the riches of the 1849 California Gold Rush; Wells Fargo became a pioneer in money transport and shipping goods across the country bound for the West; in 1905, it separated its banking business from the express (transport) business; in 1995,

	Wells Fargo was the first major bank to introduce Internet banking.
1862	The Legal Tender Act authorizes the United States to print United States Notes to help finance the Civil War.
1863	U.S. Congress passes the National Currency Act, establishing a standard U.S. national currency; The National Banking Acts of 1863 and 1864 passed in order to increase federal control and influence over the disparate state banking system; the Office of the Comptroller of the Currency (OCC) created.
1865	The U.S. Secret Service is established.
1870	Emergence of cooperative banking; the first U.S. credit union was established in New Hampshire in 1909.
1873	Brinks incorporated in Chicago as a baggage transport company.
1900	U.S. Congress votes the Gold Standard Act into law; the price of gold is set at $35 per ounce.
1908	The National Monetary Commission is created by the Aldrich-Vreeland Act, following the Panic of 1907.
1913	The Owen-Glass Federal Reserve Act creates the Federal Reserve System.
Post–World War I	Hyperinflation in Weimar Germany.
1929	The stock market crash; the gold standard is abandoned.
1930	The Bank for International Settlements (BIS) is established, from the Hague Agreements.
1931	The Office of Thrift Supervision is created to monitor the financial condition of savings and loans.
1933	The Glass-Steagall Act, the Banking Act of 1933, and the Securities Act of 1933 enacted specifically to reestablish confidence in the banking system; federal deposit insurance created, and the Federal Open Market Committee (FOMC) is established.
1934	The Securities and Exchange Act of 1934 empowers the Securities and Exchange Commission (SEC) with broad regulatory power. The Federal Housing Authority (FHA) is created with the passage of the National Housing Act.
1938	FNMA ("Fannie Mae") established.
1944	The World Bank, also known as the International Bank for Reconstruction and Development (IBRD), is established; the

International Development Association (IDA) later became part of the World Bank in 1960.

The United Nations Monetary and Economic Conference is held at Bretton Woods, New Hampshire, concluding with an agreement to establish a new international monetary system (the International Monetary Fund) to encourage trade and stabilize exchange rates; the gold standard is restored.

1946   The Bank of England is nationalized.

1947   The General Agreements on Tariffs and Trade (GATT), an international trade accord, is established.

1950   Diner's Club, the first credit card, is launched.

1956   The International Finance Corporation (IFC) is created.

1957   The European Economic Union is formally established.

1958   American Express (AMEX) card is launched.

1961   Certificates of deposit (CDs) introduced.

1964   The Committee on Uniform Security Identification Procedure (CUSIP), to provide a uniform numbering system for financial instruments, is introduced.

1967   The Association of South East Asian Nations (ASEAN) is established as a regional organization in 1967; it became a regional free-trade zone in 1992.

Bank of America begins franchising its BankAmericard throughout the United States in 1970. BankAmericard was spun off from the parent and in 1976 the company announced that the name of the franchise would be changed to Visa.

1969   The first ATM is opened at the Chemical Bank branch located in Rockville Center, New York.

1970   The Federal Home Loan Mortgage Corporation ("Freddie Mac") is created.

1971   Collapse of the Bretton Woods agreement; the U.S. dollar allowed to float freely.

1973   The Chicago Board Options Exchange (CBOE) established.

1974   The Basel Committee on Bank Supervision is created in 1974; in 1988, the committee recommended establishment of minimum capital requirements for banks (known as the Basel Accord or

Basel I); subsequent policy recommendations included the 1996 amendment and Basel II in 2004.

1980 and 1982   Two major legislative acts, intended to reform and deregulate the banking industry, are enacted: the Depository Institution Deregulation and Monetary Control Act of 1980 (DIDMCA) and the Garn-St. Germain Depository Institutions Act of 1982, ultimately paving the way for the savings and loan crisis of the late 1980s.

1980s   Latin American nations see dramatic price increases in the neighborhood of hundreds of percent per year.

1986   The London Stock Exchange (LSE) changes from a trading floor–based model to a networked scheme using modern communications technology.

1987   The New York Stock Exchange experiences a collapse and incurs the largest one-day point drop in history.

1989   The Financial Institutions Reform, Recovery, and Enforcement Act of 1989 (FIRREA) passed to bail out the savings and loan industry.

Fall of Communism in Eastern Europe.

1992   The Russian government establishes an interbank currency market called the Moscow InterBank Currency Exchange (MICEX).

A provision of the Treaty on European Union, commonly referred to as the Maastricht Treaty, authorizes the European Central Bank to issue currency and coins on behalf of the European Monetary Union (EMU) member nations.

1994   The European Monetary Institute (EMI) is established.

The North American Free Trade Agreement becomes effective.

1995   The World Trade Organization is created to monitor GATT provisions and mediate international trade disputes.

1996   E-gold is established; GoldMoney and e-Bullion follow suit in 2001 and 2000, respectively.

1997   The Bank of England is assigned the power to set interest rates.

David Bowie issues Bowie bonds for future royalties from his hit music.

1997–1998   A severe economic and currency crisis grips Southeast Asia, where sudden economic collapse placed severe pressure on the region's currencies.

1998	Alternative trading systems officially defined and legitimized under the Regulation of Exchanges and Alternative Trading Systems (ATS) Act.
1999	The euro is launched.
	The Glass-Steagall Act provisions are replaced by the Graham-Leach-Bliley Act.
2002	The Sarbanes-Oxley Act (SARBOX) is enacted in response to high-profile corporate fraud cases.
2003	The Group of Thirty (G-30) recommends the elimination of paper certificates throughout the world in favor of electronic book entry.
	In the United States, several federal law enforcement agencies, formerly under the jurisdiction of the Department of Treasury, including the Secret Service, are transferred to the Department of Homeland Security.

One

The History and Evolution of Money:
A Look Back

MONEY DEFINED

Consider the following: As a society develops, trade expands, social needs become greater, and the degree of interconnectedness between different components of the society increases. Technological advances enable new products, services, and capabilities to be developed. The economic system and financial institutions become more sophisticated. Advancement adds complexity and creates the need for a formally defined financial infrastructure, standards, and regulations. The barter process, involving a simple exchange of goods or services, becomes impractical. Simple trade and barter have limitations. Standardized money provides an alternative to this form of exchange, being a convenient substitute for physical goods or promises and facilitating wealth accumulation. Money allows merchants to approach trade strategically, by taking a longer-term view rather than be confined to short-term opportunities and risks. Money can be defined as a medium of exchange; it is simply what we use to buy and sell things. Money thus serves three important functions in the economy: (1) it acts as a medium of exchange, (2) it is a standard unit of account, and (3) it has the ability to store value.

Using money as a mode of payment reduces the need for barter in an economic system. Money facilitates trade by serving as an accepted standard exchange mechanism, which simplifies the valuation and exchange aspects of trading transactions. Money has value because a society collectively agrees or trusts that it does. Trust in a currency is established when it is backed by a central authority, such as a government.

Money provides a method for valuation based upon a standard unit of account. Society agrees upon the value of monetary instruments within a country, and this standard remains consistent. Money serves as a proxy for barter by substituting the face value as a standard for pricing goods and services. It is used as a benchmark for establishing prices. Money also improves the consumer's ability to compare prices and facilitates competition. Using a standard unit of account improves communication and understanding about prices of goods and services. It acts as a level-setting mechanism so that everyone has the same basic understanding of price values.

Since money is readily accepted as a standard measure of value, it is not necessary to consume (i.e., spend) it all right away. It can be held to store value for future use. For example, if you placed a $100 bill in the back of your drawer so that nobody would find it and inadvertently forgot about it for nine years, you would be pleasantly surprised when you rediscovered its existence. The value of the $100 bill would still be the same, even after nine years. But the buying power of the $100 bill might not be the same after nine years. The buying power of a currency typically declines with time due to inflation and increases in the costs of goods and services. Consider, as an example, using gasoline. When gasoline cost $1.35 per gallon, the $100 bill could purchase about 74 gallons of gasoline. Several years later, when gasoline is selling at $3.20 per gallon, the $100 bill could only purchase about 31 gallons. Clearly, the purchasing power of the $100 bill has been reduced over time though the value still represents $100.

CHARACTERISTICS OF MONEY

Money has five important characteristics that further define it and make it unique. In primitive agrarian cultures, a significant amount of trade was conducted following a harvest. Suppose the primary crop in a small village was yams. The yams have value because they are a source of food. If the village collectively decided to value yams by weight for trading purposes, the yams would satisfy the basic definition of money. They could be used as a medium of exchange, their weight could be used as a standard measure of account, and they could be stored for future use. But yams are not money. So, it is necessary to identify additional characteristics of money to eliminate confusion and clearly differentiate it from any alternatives. These include (1) divisibility, (2) portability, (3) durability, (4) stability, and (5) difficulty of duplication or counterfeiting.

Money is divisible because it can be broken down into smaller denominations. A $100 bill can be replaced by combinations of $50, $20, $10, $5, $2, and $1 paper currency. The values for these denominations are standardized. The $1 bill can be substituted with a $1 coin or replaced by combinations of half-dollar ($0.50), quarter ($0.25), dime ($0.10), nickel ($0.05), and penny ($0.01) coins. A yam comes in different sizes. It can be cut, but the pieces would not be standard. Divisibility is an important characteristic of money because it allows different denominations to be substituted with other denominations that can have exactly the same value. It also allows change to be given during an exchange. Later in the chapter we discuss in more detail what we call the decimalization of currency and its implications.

Money is portable, meaning that it can be easily transported from one place to another. Paper money and coins are often carried in a person's pocket or a purse. Money is exchanged frequently. Bills and coins are passed from hand to hand, often many times during a day. Money is small and relatively lightweight. Yams, on the contrary, are not very portable. A pocket full of yams would be bulky and uncomfortable.

Money is durable. It is made to last for a long period of time. Cash can also be stored. There is a cost and a risk associated with storing commodities. There may also be transportation and time constraints. Yams are perishable and have a limited useful life. Currency is replaced and reissued when it is torn, damaged, or just worn out. Paper money is flexible. It can be bent, folded, or crumbled but still retains its basic characteristics. Ripping, tearing, or mutilating paper money is not advised!

Stability of money refers to its ability to have a reliable value. Chapter Seven explains how the value of money fluctuates from one country to another. Foreign exchange is the term used to describe converting one country's currency into another's. The U.S. dollar is a stable currency. Factors affecting a currency's stability can be both economic and political. The United States has a large economy that, historically, has been strong. Also, the political system is well defined and relatively stable. If a currency was based upon crop harvest (e.g., yams), its value would be based upon the crop yield. A variety of factors such as drought, insects/pests, or agricultural diseases could affect the crops. There is little, if any, control over these factors. So, the harvest could not be considered stable.

Money must be difficult to duplicate or counterfeit. In the United States, the issue and production of money is controlled by the U.S. Treasury Department. If the market were flooded with imitation currency, the monetary control and power of the Federal Reserve Bank (Fed) would be negatively impacted and the value of the dollar would likely decline, leading to instability. Also, trust in the system would be lost. The U.S. Secret Service is responsible for enforcing federal laws related to counterfeiting and other types of financial fraud such as check fraud (especially related to government issued checks) and electronic financial crimes.

THE PSYCHOLOGICAL AND SOCIAL CONSEQUENCES
OF MONEY

Money is a product of society and culture. Every society has a unique culture, a collection of shared learning patterns, beliefs, attitudes, and values. Culture is an accepted manner in which new members are trained to perceive, think, and feel. It is an active and dynamic process that is continually evolving. Culture includes ideology, integration, rules, rewards, punishments, and boundaries. It also involves problems related to external adaptation and internal integration. Culture can be both formal and informal and can support the existence of subcultures. Considering the significance and role of culture in a society, it is apparent that it must be a dimension included when studying the social consequence of money.

Money is, in the words of one author, diabolically hard to comprehend. As Buchan describes in his fine book, *Frozen Desire*, the medieval philosopher Ibn Khaldun had given humanity gold and silver, or, as he called them, "mineral stones," and depicted them as ideals to which all earthly treasure could aspire.[1] Of course, over time gold and silver came to be treasured, not as having some deep inherent value owing to some inner secrets of the metals themselves, but in terms of what objectives of desire those metals could obtain. The worth of individuals has come in some profound sense to be linked to the possession of wealth, valued in monetary terms.

Buchan says that the desire for money arises in an individual's innermost nature, that is, his or her sense of self, or is nurtured by possession. He goes on to say that "money is incarnate desire. Money takes wishes, however vague or trivial or atrocious, and broadcasts them to the world." Buchan quotes the great historian Edward Gibbonas saying that "the value of money has been settled by general consent to express our wants and prospects, as letters were invented to express our ideas; did both these institutions, by giving more active energy to the powers and possessions of human nature, have contributed to multiply the objects they were designed to represent." Buchan goes on to use what he describes as a mechanical metaphor: money has become, in this view, a "railway shunting yard," which is forever receiving the wishes and dreams of countless people and dispatching them to unimagined locations.[2]

A prosaic example of the effect money can have on people can be seen by watching a game show when someone wins a large amount of money. It seems to many of us that the kind of response we see is not simply a result of the additional material well-being one can now expect by virtue of winning the lottery. The act of winning actually seems to transform the individual's view of his or her self-worth.

The deep psychological impact of money can also be seen in the depths of attachment to a particular currency or the visible form the currency takes. The adoption of the euro by the European Union, replacing thirteen national currencies including the German deutschmark, the French franc, and the Italian lira, was a wrenching psychological experience for many.

One's sense of national identity and pride can be caught up in the currency and the history and culture that the currency implicitly comes to represent. Just imagine the response if Americans were told that the U.S. dollar would be replaced by some new global currency. The dollar is viewed in much the same way as the American flag, or Mount Rushmore, or the U.S. national symbol, the American bald eagle. Even relatively modest modifications to the currency can draw public disapproval. Public response to the recent changes in the U.S. paper currency is just one example. The apparent failure by the U.S. public to accept the Sacajawea dollar coin, a coin that in the view of the authors is artistically and aesthetically quite attractive, is another example.

Money and the way it is used can communicate a great deal of information about a nation's culture and social structure. In many elite circles in the United States, carrying large amounts of cash on one's person is considered certainly in poor taste, if not vulgar. In these circles, expensive purchases can be made discreetly using credit cards. Even among credit cards differences in status arise, or at least card companies and banks want people to believe there are differences, between say a gold and platinum card.

Great Britain in the eighteenth, nineteenth, and even twentieth centuries maintained a rigid social-class-based pricing system differentiating upper-class and working, lower-class citizens. Upper-class pricing was typically done using a coin called the guinea, and lower-class pricing was in terms of pennies or shillings. We will discuss more about the British currency system later in this chapter.

MONEY AS A COMMODITY AND BARTER

Barter is the exchange of goods or services among parties without using a currency as a medium of exchange. Glyn Davies, in his massive work *A History of Money*, notes, "[T]hroughout the world, commodities from salt to tobacco, from logs to dried fish and from rice to cloth have been used. Natives in parts of India used almonds. Guatemalans used corn; the ancient Babylonians and Assyrians used barley. Natives of the Nicoban Islands used coconuts and the Mongolians, bricks of tea. For the people of the Philippines, Japan, Burma and other parts of Southeast Asia, standardized measures of rice traditionally served as commodity money." Davies goes on to point out that the word *salary* in fact means salt, which had been used as a medium of exchange. Native

Corn, rice, and coconuts were among the items used as money over 3,000 years ago. Getty Images/PhotoLink (top); Getty Images/PhotoLink (left); Getty Images/C Squared Studios (right).

American tribes typically relied upon string beads, or wampum, which meant white, the usual color of beads.[3]

Commodity money is not restricted in usage to ancient times or primitive peoples. It is used under a variety of circumstances in modern societies. Commodities may serve as money when inflation has devalued the currency typically used in transactions. Economies suffering from hyperinflation (a situation where the value of the currency is devalued on a daily or even hourly basis) may find citizens resorting to trade in commodities because the currency has become literally worthless. The paradigmatic example of hyperinflation is post–World War I Germany, where, at its worst, prices increased by thousands of percentage points per day. Citizens might literally have had to resort to carrying basket loads of currency to buy a modest meal or a loaf of bread. Under such circumstances, trade in commodities may be the only alternative to the use of more conventional currency instruments.

The Great Depression of the 1930s provided another occasion for commodity money to be utilized. Here the problem was not hyperinflation. Instead, drastic deflation, or rapidly falling prices, created an environment in which a dollar really was worth a dollar. Unfortunately, the lack of money in circulation meant that far too many people had insufficient funds for purchase of goods and services. Under such circumstances people may resort to a system of barter exchange.

Of course, barter-based economies do not necessarily occur exclusively under conditions of dire economic straits. Barter may also be common when individuals seek to evade those kinds of financial exchanges that can be easily tracked by authorities. This might be the case, for example, when individuals seek to avoid paying some portion of their taxes. A system of barter enables the exchange of goods or services valued by the parties involved, without the risk of these economic exchanges being discovered by the government. These underground economies can develop in any country, but they are prevalent in emerging markets. An underground economy simply refers to that array of economic exchanges that occur outside of the officially sanctioned, formal economy.

THE HISTORICAL FOUNDATIONS
OF MODERN MONEY

As discussed above, most early trade was structured as a barter system. Trade took place on the spot market. It was called so because the transaction for an agreed exchange took place immediately, or on the spot. Physical presence was a key factor influencing early trade. A financial system that uses paper currency and coins allows economies to expand because all transactions do not have to be bartered and exchanges can be made in the future because money allows value to be stored and exchanged in the future. The money also provides a place to store and accumulate excess capital.

It is worth emphasizing that many of the actual facts about money have been lost in the mists of time. Reconstructing the historical evolution of money with any precision is therefore virtually impossible. It is practical, though, to provide a broad overview of the development of money. For example, while barter was assuredly used, there are questions as to the extent of its use and whether it might have occurred in conjunction with other kinds of transaction mechanisms. Modern money functions as a medium of exchange. However, what we now know as money probably evolved from the use of various commodities to settle debts and facilitate trade.

The barter system is inefficient. The market value of bartered goods does not always match. Sometimes there are quantity and quality mismatches, too. Often, a selling merchant can have something that a buyer needs but the seller has no interest in anything that the prospective buyer has to offer. Trade is time consuming and goods have to be stored and frequently transported for inspection. The many variables and points of failure in the barter system eventually led to the development and creation of surrogates, like coins. It overcomes many of the shortcomings of a barter economy.

According to Wray, most commerce from the earliest times predating coins was based on a system of recording credits and debits. A tally was used for this purpose. A tally was a stick, notched in a manner to indicate the amount of purchase (or debit) when the buyer (debtor) accepted goods or services from the seller (creditor). When the debtor retired his debit, the two pieces of the tally were compared or matched to verify the amount of the debt.[4]

Mesopotamia established itself as an early and well-known center of trade. This center remained influential for a considerable time, ranging back to the third millennium BC. Commodities such as barley and silver were used as standard methods of payment. Eventually, silver evolved as a standard unit of account. Loans were even extended as early as the seventh century BC.

The Greek financial system began to evolve around the sixth century BC. Silver coins were used for exchange about the fourth century BC. Each city minted their own coins, and money changers emerged as the first foreign exchange traders. These early systems were quite simple and primitive in comparison to that of the Romans. The Romans established banks, which provided loans. In addition to the banks, wealthy individuals also provided loans. A system of coinage developed using precious metals. Very little innovation occurred in banking and finance until the Middle Ages. Large international trade fairs were held to create a forum for buying and selling goods. Early insurance contracts were also created to cover the shipping trade. Loans were extended to finance the shipment of goods, but the loan was forgiven if there was a disaster.

Tallies began to be circulated as instruments for an array of economic transactions. Wooden tallies were not the only physical form such transactions could take. Pieces of copper dating from 1000 to 2000 BC appear to have been used in Italy, and some of the very earliest records of tallies appear to go back to Babylonia, where clay tablets were used. Some, including Wray, believe that great trade fairs such as those that occurred at Champagne and Brie in France as late as the Middle Ages, and which brought together merchants from all over Europe, used the tally system to settle debts without the use of coins.[5]

Davies provides an extensive account of the evolution of money. Jack Weatherford's work performs a similar service, though more from an an-thropological perspective. What is very clear from both studies is the enor-mous richness and complexity of the topic. The changing concepts and notions of money reflect changing social mores, technologies, and political-economic institutions.

Weatherford, for example, describes three great mutations of money. The first revolution occurred with the invention of coins in Lydia around 1000 BC. The second system emerged during the Renaissance with the establishment of a banking system. The third, which we have briefly noted above, is the ad-vent of electronic money and the birth of the digital economy. Each of these institutions or transformations has profoundly altered the institutions of so-ciety; each helped lay the groundwork for each successive revolution.[6]

The Lydian metal coins represented a uniform value and were made from a blend of gold and silver. We do not know for sure whether they were generally available to individuals or were used primarily or even strictly for the settling of large debts. However, the weight of evidence would seem to suggest that they were initially used for relatively large commercial dealings, and only over time did their usage spread to the broader population. Moreover, many question whether coins initially possessed a precise value. Since they were uniform, merchants did not have to weigh them with a scale as one would for exchanging gold or silver. Lydian merchants established central marketplaces where goods could be purchased and sold. Trade involved barter or the use of standard coins. Ancient Mesopotamian clay tablets examined by archeologists indicated that gold and silver were used as methods of payment.

The use of coins in Turkey was apparently noticed and adopted by the Greek civilization. By the time of Herodotus, the Greek historian of the fifth century BC who wrote, among other works, *Histories*, something approaching our definition of money was in existence. The Greek coins developed an iden-tity because they were stamped with uniform and unique markings. These were a great source of nationalistic pride, a characteristic that is linked to a nation's coinage and currency, and can be observed even today. Herodotus makes many references to coins, value, gold, payment to mercenary soldiers, and peaceful commerce, and to the Lydians' use of gold and silver.

Ancient Romans used salt for trade before they began using coins. The famous Roman coins with the image of the Roman emperor are an example. The Roman coin was a small silver coin, first minted 200 years before the birth of Christ. The Roman coins survived the collapse of the Roman Empire and, by late in the first millennium AD, were the only Roman coins. Later, during the late Middle Ages and Renaissance, Italian city-states minted coins, known as florins (made of gold), ducats, and other coins with varied names.

It seems amazing that an invention dating back to nearly 3,000 years is still being used today. Every industrial society has some kind of coinage as part of their monetary system. Coins, unlike paper, are highly durable. A coin can last for decades. Indeed, a gold or silver coin may remain intact for thousands of years. Treasure hunters and others have, from time immemorial, sought and found wrecks of ships that have taken their ill-fated cargo—along with the unfortunate sailors and officers—to deep and watery graves. Gold and silver coins have often been found in beautiful, virtually pristine condition even after centuries of being submerged. Paper currency, although it has major advantages such as the ease of transport, is far more vulnerable to wear and tear and requires replacement after a few years. Paper money is thus far more costly to government and taxpayers. Paper currency is certainly more vulnerable to counterfeiting, an activity that, when carried too far, can result in ruinous inflation. The Chinese are credited with creating paper money in the first millennium.

USURY

Formal organized religion had a considerable influence on the development of banking systems. Actually, religions were historically integrated with governmental authority. During the first millennium, usury was forbidden by both the Catholic Church and the Islamic empire. After the fall of Rome, trade declined and banking languished because of conflicts concerning usury. In the Middle Ages, Christians believed that usury was a terrible sin. They defined usury as the practice of lending money or extending credit and charging a rate of interest that was unreasonably high or illegal, and, further, exploiting the debtor. The mere extension of credit was considered to be usury, a practice that was prohibited. This created challenges and opportunities for medieval entrepreneurs for centuries. Eventually, banking did develop, but the banks were often partners in business enterprises rather than creditors.

The story of the money changers being evicted from the temple deserves closer examination. Visiting Jewish pilgrims were required to pay a temple tax.

The preferred method of payment was with the half-shekel coin because it was the only coin that was not stamped with the face of a pagan. The money changers at the temple were corrupt and engaged in usury when exchanging unwanted silver coins of the pilgrims for the half shekel. The Jewish pilgrims were being charged outrageous fees for their transactions. The pilgrims were being unfairly exploited in a temple considered sacred. The excessive charges prompted the incident at the temple when the money changers were driven out by Jesus.

ISLAMIC BANKING

Many Islamic fundamentalists continue to believe that simply lending money for interest constitutes usury and is morally unconscionable. The evils of usury are considered a threat to mankind and the use of banks are to be shunned. The Quran forbids usury. Speculation and taking risks are also forbidden. Fundamentalist Muslims are critical of Western values and the perceived focus on money and materialism. Others, more progressive, have a more relaxed attitude and accept the practice of borrowing and lending as an economic reality, provided it is fair and not excessive.

The Arabic word *riba* translates into English as *usury*. The comparable biblical term *neshekh* also means usury. The payment of interest based on time deposits is prohibited as *riba*. Islamic banking was developed, it appears, to be a compromise. The methods were developed to be in compliance with Muslim doctrines, while accommodating the financial needs of the society.

Those who engage in Muslim banking manage their affairs to avoid conflict with Muslim doctrines, and consider usury to be the use of exorbitant interest. Methods for establishing deposit accounts and financing without interest were developed to be consistent with Muslim religious principles. *Mudarabah* is an equity-based approach that establishes a business partnership between the bank and the borrower (partner). Loans are prepackaged as leaselike contractual agreements. Anything that can be construed as interest is basically embedded in the payments. Both partners contribute capital and share any profits or losses from the endeavor. Mortgages involving property are purchased in partnership with the bank, and over time the bank reduces its ownership share. Also, contractual business agreements are arranged that specify payments but not interest. Banking is focused more on trading and leasing than lending. Many Muslims object to the large banking network that has emerged and believe that banking is incompatible with their faith.

Though the Muslim system of banking seems to avoid usury, the system does not have a method to securitize assets. This concept, described in Chapter Six, is necessary to support a healthy financial system and economic growth. Securitized assets are debt instruments, like bonds, that pay periodic interest to the holder. Adam Smith believed that interest was acceptable so that those in need of capital were not deprived. He indicated that there should be limits on interest rates to prevent them from becoming excessive. John Maynard Keynes held a similar position. The key factor defining the boundaries of interest and usury is excessive or unreasonable charges.

THE U.S. DOLLAR IN COLONIAL AMERICA

The U.S. dollar, which today is the leading reserve currency in international exchanges, has a fascinating history. During the days when America was a colony of Great Britain, money was in short supply. The most common coin in circulation was the Spanish silver dollar. This coin was split into smaller units. Each dollar could be split into eight units called pieces of eight. The primary source was trade between the American colonies and the West Indies. The term *dollar* was initially adopted to describe Spanish pieces of eight in 1690. The same term was used by the Scots in the sixteenth century to distinguish their own currency from that of the British, representing only one aspect of Scottish nationalism.[7] The dollar has thus had a long association with anti-British and perhaps more generally, antiauthoritarian sentiment. The term *dollar* not surprisingly was adopted in the colonies using the Spanish currency. The most common single coin in use was the pillar dollar, so named because the two obverse sides showed the Eastern and Western Hemispheres with a large column on either side.

When the early colonists traded with the indigenous Indians, furs, beaver, and wampum served as currency. Later tobacco was used in trade. Virginia used notes with a unit value of one pound of tobacco. The notes were backed in full by tobacco that was physically stored in a warehouse. Commodities, for a variety of reasons, were not a good form of money. They are appropriate for a barter form of exchange. The slang term *buck* is used to describe a dollar. This term is related to early colonial trade. Traders would often use deerskins or buckskins as trading units. The term *buck* was informally adopted as a reference to the dollar, the basic unit of currency. There is certainly more than just a little irony in the fact that the United States continued to use the currency of another nation years after independence from the British had been won.

In any event, the coins produced by European or by post–independence U.S. authorities differed dramatically from the coins the typical citizens carry in their pockets today. Most coins prior to the twentieth century contained significant amounts of silver or gold, substances that, in themselves, were valuable. The U.S. silver dollar's value was based on the amount of silver in the coin. Gold coins were also similarly used. Over time, the use of gold and silver has disappeared. Modern currency systems can be described as fiat currencies. Fiat currencies are those currencies that are not supported or based on some object of inherent value. They are supported only by the confidence that people have in the system itself. The system works as long as everyone accepts that the currency is worth what the government says it is; if that worth is called into question for any reason—political instability, war, inflation, and the like—then the currency could collapse.

Foreign coins were widely accepted as a medium of exchange until 1857. The Congress first issued paper money in 1775. It was conceived by the Continental Congress to help finance the Revolutionary War effort. In the first year, $6 million were printed. In 1793, Congress declared that all the foreign coins would be accepted as legal tender. At the time, foreign coins accounted for about 80 percent of the coinage in circulation.

THE DEVELOPMENT OF BANKING

The development of a standardized monetary system provided by coins was a crucial first step in the ultimate development of the world's financial system. The second step was the creation of banking institutions to mediate the flow of money. Enormous credit for establishing the beginning of the modern banking system belongs to the Knights Templar. This elite group, which took vows of poverty and chastity, helped create over a period of two centuries a sophisticated system of finance that would allow individuals to carry out cross-national transactions of numerous kinds.[8]

The Knights Templar were eventually brought down by their own success when the French monarchy began a long campaign of terror against them. The monarchy was motivated by greed and fear: greed, in that it sought the wealth possessed by the order, and fear, because it saw the very real possibility that the knights could challenge the monarchy's political and economic position. The knights were consequently destroyed in a series of purges and executions. The destruction of the Knights Templar did not eliminate the need for financial institutions. By the time the knights had fallen, the Renaissance banking families were taking their place.

ORIGINS OF FINANCE

Very little innovation occurred in banking and finance until the Middle Ages. Large international trade fairs were held to create a forum for buying and selling goods. Banking, though simple by today's standards, became more widely accepted and gained notoriety in Italy during the twelfth century. Trust and improved organization reinforced the system, which facilitated trade. The Bank of Venice, which was established in 1171, is considered the first significant banking institution.

An important Italian innovation in the thirteenth century was the creation of the first forward contracts. The concept is addressed in Chapter Seven. Promises of future payment for transactions made at the trade fairs were recorded as a bills of exchange, which obligated a buyer to pay a predetermined amount at a future date in their home city. These bills of exchange could be sold or traded. They avoided violating the Catholic Church's restriction on usury. The amount of interest was predetermined and built into a fixed price along with a fixed exchange rate due from the buyer. Effectively, by appearance, there was no interest charged. As a result of this new financial instrument, Italian banking expanded rapidly and networks were established.

The Romans favored banking. During the Middle Ages this form of business had fallen from favor because of religious influence and concerns about usury. Usury was not permitted by the Roman Catholic Church and the Muslim faith. Banking experienced a revival in Italy, where it initially had a foothold. Venice and Genoa dating back to the fourteenth century are considered to be the home of the origins of modern commercial banking. The development of the Italian banking system reached a pinnacle with the development of the Medici bank.

The beginnings of modern banking appear to have originated in Southern Europe beginning in the twelfth century and continuing into the height of the Italian Renaissance, notably in sixteenth-century Florence under the rule of the Medicis. As noted by Spufford in his massive study of medieval European markets, "money changers in many commercial cities extended their activities from normal money-changing to taking deposits, and then to transferring sums from one account to another when instructed by the depositors."[9] This all reads very much like the description of modern-day banking. Spufford also goes on to describe activities where records indicate that local payments could be made not only in transfer between accounts at the same bank, but also in transfer between accounts in different banks in the city—made possible because bankers maintained accounts in each other's banks.

What is perhaps most interesting is that the historical records indicate that a substantial portion of the adult (male) populate had currency accounts during the time period under consideration. Venice, around 1500, appears to have had as many as 4,000 citizens with bank accounts.[10] Florence also emerged as a major financial center during the fourteenth and fifteenth centuries. Its dominance declined during the sixteenth century. The Medici bank was established in Florence in the fifteenth century. The increasing sophistication of financial institutions' use of money was a dramatic change. Instead of being hoarded, money could be used for productive investment.

Commercial loans became an ordering and unexceptional part of North Italian economic life, which in turn led to a change in the religious doctrine of usury. Now, by the fifteenth century, the payment of interest was acceptable under certain kinds of circumstances.

During the same time that local banking was developing in scale and sophistication during the medieval and early Renaissance era, international banking was becoming an increasingly powerful force. Growth in trade led to increased confidence between merchants and increased confidence led to a greater propensity to accept new financial instruments of credit. One very important result of the increased mutual confidence was the use of instruments of payment out of which ultimately emerged the bill of exchange. By perfecting bills of exchange, prospective purchasers did not need to carry large quantities of precious metals in coins, bars of silver, or the like, which were vulnerable to theft. The bill of exchange greatly expanded the supply of money available for international transactions.

Bills of exchange were, in other words very much like checks and they had two major effects on the financial system. First, they made it much easier to carry out transactions since the requisite amount of gold or silver coins did not have to be physically transferred from place to place; second, the speed with which transactions could take place increased, hence the velocity of money, in modem terminology, was dramatically enhanced by the adoption of bills of exchange. In an important sense, the bill of exchange was an enormous conceptual breakthrough. A piece of paper, worthless in itself, substituted for some quantity of gold or silver. There was a real paradigm shift. The idea that value could be transferred from one individual or institution to another without the actual transfer of the object of wealth was immensely important for the continuous evolution of the banking system. The basic concept is a very close cousin to the millions of electronic transactions that occur daily in the modem world.

The banks that emerged in Renaissance Italy were private banks. Monarchs and Popes had to come to them to finance their various and sundry projects. Over time ambitious leaders began to realize that this reliance on others limited their freedom of action. Thus, by the sixteenth century banks and the respective governments were established, in order to finance the state. We will discuss the development of national banks in greater detail later. The development of commercial banking has been a critical prerequisite for economic growth. Similar growth in banking helped provide the impetus for the industrial revolution in Britain, then the United States in the late nineteenth century. Britain, in fact, served as an important source of capital in the 1860s and 1870s during the early stages of U.S. industrialization. As we will see later, the banking industry is today evolving new institutional forms and services to meet the needs of a global economy, just as in the 1700s and 1800s it grew to meet the needs of early industrialization.

In the seventeenth century Amsterdam emerged as a financial trade center. A major development was the establishment of the first formal stock exchange. Also, the government established a national bank, which it called the Bank of Amsterdam. Merchants used the bank because it facilitated trade by making payments easier. The bank became an important central facility for settling international trade.

The first securities exchange was probably established in Amsterdam, though it is subject to debate. The exchange was used for trading stocks as well as futures and options derivative instruments. The "Tulipmania" craze occurred during 1636 and 1637 in Amsterdam. Many people borrowed money to speculate on the frenzy to capitalize on increasing tulip bulb prices. A considerable amount of borrowed money was lost when the tulip market collapsed.

PAPER CURRENCY

Although the first industrialized currency systems were developed using coins, paper money has existed for centuries. The first paper money appeared in China sometime in the middle of the second century AD. It was originally made from the bark of the mulberry tree. By the thirteenth century, paper money was widely used throughout China. Paper money appeared to have expanded outside China around the fourteenth century; possibly clothing left behind by victims of the bubonic plague might have become a source of raw material for paper. The invention of the printing press aided immeasurably in the production of high-quality currency. The initial acceptance and use of paper currency in Europe seems to have been spotty. It was used in the 1600s by Sweden as a means of compensating for the shortage of silver coins, and was also used by the Revolutionary government in France during the 1790s to help finance the revolution. Paper money played a major role in the Mississippi Company affair, when an unscrupulous Scot, John Law, paid investors in paper money, supposedly redeemable in gold, on investments made by the French in Louisiana. The paper money was issued by the Banque Royal, which Law administered. When the Mississippi Company collapsed as a result of a massive speculative bubble, the bank also collapsed, and with it Law's reputation.

Paper money proliferated in the United States. Even prior to the American Revolution, paper money was used periodically by colonists as a medium of exchange. Benjamin Franklin was an ardent supporter of paper currency and was contracted to print money issued by Pennsylvania, although, in 1764, a colonywide ban against such printing was supported by the British parliament. Paper currency was adopted by the Second Continental Congress in

1775. The paper currency issued was supposed to be backed by gold and silver. While the continentals' value was officially set at one dollar per Spanish dollar of silver, the new currency quickly devalued, trading at two continentals per silver dollar. Their value continued to decline, and by 1780, they traded at the rate of forty continentals per Spanish dollar, and dropped to seventy-five per dollar in 1781. The phrase "not worth a continental" referred to the unhappy experience with that currency.

The U.S. government ceased printing money after 1780, and would not resume the practice until 1861. States, however, issued their own currency; which was typically paper. Indeed, virtually all paper money in circulation was in the form of state and private bank notes.

The passage of the National Bank Act in 1863 marked a major change in the currency. The Act placed a tax on the notes issued by state banks in 1866, and established a national currency. Also, the Civil War had created a tremendous demand for resources to support the war effort. As part of that effort, the U.S. government began issuing paper money or "greenbacks" for the first time since the 1780s. This paper money was not, however, redeemable in gold.

With the end of the Civil War, the issuance of greenbacks came to a halt, and for all practical purposes, the nation returned to a gold standard. The United States would remain on the gold standard until 1933 when, in the depths of the Great Depression, Franklin Roosevelt would take the nation off the gold standard, where it would remain until the creation of the post–World War II international monetary system. Still the struggle over the gold standard would surely help define the politics of the post–Civil War decades. The long price deflation of the 1870s and 1880s generated enormous political pressures to inflate the currency. Since the maintenance of the gold standard placed several restrictions on the amount of money in circulation, the populist movement based one of its key planks on radical change in the financial system by demanding that the United States adopt a policy of free silver, or bimetallism. Such a policy would allow an expansion of the money supply and a reflation of the currency, offsetting the disastrous price deflation of the time. The issue of gold versus bimetallism was fought in both major parties but primarily with the Democratic Party where by 1896 the forces of radical change finally carried the day.

RATIONALIZING THE U.S. CURRENCY: DECIMALIZATION

As scholars have pointed out, the United States is something of an oddity in that it adopted a decimalization system for its currency very early in its history, and has continued with that system to the current day with an almost absolute consensus as to its desirability. At the same time, the United States has maintained a traditional nonmetric system of weights and measures that is decidedly nondecimal in nature. What do we mean by *decimalization*? It means that the U.S. currency system is structured in decimal units, by fractions of 1/100 (0.01) or 1/10 (0.10). A hundred pennies equal a dollar, ten pennies equal a dime, and ten dimes equal a dollar. Of course, the United States also has the nickel (1/20 of a dollar), quarter (1/4 of a dollar), and fifty-cent piece (1/2 of a dollar), but this is primarily to promote transaction convenience. The fundamental units can be conceived in decimal terms.

A decimal system of currency was proposed back in 1792 by the U.S. superintendent of finance and it advocated that the dollar be divided into a hundred equal parts. It was none other than Thomas Jefferson who proposed that the smallest part be referred to as a cent, from the Latin word meaning hundred, and a tenth of a dollar as a dime, from the Latin word meaning tenth.[11]

Virtually every other nation today has adopted a currency system based on the decimal system, including the euro that succeeded the traditional European national currencies, the Canadian and Australian dollar, the Mexican peso, and the like. Great Britain is one of those few countries that had a nondecimal currency system for centuries. It was under King Henry III in 1266 that the sterling system, linking weights to coinage, was established. Under the traditional British system twelve pennies equaled a shilling, twenty shillings equaled a pound, and twenty-one shillings equaled a guinea. The smallest currency unit was the lowly farthing, which was valued at one-fourth of a penny. Indeed, the phrase "I don't give a farthing" communicated the opinion that the object or subject under discussion was worthless. Only with the efforts in the 1970s to rationalize the British currency and to bring it more in line with European Union standards did Britain abandon its traditional currency and move toward a decimalized system in which one hundred pennies equaled a British pound. Under the new system, the shilling and guinea, not to mention the farthing, have disappeared from use.

The decimalization of a nation's currency certainly makes accounting an easier task, but when one thinks about it for a moment, the advent of computers and electronic accounting systems would have made decimalization virtually mandatory. It is difficult to imagine financial accounting systems today, with the requirements for the transfer of vast amounts of financial information, being based on anything other than a decimal system.

CURRENCY DEVALUATION AND DEBASEMENT

Throughout this chapter, one of the implicit themes has been the role that the government plays in determining worth. Government actions can either enhance or damage the value of the currency. Currency can be debased or reduced in value in several ways. The first is through counterfeiting: counterfeiting occurs when private individuals produce fake currency that looks like legal currency, and the fake currency is used for transactions such as the buying and selling of goods and services. Such actions, if carried too far, may create inflation in the selling of goods and services.

Typically, the most serious kind of currency debasement occurs when governments themselves act, in the interest of governing elites, to reduce the value of the money in circulation. European governments in the sixteenth and seventeenth centuries intentionally debased the value of gold and silver coins in order to finance various schemes including wars. The practical effect, of course, is not that different from counterfeiting but simply on a much grander scale. Readers may recall our earlier brief discussion of the hyper-inflation in post–World War I Weimar Germany. Political leaders intentionally printed huge quantities of money in order to pay off reparations imposed on Germany by the allies' victors after World War I. Of course, the reparations were paid in worthless currency, which was their aim. The German experience has, it seems, been burned into the German psyche with a dread of inflation that remains to this day.

Other countries have experienced severe inflation, though nothing quite like the unhappy German experience. Latin American nations in the 1980s also saw dramatic price increases on the scale of hundreds of percentage points per year. For instance, Bolivia in the 1980s and 1990s had much higher inflation for various reasons, although at its core was a complete lack of faith in the real worth of the currency. Thus a kind of self-fulfilling prophecy takes over; citizens believe the true value of the currency is not reflected in the face value, resulting in wages and so forth constantly being bid up in an often fruitless attempt to stay ahead of the inflationary surge.

The economic laws of supply and demand work to explain the value of a currency, as well as other goods and services. If governments (operating through central banks) or currency traders (operating in the private markets) sell one currency in exchange for another, the value of the currency sold (other factors being equal) will decline relative to the currency being bought. Governments and currency traders will sell a currency if they believe that the currency's value is under attack whether from inflation or some misconceived government policy. Governments will sometimes act to intentionally devalue their currency.

Economic troubles in England in the 1960s and 1970s created pressure to devalue the British pound. Such actions are not taken lightly; devaluation is often viewed as a blow to national pride and prestige. A strong currency, conversely, very often connotes strength. Since the 1980s West Germany (and now Germany since reunification) has maintained a strong mark, the reasons being the powerful tendency in Germany to eschew inflationary policies, a monetary agenda dominated by the Germany central bank (the Bundesbank), and the robust German economy with its exporting capability.

In late 1997 and early 1998 a severe economic and currency crisis gripped Southeast Asia, where a sudden economic collapse placed severe pressure on the region's currencies. In one instance, the Indonesian government was forced to devalue its currency, the rupiah, as a condition for support from the International Monetary Fund (IMF) to alleviate the crisis. The Southeast Asian crisis has sent shock waves through financial markets both here and abroad out of concern that the financial collapse could spread to the United States and even Europe.

Why would a nation devalue its currency? Devaluation does several things, but the most immediate effect is to raise the prices of foreign imports and to lower the price of the devaluing country's exports. The bottom line is that this serves to improve that nation's balance of trade. Devaluing a currency can dramatically improve the tourist trade, since foreigners find that the charged conversion rate means that a certain amount of the money being converted will go farther. In 1995 Mexico devalued the peso by 25 percent. This meant that Americans visiting Mexico following the devaluation found that when they converted, say, $100 to pesos the amount received in pesos increased by 25 percent, thus increasing this purchasing power. At the same time, devaluation can have a corrosive effect on a nation's economy since it reduces competition. Domestic manufacturers are placed in an advantageous position since, all else being equal, their goods will cost less.

It is important to note that among international bankers, central bankers, and other leading monetary authorities there has been debate for decades about the advantages and disadvantages of devaluation. Some of these topics will be explored later in this book.

CONCLUSION

The United States today, like other advanced nations, possesses a complex currency and monetary system. That system consists of traditional currencies including coins (the penny, nickel, dime, quarter, fifty-cent piece, and Susan B. Anthony dollar) and paper currency ($1, $5, $10, $20, $50, and $100 bills). Money today, however, includes not just physical objects like a coin or paper that one can touch. It is defined to include much more than coins or paper currency in circulation.

Indeed, the terms *money* and *money supply* are typically used rather loosely. However, a critical point to be emphasized is that there exist different measures of money. We also, we need to realize that as financial markets and institutions become more sophisticated and complex, so does the definition of money. Basically, the money-supply measures reflect different degrees of liquidity in the economic system.

NOTES

1. See the discussion in James Buchan, *Frozen Desire* (New York: Farrar, Straus, Giroux, 1997).

2. Ibid., p. 19–20.

3. Glyn Davies, *A History of Money from Ancient Times to the Present Day*, 3rd ed. (Cardiff: University of Wales Press, 2002), pp. 39–40.

4. See L. Randall Wray, *Understanding Modern Money: The Key to Full Employment and Price Stability* (Cheltenham, UK: Edward Elgar, 1998).

5. Ibid., p. 42.

6. Jack Weatherford, *The History of Money* (New York: Crown Publishers, 1997), foreword, pp. xii–xiii.

7. Ibid., pp. 116–118.

8. See ibid., pp. 64–71; also see Peter Spufford, *Power and Profit: The Merchant in Medieval Europe* (London: Thames and Hudson, 2002), for an excellent general discussion of medieval trade and early banking (especially chapter 1).

9. Spufford, *Power and Profit*, pp. 38–41.

10. Ibid., p. 40

11. Weatherford, *The History of Money*, p. 142.

Two

Monetary Policy and Central Banks

WHAT ARE CENTRAL BANKS?

The central bank is a nation's monetary authority. Central banks can also be called reserve banks or monetary authorities. The role of each is similar, though the structure of the organization and degree of independence is different. They are responsible for monetary policy and have various financial tools that can be used to implement and manage monetary policy.

Almost all nations, including transitioning and emerging economies, have a central bank or an organization that is equivalent. There are currently 172 central banks in the world. Their goal is to support and facilitate sustained economic growth and eliminate inflation. Central banks, conceptually, are supposed to be independent of government control. In reality, each of them is subject to different degrees of government influence. Central banks are responsible for ensuring that a country has adequate reserves to maintain the integrity of the banking system. They are also involved in foreign exchange, to ultimately manage the exchange rate and provide market intervention when necessary. Central banks are the cornerstone of a country's banking system. They are the banker for all of a nation's banks. They are also considered a lender of last resort in a financial crisis. So a nation's banks, at any time, have the ability to borrow from their central bank.

HISTORY AND DEVELOPMENT OF CENTRAL BANKS

The history of central banking began with the establishment of the oldest central bank, the Bank of Sweden, which was founded in 1668. It was not officially designated as a central bank, though, until 1897. The Bank of

The Bank of England was established in 1694. Getty Images/Neil Beer.

England gained greater prominence than the Bank of Sweden. It was established in 1694 and has operated continuously for more than 300 years. The bank established its main office in London at 1734 Threadneedle Street, which is the same physical location that it currently occupies. It has acquired and maintained the moniker, "the Old Lady of Threadneedle Street." As the government borrowed more funds, the Bank of England continued to manage the debt. The aggregated loans became known as the national debt, which is the origin of this term. The Bank of England began as the government's bank and was responsible for managing its debt. Later, it became focused on managing the currency, the pound sterling.

The bank was originally organized as the Governor and Company of the Bank of England. Its members comprised a group that participated in a loan of more than 1 million pounds to the government. The government needed to raise money for its war with France. The bank also functioned as a commercial bank and would issue notes in return for deposits. It acted as "the banker for the banks," too. During the nineteenth century the bank adopted the role as the lender of last resort in order to provide financial stability to the nation. The bank was privately owned until it was nationalized after World War II, in 1946. Afterward, it discontinued its private activities. In 1997, the bank was assigned the power to set interest rates to be responsible for monetary policy and manage the money supply.

The charter for the First Bank of the United States was developed by Alexander Hamilton, who was the U.S. Secretary of the Treasury. He modeled it after the Bank of England. The bank had a twenty-year charter, which was eligible for renewal. The charter was denied for a variety of reasons, one of which was the fact that the bank had become 70 percent foreign owned. The foreign owners had no voting rights but were entitled to an 8.4 percent dividend. The opponents objected to the foreign ownership. Others felt that the Bank of the United States was an unconstitutional extension of federal power. The U.S. Constitution did not directly address the banking issue.

There were two attempts (1819 and 1824) to challenge the constitutionality of the Second Bank of the United States. In both cases, the U.S. Supreme Court upheld the constitutionality of the banks and the authority of Congress to create a central banking entity and delegate powers. The Second Bank, though, was mismanaged and there were even allegations of fraud. There was also a bitter and continuous battle with the state officials and state banks, which eventually alienated many supporters.

The Owen-Glass Federal Reserve Act of 1913 created the Federal Reserve System. Democratic Senator Carter Glass from Virginia and Democrat Robert Owen from Oklahoma crafted the Federal Reserve Act of 1913. A new form of currency called the Federal Reserve Note was created under the 1913 Act. The Federal Reserve System was to include twelve regional Federal Reserve Banks and a Federal Reserve Board was created. The board was organized to provide oversight to the Federal Reserve System and to establish and implement monetary policy. The twelve Federal Reserve Banks were independent from the government and were to be owned by the member banks in the Federal Reserve System.

U.S. DEPARTMENT OF TREASURY

The Office of the Treasurer was established before the Treasury Department. The Treasurer's role was established by Congress in 1785. The U.S. Department of Treasury was established by Congress four years later, in 1789. When the U.S. Treasury was created, it was assigned the task of managing the federal government's revenue. The government designates its coins and paper currency notes as legal tender. The Treasury prints all paper money and is responsible for minting all of the coins. The collection of taxes is also a function of the Treasury. The federal government agencies and units that are under the oversight of the Treasury Department are listed below:

Alcohol and Tobacco, Tax and Trade Bureau (TTB)

Bureau of Printing and Engraving (BEP)

Bureau of Public Debt

Community Development Financial Institution Fund (CDFI)

Financial Crimes Enforcement Network (FinCEN)

Financial Management Service (FMS)

Inspector General

Internal Revenue Service (IRS)

Office of the Comptroller of the Currency (OCC)

Office of Thrift Supervision (OTS)

Treasury Inspector General for Tax Administration (TIGTA)

U.S. Mint

In 2003, several federal law enforcement agencies, formerly under the jurisdiction of the Department of Treasury, were transferred to the Department of Homeland Security. The U.S. Secret Service was one of the agencies removed from the oversight of the Treasury Department. The Secret Service was established in 1865. It was created under the jurisdiction of the Department of Treasury. The primary responsibility was to enforce currency-counterfeiting laws because of the substantial amount of fake currency in circulation after the Civil War. The role of the Secret Service has considerably expanded. In addition to counterfeiting, it provides security for the president, vice president, former presidents and their families, and visiting foreign dignitaries. The agency also investigates government-check fraud and electronic financial crimes.

The BEP is a division of the Treasury Department. The bureau prints paper currency for the nation's money supply on behalf of the Federal Reserve Bank, also called the Fed by industry professionals. It also destroys and replaces currency that becomes unfit for circulation. The Banking Act of 1863 established a standard U.S. national currency. National bank notes were printed by private printing contractors from 1863 until 1877. The federal government took direct control of the printing function in 1877.

The BEP prints Federal Reserve Notes, the paper money for the United States. The notes are produced at the BEP's two printing facilities. One is located in Fort Worth, Texas, and the other is in Washington, DC. The BEP has other printing responsibilities in addition to paper money. It produces Treasury securities, naturalization certificates, identification cards, engraved invitations for the White House, and other specialized official government documents. The BEP printed postage stamps for the U.S. Postal Service until 1995, for 111 years.

The U.S. Mint was created as a result of the Coinage Act of 1792. The mint became an independent agency in 1799. It became part of the Treasury

Department in 1873, with the enactment of the Coinage Act of 1873. Today, the mint is responsible for producing and circulating the nation's coin supply. It also destroys and replaces coins that become unfit for circulation. The U.S. Mint does not act on behalf of the Fed. It operates three different branches that produce coins, located in Denver, Philadelphia, and San Francisco. The city where each coin was printed is identified by a unique imprint called a mint mark. The first letter of the name of the city in which each mint is located is used to designate the location in which a coin was minted. So, Denver uses a D, Philadelphia uses a P, and San Francisco uses an S as a mint mark on the coins that each produces. Fort Knox, Kentucky, is also a U.S. Mint facility. Fort Knox does not produce coins. It does, though, serve as the nation's gold depository and is used to store gold bullion reserves.

U.S. FEDERAL RESERVE SYSTEM

The role of central banks is to control the money supply and general availability of credit in a nation's economic system. The general objective of central banks is to ensure that the economy grows at a steady, sustainable pace and minimize inflation. The system and its operations are complex but vital to the nation's economic well-being.

The Fed is the central bank in the United States. It was created by the Federal Reserve Act of 1913. This act helped to stabilize the fledgling U.S. banking system. The economy was transitioning and becoming more industrialized as business empires were being established. The primary role of the Fed is to establish and implement monetary policy. The Fed is responsible for maintaining public trust and confidence in the banking system.

Developing and implementing monetary policy involves controlling the supply of money to facilitate the country's economic growth and minimizing inflation. The Fed wants the economy to grow, but not too fast. If the economy grows too fast and triggers high inflation, the Fed will attempt to slow down the growth rate. Inflation is characterized by increasing prices and interest rates. If interest rates are high, it is more expensive for businesses to borrow money. Cost increases incurred by businesses are typically passed along to consumers. The Fed tries to promote stable growth. Maintaining an adequate amount of money in the economy requires careful monitoring and sometimes calls for intervention. The Fed does both. It must also balance short-term and long-term interests.

The Fed is an independent entity but operates under a federal government mandate. It is not controlled by the government and does not receive any Congressional funding. Although the Fed is an independent body, it acts within the federal government's domain. All nationally chartered banks in the

FIGURE 2.1
Federal Reserve System Organizational Chart

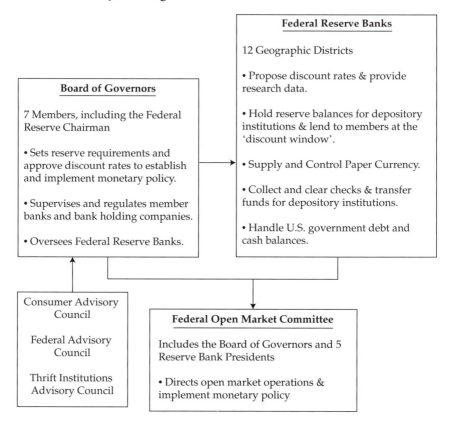

United States are the shareholders of the Fed. The Fed shares of stock are restricted and cannot be sold or traded. The Federal Reserve System consists has four related elements. They are the Board of Governors, the regional Federal Reserve Banks, the Federal Open Markets Committee (FOMC), and the banks that are members of the system (Figure 2.1).

FEDERAL RESERVE BOARD OF GOVERNORS

The Federal Reserve Board of Governors has seven members. These governors supervise the regional banks and oversee their regulatory compliance. The board also supervises the activities of U.S. banks outside the United States. The most influential responsibility of the board, though, is to formulate the U.S. monetary policy.

The Fed governors are nominated by the president and confirmed by the Senate. Each of the seven board members must be from a different Federal District. Six of the governors are appointed for fourteen-year terms. Appointments are staggered because a term begins every other year (i.e., February 1 of even-numbered years). The Fed governor's terms cannot be renewed unless a governor was appointed to serve the remaining time on an unexpired term. The seventh member of the board of governors is the chairman. The Fed chairman and vice chairman are selected from the board. They are both appointed by the president and confirmed by the Senate. The chairman is appointed for a four-year renewable term.

FEDERAL RESERVE REGIONAL BANKS

There are twelve Regional Federal Reserve Banks in the Federal Reserve System. They are geographically dispersed and divided as districts throughout the entire United States. Each of the twelve banks has a separate board of directors. The member banks can borrow funds within the system from the Fed's regional banks. The regional banks also perform a function called check clearing. Using an example as reference will make this function easier to understand. Since the Fed is comprised of twelve regional banks, observers consider the U.S. system to be more decentralized than other nations.

One of the twelve regional Fed banks has jurisdiction over the geographical location of a bank. The Federal Reserve Regional Bank serves the banks within its district.The U.S. Federal Reserve System has twelve Federal Reserve Districts (Figure 2.2). The Federal Reserve officially identifies districts by number and reserve bank city. A reserve bank is located in each of the twelve districts, listed in Table 2.1.

The Fed is also empowered to lend banks money as a lender of last resort. This allows liquidity to be added to the system and helps banks to maintain solvency. The Fed regulates bank credit. It controls the amount of bank lending through reserve requirements. The Fed requires that banks place reserves in the Regional Federal Reserve Bank. These reserve accounts enable the Fed to carry out the function of clearing checks and settling accounts among banks.

FEDERAL OPEN MARKET COMMITTEE

The 1913 Act officially establishes the long-term overall goals as guidelines for the Fed's monetary policy. They are identified as stable prices, maximum employment, and moderate interest rates (long-term horizon). The overall goal is to build and improve public confidence in the banking system.

FIGURE 2.2
The Federal Reserve Districts

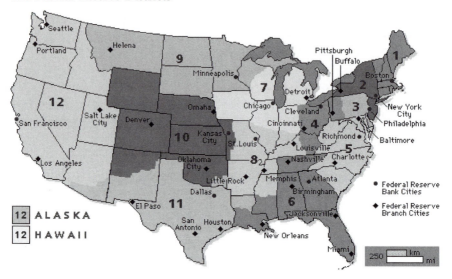

1. **Boston**	5. **Richmond**	9. **Minneapolis**
2. **New York**	6. **Atlanta**	10. **Kansas City**
3. **Philadelphia**	7. **Chicago**	11. **Dallas**
4. **Cleveland**	8. **St. Louis**	12. **San Francisco**

In the Twelfth District, the Seattle Branch serves Alaska, and the San Francisco Bank serves Hawaii. The system serves commonwealths and territories as follows: the New York Bank serves the Commonwealth of Puerto Rico and the U.S. Virgin Islands; the San Francisco Bank serves American Samoa, Guam, and the Commonwealth of the Northern Mariana Islands. The board of governors revised the branch boundaries of the system in February 1996.

Source: The Federal Reserve Board, http://www.federalreserve.gov/otherfrb.htm.

The primary tool that the Fed uses to implement and maintain monetary policy is the Fed funds rate. The Federal Open Market Committee (FOMC) meets regularly to set the Fed funds rate. The FOMC is the Fed's main decision-making entity. The Fed engages in buying or selling government securities in the open market, through the New York Regional Federal Reserve Bank. This activity is done to manage the stability of the Fed funds rate targets. The FOMC is responsible for setting national monetary policy through regular meetings to make adjustments and open market operations.

The FOMC has twelve members, including the Board of Governors, the president of the Federal Reserve Bank of New York, and four other members

TABLE 2.1
The Federal Reserve Districts

1st Reserve District: Boston	7th Reserve District: Chicago
2nd Reserve District: New York	8th Reserve District: St. Louis
3rd Reserve District: Philadelphia	9th Reserve District: Minneapolis
4th Reserve District: Cleveland	10th Reserve District: Kansas City
5th Reserve District: Richmond	11th Reserve District: Dallas
6th Reserve District: Atlanta	12th Reserve District: San Francisco

Source: Taylor, F. *Mastering Foreign Exchange and Currency Options.* London: Pitman, 1997.

chosen from the presidents of the other Federal Reserve Banks. The four members are appointed for one-year terms. The FOMC meets eight times each year in Washington, DC, to analyze, determine, and implement monetary policy. The law requires the FOMC to meet at least four times per year. The FOMC can establish and implement monetary policy within the limits set by the Fed's board of governors.

The FOMC was officially authorized with its responsibilities in 1933, under the Banking Act. It helped to open the Federal Reserve's operations to increased input from the regional Federal Reserve Banks. Analyzing and reporting economic information and research from the districts help the FOMC to make informed decisions that will influence monetary policy.

The Federal Reserve manages the currency supply in circulation, which can be expanded or reduced according to monetary policy. The Fed would be able to determine and control how much U.S. currency is in the hands of the public. It uses three tools to set and implement monetary policy, as follows:

1. Establishment of reserve requirements—regulates the availability of funds that banks have with which to extend credit

2. Adjustment of the discount rate

3. Controlling open market operations

The monetary tools of the Fed include the ability to control open market operations, establish the discount rate, and set reserve requirements. Open market operations involve buying and selling Treasury securities in the open market. Banks invest heavily in government securities and are permitted to use these securities to satisfy reserve requirements. Decisions affect the availability of money and credit as well as the cost of credit. Open market operations are conducted through the New York Regional Federal Reserve Bank.

The rate that the Fed charges its members to borrow funds is the discount rate. Sometimes banks need to borrow funds for very short periods, often overnight. They also need to borrow for a short term to meet their reserve requirements. They can borrow from the Federal Reserve System and pay the discount rate or from another member bank with excess reserves and pay the Fed funds rate. These two rates are often confused. The term *Fed funds rate*, because of the term *Fed*, seems to infer that this is the rate that will be paid to borrow from the Fed. This is incorrect. The discount rate is the rate paid to borrow from the Fed and a bank will pay the Fed funds rate to borrow from another member bank. It is less expensive to borrow from another member bank at the Fed funds rate.

There were periodic financial panics in the developing U.S. banking system. A severe panic in 1907 caught Congress's attention and thus Congress decided to create the Federal Reserve System. The Fed was intended to be the backbone of the U.S. financial system. Congress wanted to establish a more stable banking and financial system. The National Monetary Commission was created by the Aldrich-Vreeland Act of 1908. This commission identified weaknesses in the financial system. Its role was to analyze the condition of the banking industry and currency issues to make recommendations for legislation. The commission determined that the United States had no way to manage the money supply and control liquidity. The recommendations led to the passage of the Federal Reserve Act of 1913.

THE MONEY SUPPLY

The U.S. money supply is the total value of all the U.S. currency and coins in circulation. The nation's money supply is related to inflation. It is measured on several different levels, identified as M0, M1, M2, and M3. The money supply also includes financial instruments or assets that serve as a medium of exchange. They are categorized and formally defined by the Federal Reserve Board or U.S. Treasury. The levels of money supply measurement in the United States are listed below:

M0 = Base money, which includes coins, bills, and central bank deposits (bank reserve requirements).

M1 = Demand deposit balances (NOW accounts, share drafts, checking accounts), coins, currency, and traveler's checks. M1 includes M0.

M2 = Includes certificates deposit (CDs) under $100,000, savings accounts, and money market accounts. M2 includes M0 and M1.

M3 = Represents all the forms of money in use including credit. M3 includes certificates of deposit greater than $100,000, and repurchase agreements. M3 includes M0, M1, and M2.

CLEARING AND RESERVE REQUIREMENTS

The Fed provides a service for member banks called clearing. The clearing function allows banks to reconcile checking account activity. Each district provides check-clearing services for the member banks located in a geographic region. The Fed controls the amount of lending through reserve requirements. It requires that banks place reserves in the regional Federal Reserve Bank. One of the twelve regional Fed banks has jurisdiction over the geographical location of a bank. The Federal Reserve Regional Bank is the bank for the banks within its district. These reserve accounts enable the Fed to carry out the function of clearing checks and settling accounts among banks.

The following example will simplify the complex check-clearing process. Suppose that you wrote a check for $100 for a purchase at a local electronics store. You would make a checkbook entry showing the expenditure. The merchant would deposit the check at his bank. The transaction is settled between you and the merchant but not between your bank and the merchant's bank. The bank from which your check was written owes the merchant's bank $100. How do the banks transfer and reconcile this transaction?

The transfer is accomplished through the Federal Reserve Regional Banking System through the clearing process. Check clearing is a major responsibility of the regional banks. The merchant's bank presents the check that you wrote to the regional Fed bank. The regional bank would collect the funds from your bank and transfer them to the merchant's bank. When the clearing process is complete, the transaction is settled, which means that payment has been made to satisfy the obligations from each counterparty in the transaction. In this example the counterparties are your bank and the merchant's bank. The time from which a check is written until the time that it is cleared and settled is called the float.

THE AUTOMATED CLEARING HOUSE NETWORK

The Automated Clearing House (ACH) Network is a national electronic funds transfer system. The Fed processes its electronic payments through the ACH Network. The ACH was established as an electronic alternative to the previous manual paper-based collection system. The system provides for the interbank clearing of electronic payments for participating depository financial institutions. The Fed's ACH system is the nation's largest electronic payments network. The diagram and description from the NACHA Electronic Payments Association are included to explain the concept (see Figure 2.3).

FIGURE 2.3

The Automated Clearinghouse (ACH) Operational Structure

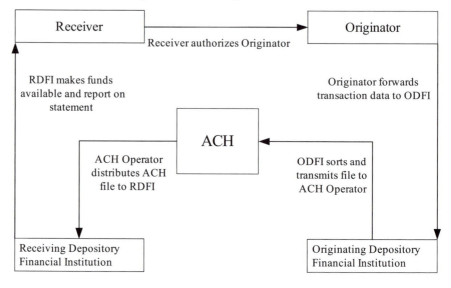

Originator any individual, corporation, or other entity that initiates entries into the Automated Clearing House Network (ACH). Originating depository financial institution (ODFI): a participating financial institution that originates ACH entries at the request of and by (ODFI) agreement with its customers. ODFIs must abide by the provisions of the NACHA Operating Rules and Guidelines. Receiving depository financial institution: any financial institution qualified to receive ACH entries that agrees to abide by the NACHA Operating Rules and Guidelines. Receiver: an individual, corporation, or other entity who has authorized an originator to initiate a credit or debit entry to a transaction account held at an RDFI.

Source: NACHA Electronic Payments Association, http://www.nacha.org.

ACH electronic payments include:

- Direct deposit of payroll, Social Security and other government benefits, and tax refunds
- Direct payment of consumer bills such as mortgages, loans, utility bills, and insurance premiums
- Business-to-business payments
- E-checks
- E-commerce payments
- Federal, state, and local tax payments
- Electronic checks
- Tax refunds

- Banks' settlements
- Check payments under Check 21

The number of ACH payments originated by financial institutions increased to 8.05 billion in 2002, with an increase of 13.6 percent from 2001. These payments were valued at $21.7 trillion. Including payments originated by the Federal government, there were a total of 8.94 billion ACH payments in 2002 worth more than $24.4 trillion. Figure 2.3, from the NACHA Electronic Payments Association, identifies the basic operation of the ACH.

CHECKS

The actual creator of the first check is controversial and a matter of debate. There is a consensus, though, that checklike instruments were used in Amsterdam, when it dominated Europe as a progressive financial and trading center in the 1500s. Merchants with excess cash placed deposits with cashiers for safekeeping. The cashiers charged a fee for the service and issued a note to the depositor, which promised repayment. The term *check* likely originated in England, during the 1700s. The first printed checks (1762) have been attributed to a British banker named Lawrence Childs. Serial numbers were printed on the papers for record keeping. This provided the ability to "check" them.

The United States is one of the few countries that remains heavily reliant on the use of bank checks as a form of payment. As described, check clearing is one of the Fed's major functions. Nations in transitioning economies and even emerging markets avoid using paper checks and are scaling the learning curve because of technological advances. The use of checks is expensive, requires a lot of extra processing time, is subject to fraud, and is inefficient overall. It is unlikely, though, that they will soon be replaced. The use of checks is part of the U.S. culture because they have been in use for so long. Older Americans, the baby boomers, have been accustomed to using checks their entire adult lives. Even though there are electronic alternatives, like debit cards and smart cards, older Americans prefer their familiar checkbooks. It is premature to predict a checkless society in the near future.

An attempt was made to streamline the check-clearing process when Congress passed the Check Clearing for the Twenty-first Century Act in 2003, which has become known as Check 21. The new law was implemented in October 2004. Check 21 is intended to reduce the time delay between when a check is written and when it is settled among banks. This time gap, known as the float, is costly to businesses. Check 21 is a method devised for the electronic exchange of checks in the banking system. It allows check images, both front and back, to be electronically transmitted to speed clearing and matching. The electronic image of an original paper check is called a substitute check. The substitute check becomes a negotiable instrument and the legal equivalent of an original check within the banking system. Prior to Check 21, the checks had to be physically delivered through the Fed to collect and settle payments.

Under Check 21, the original paper check is no longer returned to the issuer. Consumers can no longer write a check and then deposit the money to cover them within a few days because the float time is eliminated. Bank customers are advised not to write checks unless the funds needed to cover the check are in the account. Banks, however, are not required to improve the processing time to make funds available from your deposits, and may place temporary holds on check deposits.

New services are being introduced by technical and software providers to expand the use of Check 21. New electronic deposit services have been introduced that enable a business to make deposits from their premises without making a physical trip to their bank. Checks can be scanned to create a substitute check, and the digital check image is transmitted to the bank remotely, from a desktop. This process is called Electronic Check Presentment (ECP). The ECP eliminates the need to submit the original check to the bank. The amounts and receipt are confirmed electronically. The process removed much of the physical interaction from the check deposit, clearing, collection, and reconciliation process. This transaction can be done using the Internet from virtually any location. It is easy and saves time and money. New commercial applications and tools for Check 21 continue to reduce the amount of paper documents that are handled and transported for processing.

THE GOLD STANDARD

Banking reform was at the forefront of Congressional action at the turn of the twentieth century. In March 1900, the U.S. Congress voted the Gold Standard Act into law. The gold standard functioned as a monetary system and became globally accepted, especially among industrialized nations. Nations participating in the gold standard were ready to redeem currency for gold and were required to hold an adequate supply of gold reserves. This led to global acceptance of these currencies because of their perceived value.

Coins made of gold or silver have an intrinsic value, which is the value of the metal. Paper currency that is backed or payable in gold or silver also has an intrinsic value. Gold was linked to the value of coins and paper currency.

The notes represented a corresponding amount of gold that, in principle, could be redeemed by presenting the note for payment. The gold standard was set at $35 per ounce and the central bank of each participating country established and maintained a gold reserve. The fundamental purpose of the gold standard is to provide economic stability. As a result, international trade expanded. As a nation's economy grew, it was necessary to add to the reserves and procure more gold. This could be accomplished thereby increasing international trade exports or finding, a source or way to mine additional gold.

In the post–World War I economies, the countries involved in the war had enormous debts and their central bankers adopted policies to increase the money supply. This led to spiraling rates of inflation. Maintaining the link with the gold standard was becoming increasingly difficult. If there were imbalances of trade, a country could experience a considerable loss in gold reserves being transferred out. The stock market crash of 1929 led to a run on banks. This panic led to a liquidity crisis and many banks failed. Depositors lost all their money and a severe depression followed. The depression, formally called the Great Depression, had international repercussions and led to a global financial crisis. As a result, most nations could no longer be a part of the gold standard.

As the United States was emerging from the Depression, another major war broke out. Nations again accumulated large amounts of debt by financing the war effort. Wars adversely affected the gold standard. During wartime, participating nations encountered difficulty maintaining adequate reserves and, as a result, economic growth was constrained. Toward the end of World War II, the Allied nations tried to return to the gold standard but reserve requirements were substantially reduced.

The United States and England decided to approach foreign exchange from a strategic perspective. They determined that international trade and monetary stability could be coordinated internationally. Since using an established international institution like the United Nations was impractical because of political and ideological differences, a special meeting at Bretton Woods was organized.

In 1944, the United Nations Monetary and Economic Conference was held at Bretton Woods, New Hampshire. The conference concluded with an agreement to maintain major currency exchange rates with a narrow boundary range. The Bretton Woods Agreement was a consensus that steps must be taken to help rebuild the war-ravaged European nations and their corresponding economies. International trade must be reinstated and monetary stability is an imperative. To accomplish these objectives a new international monetary system was established to encourage trade. Formal rules were established for financial activity and monetary interactions among nations.

The International Monetary Fund (IMF) was created and comprised of member nations.

The Bretton Woods Agreement restored the gold standard in 1944. Nations began to maintain fixed currency exchange rates according to the gold standard. Gold was assigned a fixed price of $35 (U.S.). The U.S. dollar was chosen as the key international benchmark currency standard. Central banks established their monetary policy accordingly. If any nation wanted to make a change in the related value of its currency, the permission of the IMF was required.

This international agreement remained in effect until August 15, 1971. The system worked well for about twenty-seven years. Economic instability, which emerged in the 1960s led to some instability in the gold market. The United States accumulated a considerable amount of debt from financing the Vietnam War.

Central banks, in order to implement monetary policy, influence foreign exchange rates. Their objective is not profit-oriented; rather, it is based upon a political or economic agenda. Central Banks have an important role and influence on the foreign exchange markets. After the collapse of Bretton Woods and the subsequent devaluation of the dollar at the Smithsonian meetings, the U.S. dollar was allowed to float freely without the boundaries that previously constrained valuation. Central banks, in order to implement monetary policy, engage in market operations to influence exchange rates. The central banks regularly intervene in the cash markets to influence valuation and exchange rates to correct disparities. Central banks also use gold for reserves. Gold is used to manage risk in the event of a financial crisis.

Historically, the demand for gold has always been strong. It is considered a hedge against inflation. A hedge is a method to reduce risks. Usually, the price of gold increases with higher inflationary price levels. Gold is used in the manufacturing industry, financial markets, monetary policy, coinage, and for jewelry. The World Gold Council reported that the global demand for gold jewelry reached a record high of $38 billion in 2005.

Three

Banks, Banking, and Financial Institutions

HISTORICAL OVERVIEW: COLONIAL UNITED STATES TO THE PRESENT

The modern term *bank* is derived from the Italian word *banca*. *Banca* is taken from a German term meaning "a bench." Banks were initially developed to facilitate trade. They were responsible for institutionalizing a system for payment transfer. They also provided a central point of exchange and functioned as a place to deposit funds for safekeeping as well as a lender from whom to obtain financing.

The National Mint was established by the Coinage Act of 1792. The act also created a formal and standard federal government coinage system. Previously, the colonies minted their own coins. The official and formal term sometimes used in place of *coin* is *specie*. The use of foreign currencies, especially Spanish coins, was widespread. The Spanish dollar, also known as a piece of eight, was assigned a value of $1 to make it equal to the U.S. dollar. The practice of dividing the currency into eighths was abandoned and replaced by equivalent decimal values. The act prescribed a denomination scheme using decimal points (100 cents) expressed in terms of dollars.

The mint was established in Philadelphia, which at the time was the center of the federal government. It began producing coins in 1793 and the first coins minted were the one-cent and one-half-cent copper coins. Silver coins were first produced the following year and gold coins were first produced in 1795. In 1793, Congress also allowed all foreign coins in the United States to be accepted as legal tender. The mint became an independent agency in 1799. The agency was responsible directly to the president. In 1873, the mint was transferred to the Department of the Treasury and its headquarters was moved to Washington, DC.

The use of foreign coins was limited and, incrementally, ultimately eliminated. Foreign coins, primarily Spanish coins, were still accepted for several years after the legislation. Eventually, in 1857, Congress passed legislation eliminating the legal tender status of all foreign coins.

All the colonies issued paper money by the middle of the eighteenth century. This paper currency was called bills of credit and was issued to pay military expenses. The Continental Congress also issued paper money when the Revolutionary War began. Both the states and the federal government issued paper money to finance the war effort. After the war, the currency depreciated substantially in value to the point that a gold or silver $1 coin was worth about 1,000 continentals. This depreciation in value led to the popular expression "not worth a continental." The Congress subsequently stopped issuing paper money.

Paper money lost its value and its general use and acceptance declined. Gold and silver coins, again, because of the intrinsic value of the metal, familiarity, and abundant supply, became dominant. The most popular was the Spanish silver dollar and the dollar became the agreed-upon de facto standard unit of currency. Because it was a recognizable, widely accepted unit, it made sense to adopt it. In 1792, Congress passed the legislation designating the dollar as the U.S. standard. The original dollar that was envisioned would be a coin that was either gold ($10 eagle) or silver (silver dollar). The coins would be minted by the United States as legal tender.

The first modern, private commercial bank in America was chartered in 1781 and located in Philadelphia. It was authorized by the Continental Congress and called the Bank of North America. It opened in January 1782. Since the Continental currency was no longer being issued, the Bank of North America was able to issue its own paper currency. After the Civil War, however, the states were prohibited from issuing their own currency.

Ten years later, in 1791, Congress granted a charter for the First Bank of the United States. The First Bank of the United States was based in Philadelphia and established branches in eight cities. It was authorized to operate as a commercial bank and was empowered as the fiscal agent of the U.S. government. The bank was permitted to issue notes as paper money. Congress also passed legislation mandating that no other banks were allowed to exist, making this bank a central bank. The bank would lend money directly to the government and be repaid with proceeds from government tax collections.

The bank's twenty-year charter was subject to renewal in 1811. There was considerable opposition to the renewal. Some felt that the Bank was a tool for insiders and elitists; others felt that it ignored the agricultural sector of the

Historically, the U.S. dollar and gold have served as standards by which world currencies are valued. Corbis (top); Getty Images/PhotoLink (bottom).

economy; and still others were concerned that a majority of the bank's stock was foreign owned. By 1811, two-thirds of the bank's stock was controlled by British owners. So, in 1811, Congress voted against renewing the charter for the Bank of the United States. One year later, the central bank concept ended and competition emerged. Regional banking powers grew to control in geographical regions. The Bank of New York and the Bank of Massachusetts in Boston emerged to become prominent and influential institutions.

The Civil War created an enormous amount of government debt and, as after the Revolutionary War and the War of 1812, the monetary system was left in disarray. U.S. banks entered a period of transition and accelerated growth near the end and after the War of 1812 (1812–1815). Although there was financial turmoil, banks were allowed special concessions and were not required to meet their contractual obligations. The U.S. government recognized the need for a central bank because of the difficulty encountered in financing the War of 1812. The Second Bank of the United States was chartered in 1816. It was also called the Bank of the United States. The charter for this Second Bank expired in 1836, but the bank applied for an early renewal in 1832. U.S. President Andrew Jackson, however, vetoed the Congressional act for the renewal of the charter. The charter expired in 1836 and the bank was closed. President Jackson was not opposed to the central bank concept. He objected to the manner in which the Second Bank of the United States was managed. Regardless, the United States would not have another central bank for more than eighty years, until 1913.

One year after the demise of the Second Bank of the United States, in 1837, there was a banking panic, which resulted in a number of bank failures. A fundamental change in the developing banking system followed: individual state governments started to assume more responsibility for bank oversight. The trend began in 1838, when the state of New York enacted legislation to promote free banking. The first U.S. banks were required to have Congressional approval in order to receive a legal charter. This charter was issued for a fixed time period and required renewal, which was sometimes more difficult to obtain than the original charter.

In 1838 New York passed legislation intended to reform and promote standard regulated banking practices. The law was called the Free Banking Act and it authorized state-chartered banks. The period from 1837 to 1862 was known as the Free Banking Era. The state-chartered bank trend spread among states. For the next twenty-five years, virtually all of the nation's banking was conducted by banks chartered by the various states. At this time it was a common practice for banks to make loans by issuing their own currency (i.e., bank notes). Sometimes, a bank would not have adequate reserves to cover all the notes that it issued. The counterfeiting of these notes became a problem. Furthermore, the state banks were not regulated by the U.S. government; rather the individual states were responsible for regulating the banks that they chartered.

Fraud, abuse, and multiple bank failures accompanied the expansion of banking among the states. Many bank investors lost their investments because bank deposit insurance had not yet been introduced (federal deposit insurance was created by Congress in the Banking Act of 1933). Also, existing laws among states varied and, as a result, supervision was often weak and enforcement was inconsistent. Banks issued their own money (bank notes) and it is estimated that there were more than 10,000 different issuers. Default was high, valuation and reliability were difficult to determine, and counterfeiting was rampant. Often the notes had to be exchanged for less than face value. Using them for payment frequently involved negotiating the value with the other party in the transaction.

The National Banking Acts of 1863 and 1864 were intended to increase federal control and influence over the disparate state banking system. The U.S. government was also accumulating considerable debt as a result of the Civil War. When the Civil War began in 1861, there were 1,562 state-chartered banks. The administration wanted to establish a system of federally chartered national banks, rather than rely upon the decentralized state banking system. By 1865, there were about 1,500 national banks. Many of these banks were formerly state banks that converted their charter.

In 1863, Congress passed the National Currency Act. Despite the great demand, the United States still did not have a standard national currency. The Act was an attempt to establish a standard national currency system. The federal government was also authorized to issue Treasury debt securities to help finance the war debt. This financing was intended only to cover the Union's debt, not the Confederacy's. Prior to the Act, the state-chartered banks issued their own currency referred to as bank notes. The Act intended to eliminate all the problems that accompanied the bank note conundrum by replacing them with a single U.S. currency. Historians estimate that the United States had as many as 30,000 different types of bank note currency. There was no real restriction on currency issuance, so, in addition to states and banks, even merchants were issuing their own currency. Initially, currencies issued by the states were in competition with those issued by the federal government.

During the same year, 1863, Congress also passed the National Bank Act, which was an attempt to resolve the increasing problems with state chartered banks. The law was intended to create a national system of banks that would be government chartered. The law also created a government agency, headed by the comptroller of the currency, which was authorized to establish the new national banking system and provide regulatory control. The creation of the Office of the Comptroller of the Currency (OCC) as a part of the U.S. Treasury Department was a milestone in banking regulation. Also, the establishment of a national currency was encouraged. Banks that were part of the new system received U.S. national bank notes.

In 1864, the U.S. Congress passed amendments to the act. One of the amendments introduced a tax on state bank note issues. The number of state-chartered banks declined substantially following this amendment as a direct result of the tax. State banks responded with an important financial innovation—demand deposits. Demand deposits are payable to the depositor "on demand"—checking accounts are an example of a demand deposit. Following the introduction of this concept in the 1870s, state banks again flourished.

The National Banking Acts of 1863, 1864, and 1865 effectively nationalized banking and eliminated the decentralized, increasingly unstable state banking system. Under this legislation, the OCC was authorized to charter national banks. The number of state banks declined as the nationally chartered banks grew. The national currency was also successfully displacing state currencies. The 1864 act gave the OCC the necessary authorization to provide regulatory oversight to the nationally chartered bank system. During the following year, in 1865, Congress passed another law that addressed the bank note problem. A tax was imposed on the state bank notes, which in effect reduced their number until they were eliminated, eventually. The act also increased the number of nationally chartered banks.

THE OFFICE OF THE COMPTROLLER OF THE CURRENCY

The new legislation enabled the U.S. government to assume regulatory control over the federal banks. The OCC was created to help fulfill this objective. The comptroller was given responsibility for printing all the bank notes issued. The uniform currency was intended to eliminate the instability, counterfeiting, and volatility problems encountered by the state-chartered banks. All the national banks were required to accept the standard bank notes issued by the Comptroller at their face value.

The director of the OCC, the comptroller, is appointed by the president and approved by the Senate. The comptroller serves a five-year term and also acts as a director of the Federal Deposit Insurance Corporation (FDIC). The responsibilities of the OCC are listed below:

- Examination and regulation of national (federally chartered) banks: supervision of operations with periodic reviews including on-site visits
- Regulation of the issuance of national bank charters: reviewing and making decisions related to bank charter applications and requests for additional branches and changes in corporate or capital structure

- Taking action against banks that break the rules or are noncompliant with requirements
- Development of rules to regulate bank lending and investment practices

THE TWENTIETH CENTURY

The Civil War created additional problems for the banking system as war debts and inflation increased. Congress intended to bring banks under federal oversight, but state-chartered banks continued to exist and proliferate, resulting in a dual banking system. State-chartered and federally chartered banks were able to coexist. This dual banking system exists today. Banks can choose to be chartered at the state or federal level. Post–Civil War banking abuses and mismanagement continued as the dual banking system expanded.

The banking system was still unstable and was subject to periodic financial panics. A severe panic occurred in 1907. The 1907 financial crisis became known as the Wall Street Panic. The crisis was based in New York City and was triggered by a stock market crash. The panic next spread to Chicago. It all led to a run on the banks. The banks were unable to meet withdrawal requests from depositors and many were forced to close. The experience clearly identified liquidity problems because of inadequate reserves in the developing banking industry. Millions of people lost their deposits because federal bank deposit insurance did not exist yet. Many banks collapsed and the economic impact spread throughout the country. The rate of unemployment reached 20 percent and millions of people lost their bank deposits. The collapse of reputable major banks led to a lack of confidence and distrust in the banking system. The result of this panic was a severe economic depression. Another growing problem was related to a variety of different bank notes issued by all the state-chartered banks.

The 1907 depression conveyed a strong message that economic reform was necessary. In 1908, Congress enacted the National Bank Act, which created the National Monetary Commission (NMC). The 1908 National Bank Act is also known as the Aldrich-Vreeland Act. The NMC was authorized to examine the status of the banking environment and evaluate the state of money and currency. It was expected to make recommendations concerning banking and currency, which it did.

The recommendations of the NMC influenced the passage of the Federal Reserve Act of 1913. The Federal Reserve Act of 1913 was also called the Currency Act and the Owens-Glass Act. The Fed that was conceived in 1913 is not identical to the original. As the Federal Reserve System developed, some changes were necessary, especially during the Great Depression following the

1929 stock market crash and during the 1970s following the removal of the gold standard and currency valuation problems.

FEDERAL RESERVE NOTES

A popular term used interchangeably with a Federal Reserve Note is the U.S. dollar. The Federal Reserve Note was authorized by the Federal Reserve Act of 1913. The notes are issued in various denominations, described in dollar units (e.g., $5 bill, $10 bill, $20 bill, etc.). The predecessor to the Federal Reserve Note was the United States Note, which was first authorized in 1862. For most of the twentieth century, Federal Reserve Notes and United States Notes were both produced.

THE GREENBACK

United States Notes represent the first paper currency issued and are the original greenbacks. The Legal Tender Act of 1862 authorized the United States to print United States Notes to help finance the Civil War. These notes were known as greenbacks and are the predecessors of modern currency. They were called greenbacks because of the green ink used to produce the notes. The greenback is an American icon and a cultural symbol. The description of legal tender, as worded in the Legal Tender Act of 1862, is "legal tender for all debts, public and private, except duties on imports and interest on public debt, which from that time forward should be paid in coin."

United States Notes started to become obsolete in 1963, when they were no longer able to be redeemed for precious metal. The issuance of United States Notes ceased in 1971. As the United States Notes became obsolete, Federal Reserve Notes remained as the nation's main paper money.

DEPRESSION ERA BANK REFORMS

The stock market crash of 1929 led to the biggest financial crisis in the history of the United States and triggered a run on banks. This panic led to a liquidity crisis and many banks failed. Depositors lost all their money and a severe depression followed. The depression had international repercussions and led to a global financial crisis. The number of banks fell by 40 percent because more than 11,000 failed or had to merge in order to remain solvent. The Great Depression left about 25 percent of the once working population unemployed. Congress passed legislation in the early 1930s that helped restore trust in the banking system and led the country out of the depression.

The legislation that became popularly known as the Glass-Steagall Act is actually the result of two separate Congressional actions. Both acts were sponsored by the same two parties and bear the same name. The acts are similar; both address banking and monetary reform. The main provisions of each act, however, are fundamentally different. The first was the Glass-Steagall Act. The second was the Banking Act of 1933. The 1933 act contained important provisions that were intended to restore trust and confidence in the banking system.

The Glass-Steagall Act provided access to $750 million of the nation's gold reserves to provide loans to assist industries and businesses with good credit. It removed the gold-related restrictions on the Fed's collateral requirements. Congress provided the Fed with greater authority by increasing its ability to exert influence on the nation's money supply. The Fed was authorized to use government securities (Treasury bills, government notes, and government bonds) rather than gold as collateral in order to issue U.S. Bank Notes (paper money). This allowed the Fed to issue dollars according to its monetary policy. Previously, Federal Reserve Notes could be issued only if they were backed by gold. Removing this gold requirement provided the Fed with the power and authority to implement policies. Congress also reduced the amount of collateral that national banks were required to deposit with the Fed.

Another banking act, the Emergency Banking Relief Act of 1933, is sometimes confused with the Glass-Steagall Act because it was also enacted in 1933. The Emergency Banking Act officially removed the gold standard. The act also created a plan for closing insolvent banks and providing support so that the banks capable of surviving could be reorganized. The Secretary of the Treasury was given the authority to force those who were holding gold to sell it to the government.

Both the 1933 acts, the Glass-Steagall Act and the Emergency Banking Act, were sponsored by Carter Glass and Henry Steagall. Carter Glass was a Democratic Senator from Virginia and Henry Steagall was a Democratic Congressman from Alabama.

The Banking Act of 1933 is also called the Glass-Steagall Act and was passed after the Emergency Bank Relief Act. It amended the liberal operating extensions allowed by the McFadden-Pepper Act of 1927. The 1927 act liberalized the securities underwriting activity of national banks. The Securities Act of 1933 was enacted specifically to reestablish confidence in the banking system. Initially, banks and their investments were blamed for the stock market collapse. The myth was later dispelled and researchers determined that the stock market was overvalued, a scenario that repeated itself, notably in 1987. The Banking Act of 1933 created federal deposit insurance to protect the depository assets of bank customers. Accounts were originally covered for up to $2,500 per depositor. Another reform introduced by the 1933 act was a restriction imposed on banks forbidding them to pay interest on demand deposits (e.g., checking accounts).

The 1933 act specifically addressed the type of financial services and business segments that banks would be permitted to enter. Banks were restricted from purchasing securities for investment, with the exception of government securities. The enterprises that engage in the business of taking deposits and those that underwrite and issue securities were intended to exist separately. The act prohibited banks from underwriting securities (investment banking). Banks were also not allowed to own securities brokerage firms and insurance companies. Basically, banks were restricted to the commercial banking business. The act also legitimized the Federal Deposit Insurance Corporation, which provided insurance protection to bank depositors. The 1933 act prevented banks from paying interest on demand deposits (e.g., checking accounts) for commercial enterprises. It also imposed a cap on the amount of interest that banks were permitted to pay on savings deposits. This provision is commonly called Regulation Q.

The Securities Exchange Act of 1934 empowered the Securities and Exchange Commission (SEC) with broad regulatory power. The 1934 act provided greater protection to the investing public. New requirements and registration procedures were established for the issuance of new securities. The act initiated regulatory reporting requirements for companies whose stock was publicly traded. The securities exchanges were also placed under the jurisdiction of the SEC. The SEC was authorized to enforce the provisions of the Securities Act of 1933 and the Securities Exchange Act of 1934. The Banking Act of 1935 was enacted to complement the Glass-Steagall Act and empowered Washington, DC, to have centralized control over the national banking system. The act also codified the temporary banking rules imposed by the Democratic administration's New Deal initiatives.

The passage of the Gramm-Leach-Bliley Act (GLBA) in 1999 repealed the Glass-Steagall Act. Effectively, it allowed banks, securities brokers, investment banks, and insurance companies to enter each other's industry segments. The GLBA removed the restrictions imposed by Glass-Steagall. Gradually, these restrictions had become relaxed. Also, financial services institutions from other countries were not subject to the Glass-Steagall restrictions, thus putting U.S. institutions at a competitive disadvantage. The GLBA enabled U.S. banks to compete with large overseas financial institutions, which were not subject to the restrictions imposed by the Glass-Steagall Act.

COMMERCIAL BANKS

The U.S. financial system is made up of firms that fall into two main categories: depository and nondepository institutions. Examples of depository financial institutions include banks, credit unions, savings and loan associations (S&Ls), and savings associations. Nondepository financial institutions include credit card companies, finance companies, insurance companies, and pension funds. Incrementally, though, the boundaries of these financial organizations are becoming blurred because of technology, financial innovation, and competition. Also, large multinational financial institutions are blurring national borders and expanding globally.

Commercial banks, as depository institutions, have the unique ability to "create money" in the U.S. economic system. How do banks create money? Money was first created because all the deposits made to the bank were held in safekeeping, but remained idle. Enterprising bankers realized that this money could be loaned to other borrowers, who would pay a fee (i.e., interest) for the use of the money. The funds from the existing deposits are loaned to borrowers. In principle, the depositor still has funds by way of deposit with the bank and is entitled to them. The new borrower also has funds that can be used. When the money supply is compiled, the borrower's funds will be included and so will the depositor's. Effectively, the bank creates "new money" from the existing deposit. This new money has purchasing power. The depositors are informed of the practice and usually pay a fee for the use of their deposits which are normally excess assets. The bank keeps the fee for lending the money but often shares it with the depositor.

Commercial banks are depository financial institutions. They function as financial intermediaries. Commercial banks accept deposits, and offer a variety of services such as checking accounts, savings accounts, time deposits, and extending credit. The deposits, like certificates of deposit (CDs) are placed with a bank for a fixed period of time for a guaranteed rate of return. Usually, the interest rate paid for CDs is fixed, but sometimes it is variable. Commercial banks also make loans to business clients and individuals. These banks are usually categorized or segmented according to size.

Banks were formally called commercial banks to differentiate them from investment banks. The investment banks serve specific business needs such as helping both public and private corporations to raise money in the capital markets. They are typically involved in securities underwriting and funds are often raised by issuing debt and equity securities. The bankers provide consulting, research, and advisory services, too. They can also be involved in direct investment, mergers, acquisitions, and other business combinations.

Organizing syndicated loans for their clients is another service of the investment bankers. Syndicated loans involve a group of banks collectively lending a large sum of money. By working as a group, the lending banks are able to share the risks among the members of the syndicate. Investment bankers will also act as intermediaries for securities trading. Investment banks are different from brokerage firms. Many brokerage firms, however, have organizational divisions that engage in the investment banking business. The Glass-Steagall Act prevented banks from participating in the investment banking business until its repeal, in 1999.

Banks are typically identified by their primary business functions. There are multiple ways to categorize banks. In this work, banks are categorized according to their asset size. The first tier includes the top twenty-five banks, ranked by total assets, and this is the first commercial bank category. The largest banks in the country are often called money center banks and are typically organized as bank holding companies (BHCs). The second tier represents a large group. It includes all the banks within the top twenty-five and the banks with $1 billion or less in assets. The asset size ranges from $1 billion to approximately $45 billion (the size of the smallest of the top twenty-five BHCs). The third tier banks are called community banks and have assets of $1 billion or less. There are other types of financial institutions included in this chapter. They are savings and loans, credit unions, and merchant banks. All these, except merchant banks, are considered depository institutions. Merchant banks are more significant in other countries, especially in the European nations than in the United States. The top twenty-five U.S. banks in terms of assets are listed in Table 3.1.

Commercial banks can be federally chartered or state-chartered. Many banks are chartered only at the state level. They are regulated and restricted to operation only in their home state. They can become part of the FDIC insurance system and must comply with the appropriate regulations. FDIC participation is optional for state-chartered banks. The state banks also pay fees to obtain FDIC deposit insurance. Federally chartered banks are regulated by the U.S. Comptroller of the Currency, the FDIC, and the Fed.

The GLBA removed many of the restrictions encumbering bank expansion. In addition, the earlier Riegle-Neal Interstate Banking and Branching Efficiency Act of 1994 triggered bank expansion beyond state geographical boundaries. As banks grew, there was a wave of mergers and acquisitions among banks, which created larger and stronger institutions.

After the Glass-Steagall provisions were finally repealed by the GLBA, banking conglomerates were assembled. Banks were allowed to enter the securities and the insurance business. BHCs emerged after the Glass-Steagall provisions restricting the scope of their business were removed. There has

TABLE 3.1
Largest 25 Banks in the United States (in Millions of U.S. Dollars)

Rank	Name (city, state)	Consolidated Assets
1	Bank of America Corp. (Charlotte, NC)	$1,082,243
2	J. P. Morgan Chase & Company (New York)	$1,013,985
3	Citygroup (New York)	$706,497
4	Wachovia Corp. (Charlotte, NC)	$472,143
5	Wells Fargo & Company (San Francisco)	$403,258
6	U.S. BC (Cincinnati, OH)	$208,867
7	Suntrust Banks, Inc. (Atlanta, GA)	$177,231
8	HSBC North America, Inc. (Buffalo, NY)	$150,679
9	Keybank (Cleveland, OH)	$88,961
10	State Street Corp. (Boston, MA)	$87,888
11	Bank of New York Company, Inc. (New York)	$85,868
12	PNC Financial Services Group, Inc. (Pittsburgh, PA)	$82,877
13	Regions Bank (Birmingham, AL)	$81,074
14	Branch BKG&TC Corp. (Winston-Salem, NC)	$80,227
15	Chase Bank USA (Newark, DE)	$75,052
16	Countrywide Bank (Alexandria, VA)	$73,116
17	LaSalle Bank (Chicago)	$71,061
18	National City Bank (Cleveland, OH)	$69,482
19	Bank of America USA (Phoenix, AZ)	$62,983
20	MBNA Corp. (Wilmington, DE)	$58,517
21	Fifth Third Bancorp (Cincinnati, OH)	$57,613
22	North Fork Bank (Mattituck, NY)	$57,045
23	Bank of the West (San Francisco)	$55,158
24	Manufacturers and Traders TC (Buffalo, NY)	$54,391
25	Comerica (Detroit, MI)	$53,577

Source: Federal Reserve System, National Information Center.

been considerable consolidation and merger activity among financial services firms to form multidisciplinary BHCs. Powerful financial organizations comprised of bank, brokerage, investment banking, and insurance subsidiaries emerged. Examples include Morgan Stanley Dean Witter, CitiGroup, Chase, and Bank of America.

In emerging markets, traditional banking dominates the early stage of economic development and is less critical as an economy becomes more advanced. A traditional banking system, though, can impede as well as support development because it tends to be resistant to change out of a desire to protect its business domain. The development and growth of a free-market financial infrastructure is a process of transformational change, and the nature of that change will affect the resource allocation decisions of investors. The financial sector in an emerging market should develop in response to market incentives.

SAVINGS AND LOAN ASSOCIATIONS

S&Ls exist for the primary purpose of lending money for home mortgages. The term *thrifts* is often used to describe these depository institutions. During Ronald Reagan's first term as president, many restrictions limiting the activities of S&Ls were removed. So more risk was added to the system. Also, as a result of financial innovations, the growth of money being deposited at these institutions was explosive. Unfortunately, the size of the underlying federal insurance program was not.

The Office of Thrift Supervision was created to monitor the financial condition of S&Ls. The first S&L opened in 1931. The Federal Home Loan Bank System was introduced as their regulatory authority in 1932. Deposits were to be insured by the Federal Savings and Loan Insurance Corporation (FSLIC) for up to $40,000. The government began chartering S&Ls in 1933. The S&Ls were not required to be national and many were registered at the state level. S&L banks accept deposits and pay interest to the savings depositors. They use the deposits to make loans to borrowers. Many of these loans are for home mortgages. These mortgages are sold to investors and the S&Ls can make additional loans.

S&L depositors were protected by the FSLIC, which was chartered to perform the same role as the FDIC. The FSLIC was grossly underfunded and was unable to handle a systemic catastrophe. Since such a catastrophe seemed unlikely, at least in the early 1980s, federal regulators largely ignored the problem. The regulations governing the types of accounts and rates of interest that could be paid by S&Ls were liberalized. Also, the early 1980s were characterized by economic problems caused by high oil prices under the Carter administration and runaway inflation. Interest rates for time deposits were still high and the banking environment was very competitive. Banks and S&Ls began more direct competition and it was often based on interest rates that could be offered to the customers. Interest rates were so high, that it was often worthwhile to pay the penalty for withdrawing a CD early and placing it with a different financial institution paying a higher rate of interest. After all, either the FDIC or the FSLIC guaranteed these deposits up to $100,000.

Two major legislative acts intended to reform and deregulate the banking industry were enacted in 1980 and 1982. The first is the Depository Institution Deregulation and Monetary Control Act of 1980 (DIDMCA). The other is the Garn-St. Germain Depository Institutions Act of 1982. Both had considerable influence and impact on the financial services industry during the 1980s. Their impact is discussed in the next section, which describes the S&L crisis. The main elements of the two acts are listed below.

Depository Institution Deregulation and Monetary Control Act of 1980

- Phased out Regulation Q (from the 1933 act), which limited the amount of interest that could be paid on time deposits such as CDs. Increased FSLIC deposit insurance to $100,000 at S&Ls.
- Allowed S&Ls to make commercial loans.
- Made reserve requirements the same for banks and S&Ls.
- Authorized NOW accounts on a national basis.

A Negotiable Order of Withdrawal (NOW) account was introduced before bank Money Market Deposit Accounts (MMDAs). NOW accounts are deposit accounts and include a check-writing privilege. The deposit account pays interest but the rate is typically low. There are no legal criteria for minimum balances, but banks usually impose them in order to maintain an account without incurring penalty fees. The check-writing policies for NOW accounts are not as restrictive as for MMDAs. The MMDA, though, usually pays a higher rate of interest on account balances.

Garn-St. Germain Depository Institutions Act of 1982

- Commercial banks were permitted to acquire failing savings banks.
- Gave S&Ls that were federally chartered more power and loosened the restrictions and limitations on their activities.
- S&Ls were given broader lending capabilities.
- Expanded powers to accept demand deposits.
- Banks were allowed to sell MMDAs.

MMDAs are offered by commercial banks. The MMDA is a savings deposit account but funds can be accessed by writing a check. It requires that the depositor maintain a relatively high account balance. Bank MMDAs typically pay a higher rate of interest than simple savings accounts. Usually the bank imposes some restrictions on the check-writing privilege. For example, many banks restrict the amount of the check written by imposing a $1,000 minimum. There is also a restriction on the number of checks—usually six—that can be written within a defined monthly time period. MMDAs were created to compete with the money market mutual funds offered through securities brokerage firms. Unlike the money market mutual funds, bank MMDAs are covered by FDIC insurance. The law treats the account as a savings account rather than a checking account. Banks apply high penalty fees to customers who exceed the check-writing limits and may also close the accounts.

SAVINGS AND LOAN CRISIS

The DIDMCA was intended to provide comprehensive banking and monetary reforms. S&Ls were basically deregulated by this act in 1980. The DIDMCA also changed regulations for reserve requirements so that they would be applied uniformly to all depository financial institutions. The FSLIC insurance for deposits was increased to $100,000. The 1980 act also authorized NOW accounts. This act marked the beginning of a government initiative to reduce regulatory constraints in the financial services industry. By the end of the 1980s it was clear that the legislative reform efforts produced unintended consequences that were exacerbated by the S&L crisis.

The economic environment of the early 1980s included an energy crisis, a recession, and record-high mortgage rates. The high mortgage rates were prohibitive and home buyers were reluctant to commit to such high interest rates during a period of economic uncertainty. In 1981, S&Ls were permitted to issue adjustable rate mortgages (ARMs) in which the interest rate on the unpaid mortgage balance would be adjusted at fixed periods upon an established benchmark to reflect current interest rates.

Ronald Reagan became president in 1982. His administration believed in the power of free markets and engaged in the process of deregulation in many different industries. For example, the telecommunications industry became deregulated in 1984 with the breakup of AT&T into eight regional Bell operating companies. This breakup created new entities and increased competition, which eventually led to new telecommunications innovation and a better understanding of consumer needs and preferences. Ultimately, the Internet emerged as a viable commercial enterprise and whole new industries were created. An interesting anecdote is that because of a series of mergers and acquisitions, the original AT&T has almost been reassembled. The liberalization of the S&L industry demonstrates a need for government oversight in some industries.

Further legislative relief was provided by the Garn-St. Germain Depository Institutions Act of 1982. The Act was intended to help deregulate the S&L industry. It permitted S&Ls to offer interest-bearing MMDAs in order to be more competitive with banks and other financial institutions. The NOW accounts were authorized in the 1980 Act. An abundance of funds were being deposited at S&Ls to earn the high prevailing interest rates. The 1982 act permitted S&Ls to invest in areas that had been historically prohibited in order to earn higher rates of return on investments. It also reduced reserve requirements. Essentially, it gave S&Ls the ability to speculate. It was a no-lose deal for the S&Ls who were, of course, insured by the FSLIC. They were permitted to invest in almost anything with federally insured deposits. This provision proved to be a terrible mistake.

Many S&Ls moved into speculative and risky commercial real estate development investment deals, including buying raw land, which did not produce a cash flow. This influx of capital along with declining interest rates led to a real estate boom. S&Ls entered a risky business that many knew nothing about. A high percentage of the investments that were made turned out to be high risk and irresponsible, but for the most part, legal practices. S&Ls were permitted to invest in these speculative high-yield bonds.

In the early 1980s the stock brokerage firm Merrill Lynch encroached upon the boundaries between the traditional banking and brokerage business, which were required to be separate under the Glass-Steagall Act of 1933. Merrill Lynch financial engineers created an innovative new account for its clients called the cash management account (CMA). This account combined a traditional brokerage account with an interest-bearing account for idle or excess funds. In addition, the account included a "sweep feature." If dividends were paid from a stock holding or the proceeds of a sale were received, they were automatically "swept" into an interest-bearing account. Soon all the major brokerage firms mobilized their resources to develop and provide similar account offerings. Merrill Lynch, along with the other major brokerage firms, began brokering or directing MMDAs deposits to S&Ls. These deposits were typically $100,000, the same amount that FSLIC provided as deposit insurance. On the surface, it appeared to be a good deal for all the parties involved. The customers received a high rate of interest, the deposits were guaranteed by the FSLIC, and the S&Ls received a huge inflow of capital.

The S&Ls also issued CDs that the brokerage firms sold to their customers. This money, too, went straight to the S&Ls. These CDs were different from traditional CDs. With a traditional CD, the customer deposits money for a fixed period of time for an agreed rate of interest. The rate of interest may be variable but the CD remains with the bank and is nontransferable. The brokerage or brokered CDs, on the other hand, were marketable and ownership was transferable. As a result, a large secondary market for these brokered CDs emerged. It was an over-the-counter market among the brokerage firms.

These CDs, like bonds (which are discussed in Chapter Six), will fluctuate in value. Changes in interest rates will affect the prices or market value of financial instruments that are sensitive to these rates. When interest rates increase, the prices decrease, and when interest rates decrease, prices increase. The price or market value of a traditional bank CD is constant. If you deposit $10,000, the value is constant, unless you pay a penalty for withdrawing the time deposit early. The brokered CDs had no early withdrawal fee. They were bought and sold in the open market based upon prices that investors were willing to pay. Since S&Ls did not have to worry about redemptions, they issued a substantial amount of these CDs and paid very high rates of interest to attract customers. Many clients did not realize that the value fluctuated and were surprised when they sold their CDs and received less than their original investment.

Soon, interest rates were declining and the S&Ls were still obligated to pay the high rates on these CDs. The traditional business of S&Ls was to provide home mortgages at competitive rates. As rates declined, so did mortgage interest and it became more difficult for S&Ls to earn high rates of return to pay their interest obligations.

Merrill Lynch and the brokerage firms were earning high fees for brokering deposits, and the S&Ls often paid higher interest rates than the prevailing market to attract deposits. The higher the rate paid on the deposits meant that the S&Ls had to earn even more from investing these funds to pay the interest and related expenses. Wall Street was hawkishly promoting debt instruments in the 1980s politely referred to as high-yield bonds. These bonds were actually high yielding because their credit quality was very low. Many of the bond issues financed real estate development projects. S&Ls were not restricted from purchasing these bonds, and many did in an attempt to earn higher yields on their invested capital. Unfortunately, many of these junk bonds defaulted, causing even more solvency problems for many S&Ls.

The stock market values were increasing and a merger mania emerged. There was a substantial number of takeovers. Following a takeover, the assets of a company were often sold. It became clear that the value of the parts of many companies was greater than the price of the whole company when broken apart and sold. So, many companies were bought and divisions were sold off to pay for the debt incurred to buy the company. After all, many of the corporate takeovers were financed and called leveraged buyouts.

Investment bankers would help an investor or investment group trying to buy a company by organizing the debt financing and issuing bonds. Many of these bonds had high yields and low credit quality. Some of the buyout investors were called predators because they would take over a company and sell off parts to make as much money as possible on the deal. These predators were not interested in the long-term success and viability of the target company; they were only interested in turning a quick and large profit.

The financial environment also included a plethora of new financial derivative instruments, including futures on the Standard and Poor's 500 Stock Index. Traders used this product and computers to automatically buy and sell large quantities of an index and a basket or group of stocks representative of the index to lock in a profit. This practice was called program trading and these transactions were very large. Effectively, they drove the direction of the market and were a powerful investment tool. Financial derivatives are discussed in greater detail in Chapter Eight.

The S&L problems began to emerge in the mid-1980s and were a serious concern by 1986. On Friday, October 19, 1987, the New York Stock Exchange (NYSE) experienced a collapse and incurred the largest one-day point drop in history. The regulators acted quickly to restore market confidence and avoid another market meltdown like the 1929 crash. They instituted a set of policies known as circuit breakers. The regulators recognized the impact of program trading and the ability to influence the market. So, a series of rules was established requiring that trading be halted if the NYSE experienced increases or decreases to a certain level. This trading halt was intended to restore order back to the system and prevent an emotional frenzy. The plan worked and these circuit breakers are still in place. They have been modified, though.

Mismanagement, bad loans, and bad investments were the ultimate cause of the S&L debacle, but inadequate regulation was the catalyst. Loan default rates were high. Credit was often extended to friends, fraudulent loans were widespread, and credit was frequently granted to poor credit risks. This collapse, though, had economic repercussions. Investors started looking for safer instruments for their investments and most S&Ls were holding portfolios of high-risk investments. Defaults and insolvency were inevitable and a crisis ensured. It was compounded by the fact that the FSLIC insurance was grossly underfunded.

By 1989, the S&L problems had risen to crisis proportions. It was the biggest financial failure since the Great Depression. The Financial Institutions Reform, Recovery, and Enforcement Act of 1989 (FIRREA) developed a scheme to bail out the troubled industry. An Office of Thrift Supervision was established to supervise S&Ls. It was under the jurisdiction of the U.S. Treasury Department. The FSLIC was replaced by a new Savings Association Insurance Fund that was to be controlled by the FDIC. The FDIC basically absorbed the FSLIC. The FDIC was given broad oversight authority over S&Ls. Congress had to appropriate money to finance the bailout, which they did after much debate.

The Resolution Trust Corporation (RTC) was also created to buy and sell S&Ls that were in default. It was authorized to liquidate the assets and dispose of the property from failed thrifts. In an effort to alleviate the crisis, the government turned to Wall Street. After all Wall Street had facilitated the crisis and it had money. The federal government, through the RTC, sold insolvent S&Ls at fractions of their value. The Office of Thrift Supervision replaced the Federal Home Loan Bank Board. This office regulates both the state and federally chartered institutions that are members of the Savings Association Insurance Fund (SAIF). Though the aftermath and reorganization lasted several years, the crisis was ultimately controlled, albeit at an enormous cost to American taxpayers.

The S&L crisis attracted considerable attention. There have been many books written on the subject. The title of one popular book by William Black is *The Best Way to Rob a Bank Is to Own One*. For many S&L owners, in hindsight, it was apparently true. Critics referred to the 1982 act as a license to steal. Some of the decisions made by S&Ls seemed ridiculous and excessive. For example, a Texas Savings and Loan, Lamar Savings, even had plans to open a branch on the moon.

CREDIT UNIONS

Credit unions are financial institutions organized as cooperative mutual organizations. They are owned and governed by their members, who are the account holders. Only members can have a credit union account and be authorized to use the services. Credit unions are organized as nonprofit corporations established for the benefit of the members. In order to belong to a credit union, a person must meet the membership criteria. Credit unions have been established by churches, fraternal organizations, labor unions, corporations, communities, and even the federal government.

The concept of cooperative banking in the United States appeared in 1870. The concept of a people's bank as a cooperative entity has its origins in Germany. Interest in the concept increased before the turn of the century. A formal, regulated banking system was needed to support the needs of individuals rather than businesses. Individuals were being charged exorbitant interest charges to borrow money. When borrowing from a pawnshop or wealthy lenders, an individual would often be charged 40 to 50 percent interest fees. There was a demand for a financial institution to serve the needs of the blue-collar labor force.

Credit unions are regulated by the National Credit Union Association (NCUA), which is a government agency. The NCUA evolved from the original regulatory agency called the Bureau of Federal Credit Unions. The deposit insurance for a credit union is similar to the FDIC. The credit union deposits are insured by the National Credit Union Share Insurance Fund (NCUSIF), which is overseen by the NCUA.

Credit unions are mutual or member-owned organizations. The first credit union in North America was established in 1900. Several years later, the first U.S. credit union was established in New Hampshire, in 1909, four years before the Fed was authorized. The theory behind the credit unions was to satisfy the needs of both savers and borrowers.

The first local authorization to establish a credit union was in New Hampshire. It was specially crafted for the specific purpose of allowing the creation of the Saint Mary's Cooperative Credit Association in Manchester, New Hampshire. This is the first credit union established in the United States. Credit unions were slow to gain mass appeal and the early growth was slow.

The first general state legislation concerning the incorporation of credit unions (1909) was enacted at the state level in Massachusetts. It was more comprehensive than the New Hampshire law. The law, named the Massachusetts Credit Union Act, formally defined credit unions and created formal rules for their establishment as membership organizations. Credit unions were to be governed democratically and owned by the members. They were to operate for the benefit of the members and were intended to be not-for-profit organizations. The growth of credit unions increased slightly after the creation of the Massachusetts Credit Union Association (MCUA) in 1914. The MCUA became a master credit union and provided advice and information to help other credit unions.

After World War I, the U.S. economy was prosperous and the savings rate increased during the 1920s. The growth of credit unions was adversely affected by the 1929 stock market crash and the Great Depression, but all financial institutions were affected. The first national legislation affecting credit unions was called the Federal Credit Union Act, and was signed into law in June 1934. Credit unions went on to become a permanent fixture in the U.S. financial system. As their popularity increased, the credit union movement became coordinated on both the state and federal levels. The act was among a substantial number of U.S. financial system reforms passed during 1933 and 1934. Bylaws were soon drafted for a new national organization created to promote growth and represent the interests of the credit union industry. It was called the Credit Union National Association (CUNA). The organization continues to fill this role.

COMMUNITY BANKS

There are multiple ways to define a community bank but the size is generally a key characteristic. Community banks are usually defined and identified as small institutions. They are typically locally owned and operated. They are often called independent banks because they are not part of a larger BHC. Community banks' status is determined by the asset size of the institution. Community banks are deposit-taking and -lending institutions with assets less than $1 billion.

The number of community banks is significant. About 90 percent of the banks in the United States are community banks. Their numbers, though, appear to be declining because of competitive pressures from larger financial institutions, technological advances, and a trend toward consolidation in the banking industry. Community banks have, historically, been important as depository institutions. They are also important as reliable credit sources for local residential mortgage lending, small business loans, and agricultural lending, and have a retail banking orientation.

INDUSTRIAL LOAN CORPORATIONS

There is a current debate concerning the combination of banking institutions and commercial enterprises. At the center of this controversy are industrial loan corporations (ILCs). The ILCs are special-purpose banking entities. Nonbank commercial enterprises can establish an ILC. They have banking powers and are chartered by state regulators. ILCs are FDIC insured and subject to its oversight on the federal level. Also, there are legal restrictions concerning the size and scope of services that an ILC can offer including deposits and lending. ILCs are typically established to support the financing business of a parent company. Consumer finance companies and credit card processing organizations have historically been the primary sponsors of ILCs.

There are currently about sixty ILCs in the United States. Collectively, their assets are in excess of $140 billion. Many of these ILCs are controlled by large commercial enterprises. Some examples include Target, General Electric, General Motors, General Motors Acceptance Corporation (GMAC), and Harley Davidson. Corporations in the consumer finance industry often establish these special purpose entities.

Wal-Mart attempted to purchase an existing California ILC in 2002, but withdrew its application when the California legislature enacted law changes to prevent the move. Wal-Mart submitted an application to establish an ILC in Utah. It is currently under review by the FDIC. There is considerable controversy and opposition concerning the pending Wal-Mart application. There is no evidence that there will be a problem. Those opposed indicate that they feel that Wal-Mart will exploit the ability to expand branches and gain an unfair competitive advantage.

The Federal Reserve has expressed reservations and concern about ILCs. The Fed has maintained a policy that keeps banking and commerce separate. It would like to maintain the separation between commercial firms and banks, which has historically existed in the United States. The Fed is concerned that the banking and commercial business relationship would challenge the legal boundaries separating the two. If the relationship between banks and a commercial firm were too close, it could cause the financial system to be weakened and the regulatory power of the administrators could be impaired.

The FDIC has a different, opposing position on the subject. It indicated that, as a regulator, it does not believe that the ILCs present risks any different from other banks. Further, the FDIC's position indicated that preventing commercial enterprises from establishing ILCs would stifle financial innovation.

There has been widespread criticism of allowing new ILCs, especially from the banking industry. One concern is that there would not be any regulatory barriers from the states to expanding branches throughout the nation. Further, there is concern that new ILCs affiliated with national commercial businesses may decide to compete directly with commercial banks. The relationship, without the existing regulatory boundaries, could lead to conflicts of interest that would threaten the stability and soundness of the ILC financial institution. Another argument is that regulations concerning commercial banks exist and loopholes related to ILC laws should be closed. If Wal-Mart and others are granted ILC charters, a review of how to control risks and provide adequate safeguards should be undertaken at both the state and federal level. Also, a revised regulatory approach should be considered.

MERCHANT BANKS

Businesses that grant credit have existed in some form since ancient times. They were actually considered lenders rather than bankers because they extended credit using their own assets. Deposit banking can be traced back to ancient China during the eighth century AD. Merchants accepted valuable items as deposits in order to hold them for safekeeping. The depositors paid the merchant a fee and in return the merchant issued receipts to the depositor. Eventually, depositors began to trade these receipts as forms of payment. The receipts were accepted as money and merchants began issuing more receipts than collateral on deposit.

The original merchant banks were not involved in investment banking activity. Their primary role was trade finance. Merchant banks expanded as trade with America expanded during the 1800s. Merchant banking was often risky but the potential for big profits helped to offset the risk. The practice of merchant banking originated in Europe. The first merchant banks appeared in Italy in the twelfth century. They developed to facilitate trade at the Champagne Fairs. Merchants began using their excess funds to finance trade and charged fees for the service, which came from the profits. Merchant banking operations were typically small, although several very large partnership networks were established. They were often family businesses and focused upon managing their wealth. Following their decline in Italy, merchant banks again gained prominence in Amsterdam when it emerged as a financial center in the early seventeenth century. Merchant banking expanded to London as England's global trade increased.

Merchant bankers were wealthy businessmen. Wealthy merchants or groups of wealthy merchants facilitated trade by creating businesses that would lend money to finance trade. Many made their fortunes in textiles or clothing. Lending money provided an outlet for their extra money. Wealthy merchants would keep their gold in safekeeping. The merchants made loans against their reserves, often the loans would be substantially in excess of these reserves. The merchant bankers were not just lenders; they were actively involved in the trade process. They also analyzed an opportunity to determine the profit potential and the ability to collect proceeds. It was not uncommon for the banker to be a key participant in the trade negotiation process. Merchant bankers followed a transitional path from trading in commodities to banking. When a merchant established a good reputation and wealth, banking offered an alternative to trading. Financing trade and advisory services involved lower risks and provided greater profit potential.

The role of the merchant banker expanded during the 1920s and adopted an increasingly broad financial advisory role. European merchant banks generally offer a complete range of capital markets services, especially debt or equity financing. The banks perform many of the functions that an investment banker performs in the United States. Merchant banks are not formally defined under U.S. securities and banking laws. Traditional merchant banking functions are often considered as part of investment banking, though they are distinct. The merchant bankers were traditionally a source of capital. Their business was concentrated in financing the shipping of cargo and trading commodities.

Merchant bankers in the United States concentrate on the private equity market. Private equity dealings are not publicly disclosed. They are often less expensive and bypass the regulatory filing requirements for public equity financing. Merchant banks often provide services to public companies that want to become private. The requirements for public companies imposed by the Sarbanes-Oxley Act in 2002 made compliance very expensive. Several public corporations decided that it was more strategic and economical to privatize and avoid the high cost of compliance.

CONCLUSION

Beginning in the 1980s, there was an incremental and gradual easing of the Glass-Steagall Act. As noted earlier in the chapter, Glass-Steagall was a

Depression era, post-Crash (1929) law intended to separate the business of banks, brokers, and insurance companies as a safeguard to the nation's financial system. It was also meant to rebuild confidence in the battered system. As technology advanced and multinational banks began expanding and competing internationally, U.S. financial services organizations were unable to compete effectively with European financial services firms, who were able to offer all three of these services. Many insurance companies demutualized in anticipation of opportunities that would be present in the changing business environment. The Glass-Steagall Act provisions were replaced by the GLBA in 1999 and it removed the restrictions concerning bank ownership of other types of financial services companies.

Four

Currency and National Sovereignty

THE DEMISE OF BRETTON WOODS

The United States maintained a strong economy and was able to post annual trade surpluses until 1970. The United States was in the Vietnam War and accumulated debt, too. Concerns arose that the dollar was overvalued and confidence in the dollar's strength began to deteriorate. In 1971, Richard Nixon discontinued the dollar's link to the gold standard established at Bretton Woods. The announcement came as quite a surprise to the international community. The International Monetary Fund (IMF) was not informed, and neither were the key U.S. policy advisors, notably from the U.S. State Department. This move led to nations adopting floating currency values in the foreign exchange market.

Following Nixon's declaration, a special meeting to discuss international monetary policy and exchange, called the Smithsonian meeting, was convened in Washington, DC, to reset the standard price of gold, eliminate gold convertibility requirement for Bretton Woods, and establish currency fluctuation ranges. The outcome was initially positive but could not be sustained. The Bretton Woods Agreement ultimately collapsed. The IMF's role changed as a result.

After the collapse of Bretton Woods and the subsequent devaluation of the dollar at the Smithsonian meetings, the U.S. dollar was allowed to float freely without the boundaries that previously constrained valuation. The central banks regularly intervene in the cash markets to influence valuation and correct disparities. The Smithsonian Agreement was the outcome of an international monetary conference held in 1971. The U.S. dollar was devalued against other major currencies and the range in which it would be permitted to fluctuate was expanded, but still limited. A severe U.S. recession began in 1973 and lasted into 1974. Floating exchange rates were adopted in 1973, which eliminated the narrow boundary range within which the U.S. dollar could move.

EXCHANGE RATE SYSTEMS

Barter is the exchange of goods or services among parties without using a currency as a medium of exchange. The goods or services exchanged neither meet the criteria nor possess the characteristics to qualify as a currency, as described in Chapter One. The use of money as a medium of exchange continues to facilitate international trade and the transfer of goods. New electronic trading tools and methods are increasing capabilities and opportunities as well as risks. The world's currencies are still mostly sovereign and the currency system, as well as currency exchange, is complex. Currency correlation relates to the observing and measuring of the movements and relationship in value between two currencies. Currencies and foreign exchange are described further in Chapter Seven. There are seven major world currencies. They are listed below, in alphabetical order:

Australian dollar
British pound sterling
Canadian dollar
Euro
Japanese yen
Swiss franc
U.S. dollar

There are three primary policy-based methods that countries use to manage their currency exchange rates, which determine the relative value of their home currency:

1. The free float
2. The peg
3. The managed float

The choice among the three is a matter of policy and preference and can change. A basic description of each follows.

The *free float* allows a currency value to be variable. It is permitted to fluctuate without boundaries and there is no government intervention. In a free-floating rate system, the market determines the exchange rates of currencies. Supply and demand factors in the market determine prices.

A *pegged* or *fixed-rate* currency is linked to the value of a currency of another country or a basket of currencies. There is usually a narrow trading range established with an upper and a lower boundary, between which the currency could fluctuate. Usually, currencies from countries that have a pegged exchange rate trade openly on the spot market. A fixed rate currency is often used by developing economies to provide stability to the financial system. It helps emerging markets to establish and maintain a more stable currency and can help to avoid a crash. The pegged exchange rate was created by the European Economic Community (EEC) in 1972.

A *managed float* is a combination of the free float and the peg. There are some restrictions on capital controls. The managed float is also called the dirty float. It is also frequently referred to as flexible exchange rates. The currency is not tied to a specific exchange rate, like the peg. Often, central banks will intervene in the open market and take action to support the nation's monetary policy. This helps to manage inflation. Central bank intervention also helps to stabilize the exchange rates and controls potential adverse appreciation or decline. The managed float is currently the most widely used system in the world. Critics believe that a managed float is susceptible to government manipulation.

DOLLARIZATION

Some countries use the U.S. dollar as their base currency because it is strong and stable. This concept is known as dollarization. Dollarization occurs when a country uses the dollar rather than its home currency. All of the home currency is purchased by the central bank to remove it from circulation. The central bank uses dollar reserves to make the purchases. The country no longer uses its own currency and the home currency becomes replaced by dollars.

There is considerable debate in Mexico about whether it should dollarize. The peso has historically been a weak currency relative to the dollar. Dollarization, though a partial and not an official policy, is occurring in Argentina, Paraguay, and Uruguay. Using the dollar as a currency adds monetary credibility to a country because of the dollar's stability, and prevents the capital outflows that would occur before a currency crash (i.e., by those expecting a crash). It also helps to control inflation. Many emerging countries experience high inflation, which often results in currency devaluations.

CURRENCY AND NATIONAL SOVEREIGNTY

The national currency is a symbol that is embraced in many countries, with the same passion as the national flag. The currency provides a sense of nationalist pride and is a symbol of their economic system. Making the decision to give up their national currency was an obstacle for many of the Eurozone countries. Many of the citizens in these countries objected to giving up a symbol of their national identity, their currency, to adopt the euro. Sweden chose not to participate for this reason. In fact, they even had a public referendum election in 2003. A majority of the people voted in favor of retaining the krona, Sweden's national currency, and against adopting the euro.

Russia is currently choosing a new symbol for the ruble, which is the national currency. The Russians have publicly expressed great pride in the ruble and consider it a national symbol. Many Russians also see it as symbolic of the nation's free market reforms and the success of the emerging financial system, especially their successful world-class securities exchange, the Moscow Interbank Currency Exchange (MICEX). The ruble recently reached another milestone toward the goal of becoming an international currency. In July 2006, the ruble became fully convertible. The search for a symbol for the ruble has been pared to four choices. Based upon national polls the people prefer a symbol that will enhance the country's image and serve as a display of Russian culture and heritage. The top choices include a design that incorporates Russian Cyrillic lettering and a Roman capital letter R with two strokes on the post. A prominent politician said that the symbol of the ruble is as important as the national anthem.

Great Britain, Sweden, and Denmark chose not to adopt the euro. The British consider themselves to be separate from mainland Europe and chose to remain independent of the euro to maintain their heritage of being a world power, as well as to maintain their political and monetary autonomy. In addition, they did not agree with all the requirements for euro compliance and wanted to retain the pound sterling currency. Public opinion supported the government's position not to participate. A majority continue to oppose euro participation. Clearly, money appeals to emotions and has social, political, economic, nationalistic, historical, and symbolic significance.

THE EURO STORY

On January 1, 1999, the euro was officially launched. This represented one of the most significant financial events of the twentieth century. The euro was a new common currency originally adopted by twelve European countries to replace their separate national currencies. They completely discontinued using their national currency and adopted this common currency. The euro was phased in over a two-year time period. Not all of the European Union (EU) countries adopted the euro. The UK and Switzerland chose to retain their national currencies, the pound sterling and franc, respectively.

Currencies are powerful symbols of national sovereignty. In 1999, twelve countries in the European Union adopted the euro as common currency. Corbis.

A provision of the treaty on the EU, commonly referred to as the Maastricht Treaty, authorized the European Central Bank (ECB) to issue currency and coins on behalf of the European Monetary Union (EMU) member nations. It was signed in Maastricht on February 7, 1992. The introduction of the euro was another step in eliminating boundaries to trade and commerce among European nations. The euro has become both a domestic and an international currency.

The EEC members decided to link their rates of exchange to each other's currency. This agreement created the European Monetary System or the EMS. The EMS agreed to use a basket of member currencies as a benchmark for valuation and rejected the gold standard and the U.S. dollar standard. In 1992, the EU member countries called their system the EMS Exchange Rate Mechanism or the ERM.

The Maastricht Treaty of 1992 represented an important modern financial milestone. The participants were the original twelve EU members. These nations agreed to cooperate with the integration of their monetary policy to stabilize foreign currency exchange and promote regional trade among the member states. The European Central Bank and The European Monetary Authority were also created. The European Monetary Institute (EMI) was established in 1994, following the Treaty of Maastricht. The EMI was a developmental step toward the establishment of an ECB and the introduction of the euro. The provisions of the Maastricht were developed throughout the

1990s and culminated in 1999. The exchange rates for the participating nations were established along with a shared monetary policy.

The EU nations established a new ECB in 1998. The ECB helped to facilitate the introduction and adoption of the euro. On December 31, 1998, official conversion rates were established for all eleven currencies eventually being replaced by the euro. These values are listed in Table 4.1.

The fifteen original EU members are listed below. Only twelve converted to the euro and are the nations that now comprise the eurozone. They are identified separately from the nonparticipants.

Eurozone States

1. Austria
2. Belgium
3. Finland
4. France
5. Germany
6. Greece
7. Ireland
8. Italy
9. Luxembourg
10. Netherlands
11. Portugal
12. Spain

TABLE 4.1
Nations That Have Adopted the Euro (Conversion Rates from Previous Currency)

Adopted the Euro	Previous Currency	Euro Conversion Rate
Austria	Schilling	13.7603
Belgium	Franc	40.3399
Finland	Markka	5.94573
France	Franc	6.55957
Germany	Mark	1.95583
Greece	Drachma	340.750
Ireland	Punt (or pound)	0.787564
Italy	Lira	1936.2
Luxembourg	Franc	40.3399
The Netherlands	Guilder	2.20371
Portugal	Escudo	200.482
Spain	Peseta	166.386

Eurozone Nonparticipants

1. Denmark
2. Sweden
3. United Kingdom

In January 1999, the euro was introduced as a common currency for participating nations. There was considerable uncertainty and skepticism concerning the introduction of the euro and whether the populations would accept the change. To date, the implementation and acceptance of the euro have been considered successful.

The euro was first used electronically in January 1999. A plan was agreed upon to eliminate the home currencies and phase in the euro. In January 2002, euro notes and coins were introduced into circulation. By July 2002, the single euro replaced all the individual national currencies for the participating EU countries.

On May 1, 2004, ten new member countries were admitted to the EU. These nations are required to establish financial controls and meet economic criteria before they are permitted to adopt the euro to replace their national currency. The newest ten nations are listed alphabetically below with their projected target year for euro adoption. There are now a total of twenty-five member states in the EU, including the fifteen original members.

EU Nations Admitted May 1, 2004, with Year Expected to Adopt the Euro

1. Cypress (2008)
2. Czech Republic (2010)
3. Estonia (2007)
4. Hungary (2010)
5. Latvia (2008)
6. Lithuania (2007)
7. Malta (2008)
8. Poland (undecided)
9. Slovakia (2009)
10. Slovenia (2007)

The Eurozone nations are a huge trading bloc. The total population in this market exceeds 300 million. The reduction in trade barriers and the ability to compete as well as pricing being more transparent because a single currency is being used will create substantial economic opportunities. Trade, travel, and investment will be stimulated in the region. The securities markets, including regulated exchanges, are beginning to consolidate and this trend is expected to continue.

WORLD TRADE ORGANIZATION/GATT

The World Trade Organization (WTO) is the successor to the General Agreements on Tariffs and Trade (GATT). GATT is an international trade accord that was established in 1947. Its purpose was to promote and liberalize international trade by reducing tariffs, removing import quotas, and over-coming other barriers to trade. The WTO rules are negotiated by and among the members. At the end of June 2006, the WTO had 139 members. Trade has been important to society since civilization existed.

The WTO was created in 1995. It monitors and enforces GATT provi-sions and mediates international trade disputes. The WTO has the power to issue sanctions and levy fines. The WTO decisions concerning disputes are binding upon members—an important change from GATT. Free trade promotes prosperity and over time can improve the quality of life. Im-provements, however may be slow and incremental. WTO meetings often attract controversy and protests. Activists for various causes use this highly visible international forum to express themselves by protesting and through civil disobedience. Environmental concerns have become a high-profile issue.

THE WORLD BANK

The World Bank was established in 1944. It is also known as the Inter-national Bank for Reconstruction and Development (IBRD). The World Bank is not actually a bank. It is an organization comprised of a group of five related entities. The core entities of the World Bank are the IBRD and the International Development Association (IDA). The IDA became part of the World Bank in 1960. Each of these two key institutions supports the World Bank's overall objective, which is to reduce poverty and work towards its eradication. The IBRD and the IDA each focus on different but related functions. The IBRD's constituents are creditworthy poor countries. The IDA serves only the poorest countries. Both work to provide grants for education and health infrastructure development programs as well as low-interest loans and interest-free loans to their target countries.

The role of the World Bank is to provide loans to governments to support and encourage economic development among nations. It provides loans that are funded using borrowed funds obtained by issuing bonds. These bonds are sold to governments as well as private investors. The World Bank has a for-profit orientation and does not subsidize the loans that it extends. There are currently 184 members. The five entities included in the World Bank Group and the year each was established are listed below:

1. International Bank for Reconstruction and Development (IBRD), 1945
2. International Development Association (IDA), 1960
3. International Finance Corporation (IFC), 1956
4. Multilateral Investment Guarantee Agency (MIGA), 1988
5. The International Center for Settlement of Investment Disputes (ICSID), 1966

The World Bank broadly defines institutions in the context of a country's economic development as the result of the formal laws, informal norms and practices, and organizational structures within a given environmental setting. This definition is especially applicable to developing countries faced with the challenge of establishing a reliable financial infrastructure and a healthy free-market economy. Institutions are the social frameworks within which humans interact. They serve to define the cooperative and competitive relationships in society and economic order. The major role of an institution in society is to establish a stable (although not necessarily efficient) structure, which reduces uncertainty in human interaction. Organizational institutions, both private and public, have ethical and legal obligations to society.

THE INTERNATIONAL FINANCE CORPORATION

The International Finance Corporation (IFC) was created in 1956, and is currently owned by 178 member nations. It is affiliated with the World Bank and functions as an independent financing entity to support the private sector in developing nations. The IFC consciously provides support to the private sector rather than to the government or public sector. The IFC will not accept any government guarantees as part of its financing operations in order to remain independent. The IFC's objective is to promote economic growth through private sector investment and market development. It provides support through loans to companies and sometimes by taking an equity or ownership stake in an enterprise. The IFC mitigates risks by providing a small percentage of the funding that an organization needs, usually about 10 percent to 15 percent. It has 178 members.

The IFC plays a key role in directing private capital flows to developing nations and transitioning economies. In 1981, it was responsible for creating the term *emerging markets*. The IFC adopted the use of syndicated loans in the

1970s to introduce new sources of capital and financing to business enterprises in developing nations. A syndicated loan involves a group of banks that collectively provide a large loan. By pooling the group's capabilities, larger loans can be issued and all the risks are shared among the banks. The IFC helped the former Soviet nations convert state-owned enterprises into privately owned businesses.

The IFC is moving beyond individual private sector enterprises and is focusing, more strategically, on development of a capital market infrastructure. It is becoming increasingly more involved in public-private partnerships, corporate governance, ethics, and stock markets. The IFC adopted a socially responsible approach and takes a long-term view of the environment and the impact of industrial development. It has had an impact on improving living standards in emerging nations and continues to develop innovative programs to help reduce poverty levels.

The IFC is presently working hard to attract investment to countries in South America and Central America. In its fifty-year existence, from 1956 through 2005, the IFC applied $49 million of its own to emerging nations to promote economic growth. In addition, according to the IFC, it coordinated $24 billion in syndicated loans to help 3,319 companies located in 140 developing countries.

THE INTERNATIONAL MONETARY FUND

The idea for the IMF was developed by representatives from forty-four governments participating in the Bretton Woods conference in 1944. The delegates determined that a program to promote economic cooperation could be developed to provide intervention to avoid financial crisis. The IMF was established in December 1945 when twenty-nine countries signed the formal articles of agreement to form the organization as a permanent institution. The IMF is based in Washington, DC. There are 184 global members who govern the organization. It is often confused with the World Bank because both organizations were conceived at the Bretton Woods meeting. The IMF's goals and objectives are different.

The IMF supports and promotes the well-being of the global economy. Its objective is to stabilize the world's monetary system. The members pledge to provide financial assistance to nations if a serious economic crisis emerges. The IMF attempts to convince countries to follow financial policies intended to maintain economic stability. The IMF is actually a fund. It provides temporary emergency financing when countries have problems with their balance of payments. The balance of payments is a measure of the total flow of money into or out of a country for a period of time. The actual number is the net total obtained by subtracting the cash outflows from the cash inflows. If the number is positive, there is a surplus. If the balance is negative, there is a deficit. A deficit is an unfavorable position.

The IMF is an important institution for international trade because of its position as the central institution of the international monetary system. The international monetary system represents the complex relationship of international payments and the interaction of currency exchange rates that function to facilitate, promote, and sustain international trade.

According to the IMF's statutory purposes, it supports global prosperity by promoting the following four activities:

1. Balanced expansion of world trade
2. Stability of exchange rates
3. Avoidance of competitive currency devaluations
4. Orderly correction of balance of payments problems

In order to support these four activities, the IMF engages in a variety of research, surveillance, advisory, technical, and intervention functions. The IMF actively monitors the policies and economic environment of its members, from a macroeconomic perspective. It also provides the central banks and governments of its member countries with consultancy assistance. It provides training support and technical assistance to help member countries develop their infrastructure. The IMF also provides emergency loans to countries encountering severe payment problems. These loans are accompanied by expert analysis to identify the root cause of the problem and develop policies for reform.

THE BANK FOR INTERNATIONAL SETTLEMENTS

The Bretton Woods Agreement initially intended to abolish the Bank for International Settlements (BIS) because the participants were suspicious and concerned about BIS activities during World War II. The European central bankers fought to keep the BIS and eventually prevailed. The BIS became an important institution and played an important role in the reconstruction of Europe. It helped to implement the Bretton Woods Agreement and proved to be a staunch defender and supporter.

The BIS was established in 1930, from the Hague Agreements. It was initially involved with German reparation payments imposed by the Treaty of Versailles. The role of the BIS was refocused to become a centralized organization for promoting cooperation among central banks. The BIS is a forum for the central banks from the largest capitalist nations.

It is known as the central bank for central banks as well as the lender of last resort. The charter for the BIS established five major objectives:

- Promoting free trade
- Facilitating interest-rate stability
- Urging cooperation among nations for monetary concerns
- Ensuring free movement of funds among nations
- Assisting nations to make debt repayments and to correct international payment imbalances

The BIS is the oldest international financial institution, with its headquarters located in Basel, Switzerland. The location was selected because of its accessibility. The BIS also maintains offices in Mexico City and Hong Kong. It is an important organization and influences the world's financial architecture. It sponsors regular meetings of international central bank officials in Basel to discuss policy. This was the source of the Basel Accord of 1988 and the revision called Basel II. Basel II is addressed in Chapter Nine. The BIS collects and conducts extensive financial research, which is available to the public.

FINANCIAL INSTITUTION DEFINED

The term *institution* is used loosely in the financial services industry and has multiple definitions. Two are used herein. The first is the practical industry jargon as applied to financial institutions, for example a banking institution. This industry business definition recognizes financial institutions as organizations. This term differentiates companies or corporate entities (such as a wholesale or business customer of a bank, broker, or securities exchange) from the level of the retail customer. Individuals are retail customers. An institutional customer is usually another institution and can include banks, brokerage firms, investment banks, pension funds, hedge funds, and corporations.

The securities exchange is established as an institution. Securities exchanges are legitimized institutions that efficiently allocate resources for the market. Securities exchanges function as an institutional mechanism within the economic infrastructure of a nation and serve as a centralized forum for raising, allocating, and accumulating capital, and shifting risks. This role is essential for sustaining a strong and stable economic infrastructure. The quasi-public securities exchanges historically were analogous to public utilities. Until the early 1970s, U.S. financial exchanges were often described as providing a utility-like function. They were also considered quasi-public organizations because of their role, registered form, nonprofit status, and regulatory responsibilities and obligations.

A major trend in the financial services industry is the privatization of securities exchanges. The transformation is called demutualization. Demutualized exchanges are changing from nonprofit organizations to for-profit private corporations. Privatization of securities exchanges is characterized by a change of legal form and status and a different or modified ownership structure. Demutualization gives exchange owners the opportunity to maximize the value of their undervalued or underutilized internal assets. In some cases, an exchange will become listed on a regulated exchange for public trading. Examples of securities exchanges that have demutualized are the New York Stock Exchange (NYSE), the Chicago Mercantile Exchange (CME), Eurex, and Euronext.

A strong system of banking and lending to facilitate business expansion and economic growth in a home country cannot be established in emerging nations with free-market economies without strong securities exchanges. Exchanges facilitate access to the capital markets and enable business to expand resulting in economic growth. This growth leads to jobs, better wages, and stability, which benefit society. A fair and efficient capital market is a public good and is especially relevant in a transitioning economy. An effective securities exchange is a core element of a nation's capital market structure. The exchange must instill trust and maintain investor confidence to be effective. Economic stability is also important, especially in emerging markets. Specialized laws governing the exchanges and designated public regulatory bodies must also be a part of a nation's economic infrastructure, but these legal elements, including regulation, are beyond the scope of this work.

COMPETITION

Now technological innovation is causing the securities industry and exchange infrastructure to change. It is also stimulating competition. The need for a physical exchange facility no longer exists. Automated computer systems can accomplish all exchange functionality quite efficiently and communication no longer needs to be face-to-face. The high cost and infrastructure barriers to entry have been eliminated because of computer and telecommunications technologies. Technological advances have also reduced the cost per transaction.

Competition, especially if it is based on greater efficiency and lower costs, presents a compelling reason for an exchange to abandon the mutual status and adopt a for-profit legal form. Technological advances enabled alternative, automated trading systems that changed the fundamental exchange architecture by eliminating the need for a physical trading floor. The physical trading floor is being rendered obsolete. New, innovative financial products and services are being introduced, too. Financial services firms are engaging in financial engineering to actively develop innovative products and services to compete more effectively.

REFERENCE WEB SITES

The Bank for International Settlements, www.bis.org.

The International Finance Corporation, www.ifc.org.

The International Monetary Fund, www.imf.org.

The World Bank, www.worldbank.org.

The World Trade Organization, www.wto.org.

Five

Financial Exchanges, Globalization, and Technology

Formal and regulated financial markets established as a centralized forum for trading securities, derivatives, or commodities are called exchanges. Financial exchanges function as a centralized marketplace for raising, allocating, and accumulating capital, and shifting risks. This role is important to a nation's economic infrastructure and to the effective functioning of the economy. Securities exchanges are an integral part of a free market economy and have traditionally occupied a quasi-public role, which is analogous to that of a utility. In the late 1980s, the interaction of technological advances, competition, and globalization changed the traditional model of exchange architecture and operation. Derivative products, primarily futures and options, have been responsible for explosive financial exchange growth since the early 1980s. They are used primarily for financial risk management.

The performance of domestic financial markets is often used as an indicator of the overall strength of a nation's economy. Financial exchanges also contribute to wealth creation. The financial services industry is extremely competitive. The exchanges in highly developed industrialized nations are more specialized than those in smaller, developing nations. The specialized exchanges are sophisticated and technically advanced, and attract high trading volumes. Competitors often adopt their successful practices and product concepts. Membership of financial exchanges is made up of bank and broker intermediaries, who seek to generate revenues and maximize their own profits.

The term *financial exchange* is a generic and generalized concept that includes all the registered, regulated, and formal exchange markets in the world. Some specialize in a specific type of financial product or instrument; others are broader and may include multiple categories of financial instruments. For example, an exchange may support stock or equities trading, but it may also

Banks, exchanges, and other financial institutions employ highly
sophisticated technologies to enable real-time transactions around
the world. Getty Images/Kim Steele.

offer options or other derivatives, bonds, commodities, and futures. There is
no standard model for the financial instruments offered by an exchange. For
example, NASDAQ is a stock exchange; the Chicago Mercantile Exchange
offers derivative instruments; and stocks and bonds (primarily stocks) trade
on the New York Stock Exchange. The instruments developed and offered
by an exchange are an area of intense competition and a catalyst for innovation.

A brief history of the present-day financial exchange is a useful reference in
understanding the reasons behind its accelerating pace of growth and scope of
change as well as its new challenges. The conditions leading to the development and rapid growth of the modern financial exchange are examined
from the 1970s to the present. The industry changes that occurred in the
United States are the primary focus and are used as a baseline. The relationship among exchanges, the impact of change, and the influence of advances on other major exchanges throughout the world are also described.

MILESTONES IN FINANCIAL HISTORY

Although widely debated, the origin of the traditional securities exchange model is believed to date back to the Amsterdam Stock Exchange founded in 1602. Regardless of the actual origin, securities exchanges evolved and proliferated into national institutions and a global industry. Exchanges were created to provide a reliable centralized forum, control access, and reduce the costs of trade. Technological advances have influenced the evolution of financial markets. Communications technology, from the telegraph, to the telephone, and to the Internet, substantially enhanced exchange accessibility and growth. The mass computerization trend begun in the 1980s has enabled broad geographical expansion while, at the same time, blurring national borders as meaningful boundaries for securities exchanges. It has also triggered intense competition. New, low-cost, fully automated trading systems are siphoning business directly from bank and broker financial intermediaries. In some markets, like the United States, they have been successful as low-cost alternatives to exchange trading.

Since the early 1970s, the pace of innovation and market growth has been increasing steadily. Historical quantitative data from exchanges in general is extremely scarce for the period prior to World War II. There are some exceptions, though, and noteworthy research studies analyzing the origins of the London, Paris, and New York exchanges have been published and widely recognized.

Trading on U.S. exchanges was limited exclusively to members until the 1970s. Members had to make a substantial investment to purchase a seat or membership entitling them to certain privileges, including access to trading. Only members of a financial exchange have been given trading privileges. Thus, membership effectively serves to limit the participants and restrict direct access to exchange trading. An exchange membership is referred to as a seat. The exchange has only a fixed number of seats available. If a party wants to purchase a seat, he or she must do so from an existing member at a price negotiated between the buyer and the seller. The price of a seat varies depending on the current economic conditions.

In 1973, the Chicago Board Options Exchange (CBOE) was established. It represented an industry milestone and was the original forum for exchange-traded stock options, which are derivative instruments. Previously, stock options were only traded on a customized negotiated basis in the over-the-counter (OTC) market. Exchange-traded options contracts were standardized and liquid. By 1985, trading for stock index futures was a growing market. They were a valuable tool for portfolio managers and nonbank financial institutions such as insurance companies, mutual funds, and pension funds. Stock index futures were used as a tool to hedge against risks and for computer-based strategies. By 1987, these instruments were being employed for a variety of investment management strategies, including arbitrage.

The financial markets have experienced unprecedented growth and an accelerated pace of change driven by the convergence of technological advances, competition, and globalization. The world economy has grown parallel to increasing demand for capital and tools with which to manage multiple complex risks.

The personal computer, introduced in 1981, contributed to the widespread improved financial analysis and new methods and strategies for trading the innovative derivative instruments and market indices. Complex strategies and optimal timing techniques were developed using computer programs, simulations, and back testing. An outcome of this capability was the proliferation of program trading, which is a term describing a variety of computer-driven trading strategies. Program trading can take place on foreign exchanges, and trading strategies often include multiple exchanges. Program trading was responsible, in part, for the highly volatile markets in the late 1980s. In fact, the market crash of October 19, 1987, was attributed to program trading. Later investigations led to the development of exchange circuit breakers to restrict program trading and, thus, to control volatility after the market has increased or decreased to a predetermined level.

In 1986, The London Stock Exchange (LSE) changed from a trading-floor-based model to a networked scheme using modern communications technology. This change is referred to in the industry as the Big Bang. The Big Bang liberalized the UK's financial services industry, including the regulations governing financial exchange trading and membership. The changes led to the development of a more competitive, modernized financial exchange infrastructure, which reinforced London's role as a major financial center.

Exchange automation has reduced the transaction costs for executing trades and eliminated the need for a physical trading floor. Competition is increasingly intense and securities exchanges are consolidating and attempting to become more competitive through demutualization. Exchanges compete for order flow and critical mass to create liquidity and fast executions. Ironically, a high degree of liquidity, created by a critical mass of concentrated and centralized order flow, attracts more order flow and leads to greater liquidity. It builds trust, confidence, and reliability, and enhances the reputation of the exchange.

FINANCIAL EXCHANGE: LEGAL DEFINITION

The Securities Exchange Act of 1934 formally defines an exchange as "any organization, association, or group of persons, whether incorporated or unincorporated, which constitutes, maintains, or provides a market place or facilities for bringing together purchasers and sellers of securities or for otherwise performing with respect to securities the functions commonly performed by a stock exchange as that term is generally understood, and includes the market place and the market facilities maintained by such exchange."[1] In the *Handbook of the World's Stock, Derivatives, and Commodities Exchanges*, securities exchanges are defined as,

Centralized markets where issuers raise capital and participants buy and sell securities. In essence, an exchange needs to offer one of four things:

1. A place (real or virtual) where buyers and sellers can meet.
2. The ability to capture pre- and post-trade information—and facilitate the widest possible dissemination of this information to all investors, efficiently and without discrimination.
3. Rules that are enforced, not so much as to stifle trade, but sufficient to provide reasonable protection for the naïve against the unscrupulous.
4. And finally, protection against counterparty risk.[2]

In general, regardless of organizational form, a financial exchange serves the public good by providing several important functions. A financial exchange, either for-profit or nonprofit, must operate with efficiency and integrity. An exchange entity is expected to act in a rational manner to protect and enhance the business of the exchange. It will also establish rules and enforce the regulations intended to protect the markets and maintain public trust. The best interests of an exchange are not always consistent with the rational interests of the individual member organizations. Actually, as a result of substantial growth and significant changes in the industry worldwide, the long-term interests of members and the exchange are divergent.

INDUSTRY TRENDS AND CHALLENGES

There are three significant factors influencing change in the financial services industry. They are competition, technological innovation, and globalization. All the major global exchanges use electronic order technologies to support their trading operations; even the trading floors are using a specialist system. Many traditional exchanges, however, have abandoned the trading floor model and have switched to screen-based automated trading systems.

In Europe, the launch of a single currency, the euro, represents another event that will impact and change the way that exchanges operate. It has eased cross-border cash flows and has been, in part, a reason for some of the exchange mergers, alliances, cooperative agreements, and joint venture initiatives.

AUTOMATION: OPEN OUTCRY (AUCTIONS) VERSUS ELECTRONIC (AUTOMATED) EXCHANGES

The world's open outcry or auction exchanges are gradually being replaced by electronic, fully automated exchanges. The automation trend provides benefits to exchanges that cannot be ignored. The benefits include improved efficiency, economic and cost advantages, the ability to optimize technological capabilities, and competitive differentiation. The traditional trading floor is being rendered obsolete by technological advances, increased automation, public acceptance, regulatory recognition, and legal legitimacy. There are no longer any major European exchanges with a trading floor employing the open outcry auction model. The United States has been slower to respond to the inevitable change. Ultimately, exchanges are adapting not only to be competitive but also, realistically, to survive.

The parties involved in the open outcry model have resisted change in the United States. Many of the parties involved in the trading floor operation are also part of an exchange's mutual ownership structure. However, the automation trend is clearly not a passing fad. It is a fundamental business requirement and a key element of strategic intent and planning. It is obviously difficult for owners of an open outcry exchange, who rely upon the trading floor to maintain their business, to embrace a change to an electronic format and, as a consequence, eliminate the current profitable system. This conflict of interest is another catalyst driving the demutualization movement. The traditional member/owner mutual structure will not necessarily result in decisions that are in the best long-term interest of the exchange. The members will act in a rational self-interested manner, which may result in short-term advantages but will not be in the long-term or strategic best interest of an exchange.

Historically, the barriers to enter the exchange industry have been high. Some governments have regulations limiting membership and preventing competition to protect national exchanges. Often, the exchange is a source of national pride and is symbolic of a country's economic system. Some exchanges are subsidized by the national government and protected as monopolies. The financial exchange function is institutionalized and has evolved into a global industry, the scale of which grew substantially from its humble beginnings as a mechanism to create orderly access to a potential trading partner. The regulated exchange was legitimized by the utility-like role it played in a free market economy.

New electronic competitors are changing the rules of trading. No longer is a physical trading floor necessary. Actually, a physical presence is no longer required. Virtually all parts of the trade, through final processing, clearing, and settlement, can be done more efficiently electronically. So, will exchanges continue to exist? The answer is probably, but not likely in their present model. Eliminating the intermediaries offers exchanges an opportunity to bypass the brokers and dealers and to establish a relationship directly with the customer end user. This mode of operation is probably not appropriate for exchanges in emerging markets. Establishing stability, trust, and integrity are critical, and, for that reason, radically changing the traditional model would prove to be quite risky. Exchanges in emerging markets should follow, instead, a traditional model that protects the interests of the intermediaries. In this way, the exchange can become a stable part of a sustainable and advanced financial infrastructure.

Technological advances have had a significant impact on financial markets. Electronic finance has existed for more than a century. The NYSE surpassed the Philadelphia Stock Exchange (PHLX) to become the most important exchange in the United States because it dominated access to the telegraph system. Fedwire, an electronic communications system, has been in use since 1918. Modern electronic communication now includes both voice and data transmissions and, because of the proliferation of the Internet, has a much broader geographical reach. The result is an opportunity to acquire new service delivery channels and expand into new potential markets. In general, technological advance is an important factor driving changes in the financial exchange industry.

ELECTRONIC EXCHANGES

Electronic trading is transforming financial exchanges. Advances in communications technology provide people around the world with massive amounts of information and the ability to respond to this information easily and quickly. There is also a convergence of communications technologies, both voice and data, with automation capabilities that create economies of scale and improve efficiency. Remote access to information in real time and the ability to have global financial markets available twenty-four hours a day, seven days a week is on the horizon.

During the 1980s and 1990s, expensive communication networks were necessary to access and share information with exchanges and trading intermediaries. The advances in computing power and affordable information technologies have contributed to the growth as well as the structural changes that have occurred at major financial exchanges since the early 1970s. The exchanges have historically demonstrated a strong appetite for consuming leading-edge technologies.

Automation and the growth of electronic exchanges present new strategic challenges. Reliance on computer automation is increasing and the role of the human participants is declining. Alternative Trading Systems (ATSs) and Electronic Communications Networks (ECNs) represent a transformational new electronic alternative trading model for financial exchanges that is changing the competitive environment and the culture of traditional exchanges. The ATS and ECN concepts have become widely accepted and are now considered mainstream in the industry. Alternative Trading Systems were officially defined and legitimized under the Regulation of Exchanges and Alternative Trading Systems (known as the ATS Act) enacted in December 1998. This SEC regulation defined the regulatory framework and requirements necessary to create a new and significant trading venue.

The 1998 ATS regulation modified the definition of an exchange. The SEC's revised description of an exchange is "any organization, association, or group of persons that: (1) brings together the orders of multiple buyers and sellers; and (2) uses, established, non-discretionary methods (whether by providing a trading facility or by setting rules) under which such orders interact with each other, and the buyers and sellers entering such orders agree to the terms of a trade."[3]

ELECTRONIC COMMUNICATIONS NETWORKS AND THEIR IMPACT

The ATS designation is a generalized category. The ECNs are an automated matching system and can execute a trade almost instantly, both efficiently and economically. ECNs have also been called virtual exchanges because they do not require a traditional trading floor and the related physical infrastructure. As a result, they have reduced overhead costs, both fixed and variable. ECNs can be described as private electronic trading systems with a for-profit motive.

The Internet's access capabilities complement automation technologies, which are increasing efficiency at exchanges and reducing costs. Voice and data communications, data processing, and the increase of personal computing power are converging technologies and are collectively creating synergy that is enabling new competition and changing the traditional financial exchange industry. The Internet, with its capabilities for wireless remote electronic communication, is changing the industry and leading to innovation. It might ultimately be a driving force behind disintermediation among financial exchanges.

DEMATERIALIZATION

Another change that has been gradually occurring in the United States and around the world is the trend toward electronic record keeping. This trend is known as dematerialization and applies to the elimination of paper documents. The industry refers to the use of physical certificates as physical form. The physical form is being replaced by book entry form, which is a computer entry designating ownership of a security. There are multiple advantages to using a computer entry. There are obvious cost savings; a computer entry makes registration and transfer much easier. It also requires less physical space than a vault for certificates. Counterfeiting is also minimized. Unfortunately, different types of fraud opportunities and security challenges exist for the book entry form of record keeping. In 2003, the Group of Thirty (G-30) recommended the elimination of paper certificates throughout the world in favor of an electronic book entry. The U.S. SEC estimated that totally eliminating paper certificates would save exchanges, intermediaries, and the customers about $265 million per year.

COMPETITION

Competition, according to George Hayek, is a discovery process and is more effective than regulation. Regulation is unlikely to be the most effective way to determine, understand, and account for all the various interests and associated complexities that will converge in a market. Competition is the most effective method to accommodate the needs of the participants in a market and is necessary for a market to operate efficiently. Competitive financial exchanges are critical to maintaining a nation's free market economic system and require some degree of regulation to protect the integrity of the exchange and to prevent abuses.

Competition is the reason most often cited as a determinant for market structure and overall exchange behavior. Consolidation is creating larger and more diverse financial exchanges. The range of securities and derivatives choices available on a given exchange is expanding. Exchanges are entering into an unprecedented number of cooperative agreements such as strategic alliances, partnerships, and joint ventures. Several aggressive exchanges, such as Eurex and Euronext, have expanded operations beyond their national boundaries to challenge and directly compete with U.S. exchanges. These exchanges have broadened and modified their product offerings to compete in the U.S. market, principally in Chicago and New York. Competition in the securities industry is globalizing and intensifying. It stimulates innovation, and the net result is greater efficiency, improved service, new products, and reduced costs.

GLOBALIZATION AND INTERNATIONALIZATION

Globalization promotes the expansion of free and open markets among nations. It encourages the transfer and exchange of knowledge because of reduced barriers. Political, legal, and economic/financial institutions support globalization. Collectively they enable society to develop common values and a civil conscience, and to improve standards of living.

Thomas Friedman suggests that globalization replaced the cold war as the main focus of the international system. The cold war drained global resources and constrained free trade. Globalization represents the expansion of trade beyond national borders and includes the integration of technology, capital, and information. Decentralization and denationalization are considered characteristics of globalization. Financial firms, especially large multinational organizations, are expanding their operations throughout the world. Exchanges, too, are crossing national borders and competing in foreign countries. The globalization trend and intense competition are resulting in strategic alliances, partnerships, and new business combinations among financial exchanges.

A recent study by the McKinsey Global Institute examined the financial assets (bank deposits, government securities, corporate debt, and equity securities) of over 100 nations and estimated the present value of the world's financial markets at $118 trillion (U.S.). They forecast that the capital markets, based on current growth trends, would increase in size to a valuation of $200 trillion (U.S.) by the year 2010. The high projected growth rate is staggering, considering that the same financial assets were valued at $12 trillion in 1980 and $53 trillion in 1993.

GLOBALIZATION DEFINED

Globalization has multiple definitions and different interpretations among contingent parties. We will use the term *globalization* in the standard context of economic globalization. According to the International Monetary Fund (IMF), it is a historical process, which is a function of innovation and technological progress. The process increases economic integration among nations throughout the world.

Globalization is a macroeconomic concept that can be more thoroughly conceptualized by identifying its key characteristics:

1. The expansion and growth of multilateral trade
2. Increased economic cooperation
3. The erosion of national borders as boundaries
4. A reduction or elimination of trade barriers

5. The growth of foreign direct investment
6. The establishment of strategic relationships, which significantly increases inter-dependence

Financial institutions and exchanges are an important part of globalization because they serve as the conduits for the exchange of capital and provide access to risk-management tools. A significant and appropriate characteristic of modern globalization is the integration of markets. Financial exchanges are increasingly competing in foreign markets and are confronted with new challenges from market entrants. Globalization also enables technology and knowledge to be transferred through trade channels and other exchange mechanisms and is, therefore, accelerating the pace of change.

A country's national financial exchange is typically a source of national pride, a barometer for economic measurement, and the nucleus of a country's financial system, as well as an institutional cornerstone representing a free market economy. Technological innovations are changing the architecture and facade of the financial exchange but, as an institution, its fundamental purpose, role, and function are unchanged.

REGIONALIZATION AND TRADE

One method of internationalization is through formal regionalization. Geographical trading blocs such as the EU, NAFTA, CAFTA, MERCU-SOR, and ASEAN were created to reduce barriers at national borders and streamline trade and economic growth among the member states of a respective bloc.

The North American Free Trade Agreement (NAFTA) includes Canada, the United States, and Mexico. The three NAFTA nations represent a population of approximately 400 million. It is the largest trading bloc in the world when measured by GDP. Although still controversial, NAFTA has had some successes. Various studies indicate that Mexico's economy has grown since joining the North American trading bloc and that the pace of growth is increasing. The NAFTA treaty became effective in 1994.

Today, the European Union (EU) is a powerful regional trading block and is the product of a transitional evolution. The modern history of the organization of the countries in Europe for economic and monetary cooperation can be traced to the European Economic Union (EEU), which was formally established in 1957. The preliminary discussions leading to the establishment of the EU were optimistic but cautious. The groundwork and agreement to proceed were accomplished at the Rome Summit in 1990. It was the basis for a full year of intense negotiations and debate among nations, which concluded in a compromise with the adoption of the Maastricht Treaty on European Union (EU) in December 1991. The EU attempted to unite all the European nations, implement institutional reform, eliminate trade and travel barriers, promote economic growth and policy coordination, establish common currency, and create a centralized financial system. It partially succeeded in issuing and converting to the euro as a standard currency unit in 2000. As of July 2005, the population of the EU totals nearly 460 million people. There are several nations that did not participate and continued to use and maintain their own national money, most notably the UK. The reasons most often cited for opting not to participate were related to concerns about threats to national sovereignty. The EU continues to work toward the integration of policy and politics and is still negotiating a common constitution.

The Association of South East Asian Nations (ASEAN), another trading bloc, was established as a regional organization in 1967, but became a regional free trade zone in 1992. Critics contend that some of the free trade bloc agreement nations have been engaging in protectionist practices and contend that being within a large trading bloc facilitates the practice.

Regional trading blocs are established for two fundamental reasons. The first is to eliminate barriers to trade among nations that are proximally located and facilitate the cross-border transfer of jobs, mobility of people, trade of goods and services, and interchange of knowledge and technical expertise. In addition, the agreements are intended to establish common goals, promote cooperation, and maintain goodwill and continued participation. The nations involved in the various blocs are often culturally similar because of their proximity and have comparable political ideologies.

The second function of these trading blocs is to create a new unified regional market and establish economies of scale. The EU, ASEAN, and NAFTA represent huge geographically linked populations. The synergy, capabilities, and global influence of the trading blocs are considerably more substantial than nations acting unilaterally.

The World Trade Organization (WTO), a global trade group established in 1995, replaced the General Agreement on Tariffs and Trade (GATT). The WTO, with a membership of 150 nations, is supposed to facilitate the reduction or elimination of international trade barriers, promote trade, establish policies, provide training and technical assistance, and mediate disputes among members.

All nations do not share the benefits of globalization equitably. According to the IMF, per capita income in developing countries increased faster than in the rich countries. The evidence indicates that globalization is causing income rates to converge and the income disparity between globalizing nations is closing. However, the income gap among rich countries and nations that have not begun to globalize has actually increased. Evidence seems to indicate that international trade is an important factor influencing improved economic performance, and increased standards of living and capital market integration. Emerging and transitioning economies are often at risk because they lack technical, economic, and legal infrastructure and institutions.

SUMMARY

The traditional securities exchange model is changing and several factors are collectively introducing challenges and opportunities. Competition, globalization, and technology are the impetus for innovation and change. Modern computer and communications technologies allow emerging markets to rapidly develop effective automated systems to support exchange-traded financial instruments. The larger, more developed financial exchanges are likely to increase their importance and significance throughout the world by growing larger, stifling competition, and providing the most liquid trading forum.

NOTES

1. I. Domowitz and R. Lee, "On the Road to Reg ATS: A Critical History of the Regulation of Automated Trading Systems," *International Finance* 4, no. 2 (2004): 279–302.

2. *Handbook of the World's Stock, Derivatives, and Commodities Exchanges* (Batchworth, Herts, UK: Mondo Visione, 2004).

3. Securities and Exchange Commission, 17 CFR Parts 202, 240, 242, and 249, release no. 34-40760; file no. S7-12-98.

Six

Capital Markets and Bonds

Capital markets include securities that take more than a year to mature and the associated markets and exchanges through which these securities are traded. When a financial instrument is created or packaged and initially sold to the public, the transaction takes place in the primary market. Following the introduction, any subsequent transactions are said to take place in the secondary market. Formal regulated securities exchanges provide a forum for secondary market transactions. The over-the-counter (OTC) market refers to transactions that occur outside of the domain of formal regulated exchanges.

There are multiple significant segments of the financial markets, each serving an important role and function. The capital markets match those with funds to invest with the net users of capital for periods longer than one year. Stocks are considered long term because they can be held indefinitely. Bonds typically have a fixed maturity date. However, there have been several perpetual bond issues recently introduced. These perpetual bonds have no fixed maturity date and pay interest indefinitely. The term *equity market* is used to define the markets in which stocks are traded. The terms *debt market* or *fixed-income market* describe the markets in which bonds are traded.

Equity securities, representing ownership, are primarily shares of stock. The shares are listed and traded on various securities exchanges. The stock market is addressed in another volume is this series. When a company's stock is issued to the public for the first time, the process is called an initial public offering (IPO). The IPOs are presold in the primary market and then listed on an exchange (secondary market) for the public to buy and sell transactions. The world's formal securities exchanges are in a state of transition driven by multiple interrelated factors. Bonds most often trade in the OTC market.

What if an organization needs funds for less than a year? If financial instruments are issued and traded for a term less than one year, the transactions occur in the money market, the forward market, or the foreign exchange (forex) market (including the spot market). Debt securities are often issued for periods less than one year to satisfy short-term borrowing. These short-term debt instruments and their related financial derivatives constitute the money market. The forward market is an OTC negotiated market that is largely unregulated. Participants contractually agree to purchase or exchange a fixed amount of a currency by a future mutually agreed upon date. The foreign exchange market includes transactions for buying and selling international currencies and the associated derivative instruments. These are discussed further in Chapter Seven. The explosive growth of consumer credit and the revolution caused by the proliferation of credit card use are described in Chapter Eight.

THE BOND MARKET

What if you need money for some purpose today, but do not have any? What are your alternatives? What if a company needs money for a big project, a purchase, or even operating expenses? How do public or governmental bodies finance expenditure when they do not have enough money to cover their projected needs? Usually, the money is borrowed, although the method may vary according to the nature and objectives of the borrower. Consumers create huge debts just by using a credit card. Automobiles and major appliances are frequently purchased with consumer credit borrowing. Corporations avoid using a bank intermediary and often borrow money directly from investors by issuing bonds. Public institutions and governmental entities frequently issue bond instruments to borrow funds. States, local municipalities, government agencies, and even the federal government issue bonds as debt to raise capital. Debt is a driving force in funding the economy. Of course, it must be repaid. Accordingly, investors of bond instruments need to be aware of the credit quality of the institution or organization issuing a bond.

A bond is a debt instrument and can be considered an IOU (which stands for "I owe you"). It represents a promise to return funds that are being borrowed from investors. The bond contractually represents an amount to be repaid. The issuer of a bond typically has two payment obligations to the investor. These obligations are the return principal and periodic interest

Bonds are issued to raise capital, often to support large-scale development projects. Corbis.

payments. The principal is the amount borrowed or the face value of a bond (par), which must be repaid on a stated maturity date.[1] The interest is an obligation that is paid by the debtor. It is payable at regular predetermined intervals and can be fixed or variable, according to the specific terms of a bond issue.

Bond markets are increasing in complexity and expanding internationally. Several U.S. regulatory bodies are responsible for overseeing and governing various aspects of the bond market. The primary regulators include the Securities and Exchange Commission (SEC), the National Association of Securities Dealers (NASD), and the individual state securities commissions. Most bond issuers are required to file regulatory documents with the SEC, although there are many exceptions. The SEC is working to provide improved oversight, greater reporting requirements for traders, and improved transparency and openness to bond-trading markets. The NASD governs the brokers and dealers who are licensed to sell securities. Each state has its own securities commission, which enforces rules and regulations that apply specifically to that particular state.

A document called an indenture must accompany a bond issue. This important document explicitly describes the terms of bond offering and is the legal agreement/contract between a bond issuer (debtor) and the investors. It specifies the rights of the bondholders and is provided to all the bond investors, by law. Potential investors, upon request, are also entitled to review the indenture. Often the important terms of an indenture are summarized in an offering circular. These documents are issued for information purposes and are not intended to be a solicitation.

The registrar is an entity, often a bank, which maintains records of the registered owners of a bond issue and also acts as the paying agent for interest payments. Bonds are usually issued in registered form, meaning that the security is legally registered in the name of the owner. Formerly, many bonds were issued without listing the registered owner's name. The holder or bearer of the bond was entitled to receive principal and interest when due just by presenting a coupon for payment or submitting the bond for redemption for the principal at maturity. These bonds were called bearer bonds. There are still some outstanding bearer bonds in circulation, but they are not really issued now because it is difficult to track profits and they were often used for money laundering, tax evasion, and other illicit purposes. Also, because the owner is not recorded and registered, these bonds are difficult or impossible to replace if they are lost or stolen.

TYPES OF BONDS

Bonds and bondlike instruments are known as fixed-income securities. These terms are used interchangeably. This is because they typically provide a regular and reliable income stream at fixed intervals. As a generalization, bonds pay interest every six months. The rate of interest that a bond pays can be fixed or variable. The fixed rate is identified in the description of the bond, along with its maturity date. At maturity, the borrowing organization or institution returns the amount that was borrowed from the bondholder. Sometimes, bonds have a "call" feature, which allows the issuer to redeem the bond early and terminate the issue by reimbursing the holder for all the owed principal and interest. Some corporate bonds have additional, more exotic features, such as convertibility into common stock, which are beyond the scope of this work. The term *bond* is used in general terms in practice. Notes are frequently identified as bonds. Bond will be used herein as a generic term referring to fixed income securities unless specifically identified. Resources for further reading are listed in the bibliography.

The rate of interest that a bond pays is known as the stated rate or the *coupon*. Prior to the proliferation of electronic record keeping in the early 1980s, most bonds were issued as paper certificates with an attached sheet of coupons. Each of these coupons represented an interest payment and was dated at six-month intervals. These coupons were literally cut from the sheet and presented to a bank or broker to redeem the current interest payment. Hence, the term *coupon* was adopted to refer to the interest rate that was paid for a particular bond. Today, records of bond ownership are primarily maintained electronically. The term *book entry* is used to describe this practice. Physical certificates are usually not issued for bonds.

Bonds are more complex than stocks because they are of many different types, with different maturity dates, various interest rates, many issuers, and customized additional features. Stocks are more standardized, which facilitates formal exchange trading. Some bonds are traded on formal registered exchanges like the New York Stock Exchange (NYSE). These bonds are described as listed bonds and indicate that the issue is available for trading transactions on a particular securities exchange. But it is expensive to list securities on a formal registered exchange and there are also strict credit and historical criteria that must be met. Most bonds therefore trade on the OTC market, outside of a formal registered securities exchange.

It is easier to understand bonds by examining the fundamental categories into which they are grouped. These are corporate bonds, municipal bonds, government bonds, agency bonds, and securitized assets, which include both mortgage-backed securities (MBSs) and asset-backed securities (ABSs).

Corporate Bonds

Corporate bonds are issued by organizations in a wide variety of industries. These bonds are typically classified according to the issuer's industry, and the terms of a bond offering are often based upon comparable issues in the market. The issuer of a corporate bond borrows funds from investors rather than using bank intermediaries because better terms are available by going directly to the capital markets. When an organization such as a corporation issues a bond, it is effectively borrowing money from investors according to fixed contractual terms. The terms and conditions of the bonds issued are customized for each bond offering.

The price of a bond is based upon the expected cash flows, term until maturity, the interest rate, and the credit quality of the issuer, including any credit enhancements. The issuer promises to repay the investor the principal value or face value of the bond upon maturity. In return for the use of the investor's money, the issuer pays interest every six months. The length or term of the bond until maturity, the interest rate, and the rating are important factors for investors to consider.

There are many reasons why companies borrow money. Sometimes it is necessary to cover operating expenses or replace aging equipment, but more often the proceeds from a bond issue are used for corporate projects or expansion initiatives. The use of leverage is a very important corporate finance tool. Leverage is the use of borrowed money to effectively make money or enhance the return to a corporation. The use of leverage can be explained by considering an example from the mortgage market. If you wanted to purchase a house and had $100,000 in savings, you would have to make some important choices: You could spend the amount on a $100,000 house. Alternatively, you could purchase a $400,000 house using the $100,000 as a down payment and use a mortgage loan for the balance. Of course, you would be obligated to make mortgage loan payments.

However, there are some important advantages to taking a loan, assuming that you can afford to make the loan repayments. First, you have the use of a much more expensive home. Second, if property values are increasing the value of your home will increase accordingly. If you purchased the $100,000 home, you could expect the value to be $150,000 after five years, with an average property value growth rate of 10 percent per year. The value of the $400,000 home would be $600,000 after five years at this growth rate. You are making money from borrowed funds. This is called leverage. Companies often identify opportunities for growth to increase revenues and issue bonds to provide the funds and leverage.

MUNICIPAL BONDS

The financial field that describes the planning, negotiating, underwriting, and issuance of municipal bonds is known as public finance. Municipal bonds (often called munis by industry professionals) encompass the debt securities issued by public institutions, including but not limited to cities, states, municipalities, school districts, corporations, and special taxing authorities. There are two basic types of municipal bonds—general obligation and revenue bonds. There are many variants, but general obligation and revenue bonds structures are representative of the majority of municipal bonds issued in the United States.

General obligation (GO) bonds are debt securities issued by public entities with taxing authorities. The ability to pay the interest and return the principal borrowed from investors is secured by the taxing power and tax base of the issuer. In addition to income taxes, if imposed, municipalities also collect property or ad valorem taxes. The credit rating of the entity is an important consideration for investors. Not all municipal bonds rely on tax revenues for repayment; some are based on other types of revenue. Examples of general obligation bonds are those issued for the development and improvement of schools, parks, sewer systems, and roads.

Municipal bonds that are issued for a special project or some income-generating operation are described as revenue bonds. The payment of the issuer's debt obligations is based upon use fees or operating cash flow from a project or facility. Revenue bonds are often used for toll road projects, stadiums and arenas, airport expansion, and new building facilities that will generate lease revenues.

Municipal bonds are often insured as a form of credit enhancement to make the issue more marketable. AMBAC, a company that insures municipal bonds on behalf of an issuer, began offering insurance on municipal bond issues in 1971. With the higher credit quality, the issuer can pay a lower rate of interest.

Investors, especially those in high tax brackets, find municipal bonds extremely attractive. The main reason is that the interest they pay is tax-free income, as municipal bonds are free from federal income tax. In addition, if an investor lives in a state in which they are issued, they can be tax free at multiple levels. In states with high taxes, bonds are most attractive to wealthy investors and corporations, such as banks and insurance companies. If an investor lives in one of the few states without an income tax (e.g., Texas), the federal tax benefit is available, but there is no state or local tax benefit. Most municipal bonds are tax free.

The issuers of municipal bonds are able to offer lower coupon rates because of the tax-free status of these bonds. Table 6.1 shows how these bonds can benefit investors in various tax brackets. The information is from the tax year 2005.

GOVERNMENT BONDS

U.S. government bonds are issued by the U.S. Treasury Department, which is the largest issuer of debt securities in the world. Congress determines

TABLE 6.1
Municipal Bonds: Tax-Exempt Equivalent Yields

Marginal Tax Rate (%)	4% Tax-Exempt Yield	5% Tax-Exempt Yield	6% Tax-Exempt Yield	6.5% Tax-Exempt Yield	7% Tax-Exempt Yield	7.5% Tax-Exempt Yield
10	4.44	5.56	6.67	7.78	8.33	4.44
15	4.71	5.88	7.06	8.24	8.82	4.71
27	5.48	6.85	8.22	9.59	10.27	5.48
30	5.71	7.14	8.57	10.00	10.71	5.71
35	6.15	7.69	9.23	10.77	11.54	6.15
38.6	6.51	8.14	9.77	11.40	12.21	6.51

Source: http://moneycentral.msn.com.

the amount of debt that the Treasury is permitted to issue. The Treasury Department is also responsible for managing the government debt. Government debt is a generalized term for the various types of government securities issued by the Treasury, in the form of bills, bonds, or notes. U.S. government securities are very liquid because of their high quality and popularity. These are sometimes considered riskless in terms of credit (default) risk because they are backed by the full faith and credit of the U.S. government. The ability to repay principal and interest is based upon the taxing power of the federal government. Treasury securities issued after 1983 are required to be in electronic or book-entry form rather than as physical certificates.

The rates paid on government securities are highly significant and relied upon as key benchmarks for other markets and economic indicators, both domestically and throughout the world. For example, the six-month U.S. Treasury bill is often used as the benchmark reference rate for many outstanding adjustable-rate mortgage loans.

Treasury securities are issued in two general forms. One type pays periodic interest and is offered at a coupon rate while the other is sold at a discount. The discount securities do not actually pay interest in cash; instead, the interest accumulates intrinsically and is paid at maturity. The U.S. savings bonds and Treasury bills are examples.

U.S. Treasury securities are issued by the U.S. government in the national currency, U.S. dollars. They can be in the form of bills, notes, or bonds. Treasury bills are short term and mature in one year or less. They do not pay a coupon interest rate and are sold at a discount from par value. Treasury notes are a medium-term debt and mature in one to ten years. They are sold with a coupon and pay interest every six months. The current maturity terms offered are two, three, five, seven, and ten years. Bonds are a long-term debt with a maturity period more than ten years. Government bonds are often sold in an auction format.

A more recent type of U.S. government security was developed in response to public concerns about inflation and rising interest rates. U.S. Treasury Inflation Protected Securities (TIPS) have their principal linked to the Consumer Price Index, which is an economic indicator of inflation. When inflation is high, based on the index, the principal is adjusted and increased. When the index declines, the principal is reduced. TIPS have a fixed interest rate that is paid every six months and is based upon the current adjusted value of the principal. At maturity, the holder is paid the greater of the current value or the original principal. TIPS are issued for five, ten, and twenty year terms and have been available since 1997. The United Kingdom issued floating rate government securities before the United States could. These inflation-linked gilt securities were first issued in the 1980s.

The U.S. Treasury's thirty-year bond was called the bellwether bond because it was widely used as the de facto benchmark indicator of long-term interest rates. The thirty-year bond is also called the long bond because of its duration. Many investors were disappointed when the U.S. Treasury discontinued issuing its thirty-year bond in October 2001. Since the U.S. budget deficit was substantially reduced during the 1990s and the nation actually realized a budget surplus, there was no longer a need to borrow funds and issue bonds with a thirty-year repayment period. So, the Treasury relied on shorter-term debt to finance government operations. In February 2006, the thirty-year Treasury Bond was reintroduced. The United States was carrying a record budget deficit, which can be partially attributed to the costs of the war on terror following the attack on the World Trade Center in New York on September 11, 2001. Since the government accumulated a budget deficit, the U.S. Treasury issues bonds, which are formal, legal, and contractual IOUs, to borrow the money to finance this burgeoning debt.

The U.S. government makes it easy for individual investors to purchase Treasury securities, especially if they have a computer with online capabilities access. A Web site, www.treasurydirect.gov, was launched during the fall of 2005. This Web site and easy access through banks and brokers provide investors with a quick and convenient method for purchasing a variety of U.S. government debt offerings. In addition to easy access, there are no fees or complicated paperwork to complete.

AGENCY BONDS

Agency bonds are issued by government-sponsored entities or enterprises. These government-sponsored enterprises (GSEs) include the Federal National Mortgage Association (FNMA), the Government National Mortgage Association (GNMA), the Federal Home Loan Mortgage Corporation (FHLMC), the Federal Home Loan Bank (FHLB), and the Student Loan Marketing Association (SLMA).

MBSs represent the largest segment of agency securities. These are bonds created from pools of first mortgages on residential properties. These mortgage backed securities are issued by a government backed enterprise or agency. The payment of principal and interest to investors is typically guaranteed by the issuing agency. The GSEs have lines of credit with the U.S. Treasury, which are guaranteed. The default risk for these securities is low. One risk related to these securities, which is often overlooked, is prepayment risk. Institutions that are not GSEs, such as banks and homebuilders, also issue mortgage backed securities.

MORTGAGE-BACKED SECURITIES

One of the cornerstones of the U.S. culture is the "American dream," the ability to own a home. The federal government plays an integral role to help provide U.S. citizens with access to affordable housing. The government, through its departments and related agencies, provides insurance or guarantees for mortgage loans to assist groups with certain demographic characteristics that have the ability to purchase a home. The government provides incentives to promote the development of low-income housing. Reviewing the MBS market from an historical perspective will help to better understand the development and significance of this market to the U.S. economy. After the 1929 stock market collapse and subsequent Great Depression, the public lost confidence in the financial system. Legislation was passed by Congress in 1933 and 1934 that helped the country recover from the crisis and also influenced the restoration of confidence in the financial system.

The Federal Housing Authority (FHA) was created in 1934 with the passage of the National Housing Act. The FHA provides important protection for lenders, called mortgage insurance. If a borrower meets certain eligibility criteria, his mortgage loan can be insured by the FHA to protect the lender from default. The FHA helped to reform and standardize the structure of residential mortgages in the 1930s. Prior to the standard conventional fixed-rate thirty-year mortgage with level payments, earlier versions had much shorter terms and often required large balloon payments at maturity. In 1965, the FHA was moved into the U.S. Department of Housing and Urban Development (HUD).

Congress authorized and sponsored the FNMA, but it is a private corporation. FNMA is pronounced "Fannie Mae." It was established in 1938. Historically, its role was to create liquidity for lenders by buying and holding mortgage pools. Congress passed legislation that essentially split the FNMA agency into two separate associations in 1968. The original FNMA was retained and the new organization was named the Government National Mortgage Association (GNMA, pronounced "Ginnie Mae").

GNMA does not issue mortgages; it guarantees pools of mortgages packaged as securities. Lenders, such as banks and finance companies, originate the mortgages. GNMA purchases the pools and securitizes the assets to create debt instruments that are sold to the public. Since GNMA is a part of the HUD, the guarantees pledged by GNMA are based upon the full faith and credit of the U.S. government. GNMA provides funds to financial institutions, from the proceeds received from selling their existing pools of mortgage loans, enabling them to issue additional VA and FHA loans. This provides liquidity to the lending financial institutions. Liquidity is a term used to describe the ability to convert an asset into cash. The origins of the MBS market can be traced back to 1970, when the newly created GNMA guaranteed a pool of mortgages, which were packaged into financial instruments that passed principal and interest from the loan payments directly to the investors. These innovative debt securities were known as pass-throughs. GNMA securities are backed by HUD and represent guaranteed mortgages backed by the Veterans Administration, called VHA loans. The VA was authorized to insure loans to eligible veterans in 1944.

Shortly thereafter, the FNMA was authorized to purchase loans that were not VA or FHA insured. FNMA's market includes conventional mortgages that are not a part of FHA or VA loans. FNMA quickly responded to the GNMA securities issuing their own pass-throughs.

The Federal Home Loan Mortgage Corporation (FHLMC, pronounced Freddie Mac) was created in 1970. Under the Federal Reserve System, mortgages are sold to the FHLMC. In 1971, the FHLMC began issuing mortgage pass-through certificates. The FHLMC is a private corporation, and like FNMA, it is listed for trading on the NYSE.

FNMA first pooled mortgage loans and issued MBSs in 1981. These are created from a portfolio of residential mortgages aggregated as a pool. They represent an ownership stake in the pool of mortgage loans. The underlying mortgages and their corresponding cash flows serve as collateral for the securitized loan pools. These securities ignited a revolution in the fixed income market and led to the development of a global market in creating debt instruments by securitizing assets, usually loans or receivables with some form of cash flow.

The ability to securitize the mortgages that banks and other lenders initiate provides a method to have access to additional funds to create new mortgage loans. Also, any potential risks associated with the mortgages are shared with the market by spreading them among the investors. Liquidity, as stated earlier, is the ability to convert an asset into cash. Securitization provides liquidity to lenders so that they can offer financing to more homebuyers. They are an important tool for supporting and sustaining economic growth.

Not all of the government intervention was successful. For example, take the savings and loan associations that were backed by government initiatives. In response to the savings and loan crisis of the 1980s, Congress passed the Financial Institutions Reform, Recovery, and Enforcement Act (FIRREA) in 1989. This act assigned HUD regulatory authority for FHLMC. FNMA too falls under the authority of HUD.

COLLATERALIZED MORTGAGE OBLIGATIONS AND REAL ESTATE MORTGAGE INVESTMENT CONDUITS

MBSs have features that investors find attractive. One, they are safe. Most bonds pay interest income every six months. MBSs provide monthly income, which many investors find desirable. Investors in MBSs have minimal credit risk exposure. The biggest risk concern is prepayment risk. To understand this risk, it is worthwhile to review some MBS fundamentals. A mortgage pool is a group of individual mortgages. When the debtor pays his monthly house payment to a bank that holds his mortgage, part of it pays the interest and the rest is applied toward the principal balance. This same breakdown will pass through to the MBS investor. Most home mortgages are granted with fifteen- or thirty-year terms. The MBS is a long-term investment.

However, most homeowners do not hold their mortgage for the full term. People sell their homes for various reasons such as job transfers or changes in family circumstances. When people sell their homes, the mortgage is typically paid in full. This principal flows through to the investors. So, rather than hold a security for income, the investor may find that principal amounts are paid back in unpredictable inventories. When the principal is reduced, the income flow is also reduced commensurately. If investors purchase MBSs with a high interest or coupon rate, they may be disappointed when interest rates decline because homeowners will refinance their high-rate mortgages with lower current rates. When this occurs, the principal is also returned to MBS holders.

An additional innovation occurred in 1983, the issuance of the first collateralized mortgage obligations (CMOs). FNMA created and issued the first CMO. The CMO structure is more complex than the pass-through certificates and thus enabled the originator to customize the payment features and risk exposure of the bonds. The CMOs were structured in various classes to protect investors from prepayment risk. The pools of mortgages represented in mortgage backed securities are often pooled again to create CMOs and real estate mortgage investment conduits (REMICs).

CMOs are issued as REMICs because of the simplified tax treatment and other advantages introduced with the 1986 tax reform legislation. The CMOs or REMICs are backed by residential mortgages and are similar in structure to agency MBSs. The first CMOs were created in 1983. The Tax Reform Act of 1986 introduced tax benefits for CMOs when issued in the form of REMICs. Effectively, the terms CMO and REMIC can be used interchangeably. They are different from agency MBSs, however, because the sponsors do not have a line of credit with the U.S. Treasury and they use other methods of credit enhancement, such as purchasing default insurance protection, to make the mortgages more marketable and attractive to investors. Fannie Mae and Freddie Mac are the largest issuers of REMIC securities.

The CMOs are issued in various class categories called tranches. Tranche is a French word that means slice. The securities in each tranche have slightly different features, such as cash flows and maturity duration and are intended to meet different types of investment objectives. However, the CMO tranches also carry different types of risk exposure. Investors must be cautious and understand the characteristics of the sometimes complex tranche structures and the associated risks.

CREDIT RATINGS AND CREDIT RISK MANAGEMENT

How does one know whether a bond investment is safe? Bond investors usually refer to the credit rating of a bond offering for insight. The accuracy and integrity of the rating agencies influence investor trust and confidence. Bonds are often evaluated by a credit rating agency so that investors better understand the risk of issuer default associated with a bond offering. The ratings also have a direct impact on the rate of interest that an issuer company must pay to attract investor interest. Bonds with high credit rating can pay lower interest rates than bonds with lower ratings. The higher interest paid on the lower-rated bonds compensates investors for taking greater risks related to a potential default by the issuer.

The credit rating agencies are under the oversight of the SEC. The SEC has been criticized for passively managing the activities of the rating agencies and for being too ambiguous. There is some question concerning the role of the SEC and the scope of its authority to regulate the credit rating agencies. Congress is expected to consider a legislation providing the SEC with explicit authority and power to govern the rating agencies.

Credit rating agencies have been criticized lately because they have been slow to respond with ratings changes for organizations encountering financial problems. Since the agencies are paid by the issuer, their objectivity has been questioned and the possibility of conflicts of interest has been raised. Elliott Spitzer, the attorney general of New York State, is an outspoken critic. The rating agencies failed to recognize irregularities at major companies such as Worldcom and Enron, despite indications of problems.

There are three main national credit rating agencies in the United States: Moody's, Standard and Poor's, and Fitch. The issuer of the bond pays to have it rated. Often, an issuer will hire multiple agencies to provide a rating. These agencies evaluate the creditworthiness of the issuer based upon public information and information provided directly by the issuer. Each uses a unique basic rating convention but the differences, as you will see, are minor.

TABLE 6.2
Credit Ratings (Comparison of Three Agencies)

S&P	Moody's	FITCH
Investment Grade		
AAA	Aaa	AAA
AA+	Aa1	AA+
AA	Aa2	AA
AA–	Aa3	AA–
A+	A1	A+
A	A2	A
A–	A3	A–
BBB+	Baa1	BBB+
BBB	Baa2	BBB
BBB–	Baa3	BBB–
Speculative Grade		
BB+	Ba1	BB+
BB	Ba2	BB
BB–	Ba3	BB–
	B1	B+
B	B	B
	B3	B–
CCC+		CCC+
CCC	Caa	CCC
CC	Ca	CC
C	C	C
		DD

Essentially, the main difference relates to the use of capital and small letters. Table 6.2 identifies the alphabetical, letter-based credit ratings assigned by the three agencies.

An important point to consider is the difference between the investment grade and speculative bond ratings. The four highest rated categories from each agency are considered investment grade. Those rated below BBB (Standard and Poor's and Fitch) and BAA (Moody's) are considered speculative. Investment-grade rated bonds are debt securities in which banks can invest. Speculative bonds have a higher default risk than investment grade and are often referred to as junk bonds. They typically pay a higher rate of interest than investment grade bonds and are also commonly called high-yield bonds. Many analysts consider "high yield" to be synonymous with high risk. Bond ratings are dynamic and are subject to change. The rating agencies monitor the creditworthiness of issuers and can adjust the rating either up or down.

The factors that influence the interest rate paid with a bond issue are the credit rating, the length of time until maturity, and the current economic

---

Primary Providers of Insurance for Bond Instruments in the United States

AMBAC Assurance Corporation

American Capital Access

Assured Guaranty Corporation (AGC)

CIFG Assurance

Financial Guarantee Insurance Company (FGIC)

Financial Security Assurance

MBIA Insurance Corporation

Radian Asset Assurance

XL Capital Insurance

Source: www.munibondadvisor.com

---

conditions. The market value of bonds will change after they are initially issued. Change is based upon the same three factors.

Credit rating is a tool that provides investors insight into the creditworthiness of an issuer to help evaluate default risk. Credit rating is an opinion provided by a credit rating agency expressing creditworthiness of the party obligated to pay a debt related to repayment of financial obligations. It is not intended to be a recommendation. Fitch IBCA ratings are also purchased by government entities at all levels including national governments for their sovereign debt.

CREDIT ENHANCEMENT AND INSURANCE

The issuer of a bond, especially for municipal and asset backed securities, can purchase insurance protection to mitigate risks, improve their credit rating, and enhance the appeal to investors. The insurance protects investors from default risk. If the bond issuer were to default, the principal and interest would be guaranteed. Bond insurance is a relatively recent innovation. The first private municipal bond insurance was developed by AMBAC in 1971.

The Association of Financial Guaranty Insurers (AFGI) is a trade group representing insurance and reinsurance companies that provide guarantees of asset backed securities and municipal bonds. Presently, there are eleven member companies. In 2005, the members of AFGI provided insurance for $540.7 billion (par value) worth of bonds issued throughout the world. The timely payment of principal and interest are guaranteed by the insurer in the event of issuer default.

Many bond issues have some form of collateral backing them rather than just the creditworthiness of the issuer. Collateral is intended to make a bond more attractive to the investor by providing extra protection against the risk of an issuer defaulting. Some bonds are even insured, to provide an investor with additional security. A list of the main bond insurance providers appears on p. 107.

BOND PRICING

Most bonds are priced and sold in units of $1,000. The price is typically based, at least in part, on the par or face value. If a bond is sold at a price below its face value, it is said to be selling at a discount. If it is sold for more than its face value, it is said to be selling at a premium. There is an important relationship between prevailing interest and bond prices. If interest rates go up, bond prices decline. If interest rates go down, then bond prices increase. The example below will make this concept more understandable.

If you purchase an investment-grade corporate bond that pays a fixed rate of 10.75 percent interest and matures in ten years for $1,000, you may feel that you made a prudent investment decision. What if interest rates increase to 14.75 percent after three years? You would probably consider upgrading the bond that paid an interest rate of 14.75 percent rather than keeping the 10.75 percent bond. But who would buy yours with a 10.75 percent rate when they can buy one with a 14.75 percent rate? If you sell your bond, you would need to reduce the price to compensate for the lower interest rate. By using a mathematical formula, a yield to maturity can be determined that would price your bond so that the overall return of both bonds, if held to maturity, would be equivalent. So, if you wanted the 14.75 percent income, you would have to sell your bond at a discount.

Conversely, if you purchased the same 10.75 percent bond and interest rates declined to 6.75 percent after three years rather than increase, you would be faced with another interesting decision. If a person wanted to purchase a ten-year bond at the prevailing rate (6.75 percent), it would cost $1,000. Suppose you considered selling your bond. You would discover that investors would be willing to pay more than the face value of the bond (a premium) to have the cash flow from the higher rate. This example is simple, but it illustrates the inverse relationship between interest rates and bond prices. The market price of a bond is calculated by determining the present value of all of the future interest payments along with the present value of the principal paid at maturity. The calculation below shows the formula used to calculate the yield to maturity and determine the value of a bond, which identifies the premium or discount price that would correspond to the comparison of the particular change in bond interest rates.

$$\text{Yield} = C \times [1 - 1/(1 + r)t/r] + F/(1 + r)t$$

Bond value = Present value of the coupons (periodic cash flows) + present
                 face value of the bond

C = the coupon paid each period
r = rate for each period
t = number of periods
F = face value of the bond

Ultimately, the price of a bond is based on what the market is willing to pay. If an issuer defaults in interest payment, the bond may still continue to trade. It is said to be trading flat. The bond price would include any accrued interest that was not paid. This interest may or may not be paid, depending on the financial condition of the issuer.

ZERO COUPON BONDS

Zero coupon bonds mature at a fixed value. They do not pay periodic interest and are sold at a price considerably below their face or maturity value. The value of the bonds accretes or increases until the financial instrument matures at its face value. Zero coupon treasury securities were a popular investment during the 1980s. Many individuals used them to fund their individual retirement accounts (IRAs) because of their attractive features. They were usually considered long-term investments; they were investment grade and default risk was low (especially the treasury securities); economic conditions were such that interest rates were high; and the maturity value was predictable. U.S. Series E savings bonds are zero coupon bonds. They are purchased at a discount.

Financial firms in the United States often create their own zero coupon bonds from fixed rate bonds. The firms will separate (or strip) the coupons from the bond. The bond will repay the principal at maturity, but in the interim, each coupon represents a fixed future interest payment due on a specific date. These future interest payments are sold as zero coupon bonds. The current price is determined mathematically to be that which will provide a yield to maturity that is representative of current interest rates. Zero coupon bonds are especially attractive when interest rates are high because they allow these rates to be locked in for a long duration until maturity.

Zero coupon bonds have been introduced by corporate, municipal, and government entities. The first zero-coupon corporate bond was issued in

1982 by the J. C. Penney Corporation, based in Plano, Texas. The bond had no interest payments; rather, the interest rate was fixed and the face value of the bond was payable at maturity.

ASSET-BACKED SECURITIES

The term *structured finance* is often used by industry professionals to describe the function of creating securitized assets. An asset that has a corresponding stream of revenues can be packaged into a debt security, at least in theory. The securitization of assets is a significant and important financing tool used to provide funds for continuing operations for institutions throughout the world. An ABS is a derivative form of financing and is different from conventional fixed income securities, which are typically direct or general obligations of the seller. An ABS represents an interest in a pool of assets, which are non-mortgage-backed instruments. These assets often include receivables, which is money that is owed to an organization. The cash flow from the pools of underlying assets, both principal and interest, are used to pay the investors. The underlying pool of assets collateralizes or backs the security that is packaged and issued to investors. Hence the general term asset-backed security is used to describe this type of debt security.

According to the Bond Market Association, a New York–based industry trade association, four asset classifications account for about 80 percent of the nonmortgage ABSs issued. These are receivables representing credit cards, student loans, automobile loans, and home equity loans. Automobile leases, equipment leases, trade receivables (especially medical service providers like hospitals), and financing automobile dealer inventory floor plan make up the rest of the ABS market.

Home equity loans (including home equity lines of credit) are the most common ABSs, representing approximately 40 percent of the market. Automobile loans are the second largest component. Credit card receivables are next. They are different from the other types because money borrowed by way of credit cards is usually unsecured, meaning there are no assets such as automobiles or homes as collateral. Also, credit cards have no fixed maturity for the borrower, like other types of loans.

The Student Loan Marketing Association (SLMA) is an agency created to facilitate the issuance of student loans to provide market liquidity. The SLMA is referred to as Sallie Mae. Student loans are issued with government guarantees protecting banks, finance companies, and investors from default. Pools of student loans are packaged and issued as ABSs. The rates of default for student loans are usually high, but the risk is offset by the government guarantees. Not all student loans come with guarantees because new borrowing programs are being introduced by private lenders. Congress is considering additional legislation to limit the amount of guaranteed student loans issued each year.

It is more economical for an organization to borrow by securitizing its receivable assets by issuing an ABS when compared to the cost of borrowing from conventional sources. ABSs provide several benefits to the originating organization, including diversifying the sources for funding for a financial institution. ABSs transfer risk from the issuer and share it with the investors. Also, the pool of securitized receivables can be moved off an originating company's balance sheet.

The first nonmortgage ABS was issued in 1985. The Sperry Corporation, which later became Unisys, created a special purpose entity (SPE) and transferred its computer lease accounts receivable, which were packaged into bonds and sold to investors. This was a large issue, which totaled over $192 million at face value (par). A global asset backed securities industry developed from this first securitization. The face value of the ABSs issued annually in the United States now exceeds $400 billion.

Sears, Roebuck, Inc., is the parent company of Discover Card services. In 1991, Sears aggregated a pool of their store credit card receivables and Discover Card receivables totaling more than $5 billion. They created a debt security from these receivables and sold it to the general public as a fixed income instrument. In return for pledging these receivables, which are assets, Sears received a cash infusion, which they used to extend additional credit. Then they securitized additional receivables and the cycle continued.

The basic concept and structure of the ABSs are similar to those of MBSs. These securities are appealing to the investors and the sponsors. They can be structured to be rather safe investments and usually provide a regular monthly income stream. Prepayment risk is usually minimal, and the ABS is typically structured so that risk is eliminated.

The mechanics and structure of a securitized asset issue are somewhat complex. If a corporation decides to borrow money against selected receivables, which are an asset, there is a process required to protect investors and be in compliance with the law. The corporation does not directly issue the bonds. So, the actual originator is commonly referred to as the sponsor. First, an investment banker is hired to facilitate the issuance of the debt securities. Once the pool of assets is identified, it is transferred (i.e., sold) to a legal entity called a special-purpose vehicle (SPV) or special purpose entity (SPE), which is created specifically for this purpose and is typically established as a corporation.

Special-purpose vehicles are established to hold assets. Funds are borrowed and bonds are issued against these assets. Some types of ABS are innovative and creative. The SPV provides a level of insulation protecting the investor from originator default. The pool of assets and their cash flows are removed from the issuer and cannot be included or used in a bankruptcy. Asset backed securities are not usually subject to the prepayment risks exposure. The SPV then sells the pool of assets to a trust, another form of legal entity. Some sponsors, such as banks, do not use an SPV and instead sell the asset pool directly to a trust. Here the debt securities are created and issued. Credit-worthiness is a function of the underlying asset portfolio rather than the issuer. The bonds are routinely insured through an outside company to enhance the credit rating of the securities. This makes the securities more marketable and provides investors with extra protection against default risk.

Banks, credit card companies, finance companies, and other organizations that originate loans are the principal issuers of ABSs. The first ABSs were issued in 1985, with a total face value of $1.2 billion. Presently, the value of ABSs issued annually in the United States is about $500 billion. According to the American Securitization Forum, more than $6.5 trillion (face value) of MBS and ABS instruments are outstanding.

INNOVATIONS IN FIXED INCOME SECURITIES

David Bowie is a rock musician with a successful career that began in the 1970s. He was able to sustain a long career because of his ability to adapt to changing music tastes. In 1997, he entered into a financial transaction in which he borrowed money against his future earnings. He issued bonds, which became known as Bowie bonds for future royalties from his hit music. The bonds were to mature in ten years and the total value of the securities issued was $55 million. This represented a nice paycheck for Mr. Bowie. The securitized collateral was the future cash flows (royalties) expected from his twenty-five previously released record albums. This ABS was issued before the technology to pay and download music was commercially developed and widely used. The growth of the digital download market will lead to additional offerings similar to Bowie bonds.

Many other successful music artists followed this path, choosing to get paid by borrowing against an expected future cash flow. Luciano Pavarotti, the famous tenor, created an ABS issue similar to Bowie's. Other unusual forms of ABS that have been introduced into the market include the licensing fees for CK perfumes, health club membership fees, and lottery winnings.

SUMMARY

The securitized financial asset market includes both mortgage-backed securities and asset-backed securities. Both MBSs and ABSs are originated by companies with assets having cash flows that are pooled to create bond instruments, which are then sold to investors. The fundamental concept for creating each are similar, but there are important differences between these two classifications of securitized assets. MBS and ABS securitization helps banks and other institutions to finance their lending operations.

Financial engineers and investment banks continually develop innovative and creative methods for borrowing money. The internationalization of financial markets and advances in technology have further accelerated this trend.

Securities are identified by name and with a CUSIP (Committee on Uniform Security Identification Procedure) number. When the owner is registered electronically, the beneficial owner's name is associated with the CUSIP number. There are primary organizations assigned the task of issuing numbers as a method to identify financial instruments and issuers. CUSIP is one of the organizations providing a uniform numbering system for financial instruments in the United States. It is a service bureau and its function is to assign unique numbers and standard descriptions of issuers and financial instruments. This information is disseminated to the public, exchanges, banks, clearinghouses, custodians, as well as any other interested party. The numbers are used to identify securities for accuracy during pretrade and posttrade processing throughout the financial services industry. CUSIP is operated by Standard and Poor's Corporation for the American Bankers Association (ABA), and it dates back to 1964.

The other major numbering scheme for financial instruments is referred to as the ISIN number. It, too, is a unique code used to identify a specific financial instrument. The organization responsible for assigning the ISIN numbers in any country is the National Numbering Agency (NNA). The ISIN number is used more internationally than the CUSIP number and some financial instruments have both designations. These identifiers are useful for minimizing errors, improving processing efficiency, and facilitating dematerialization.

NOTE

1. Many bonds have custom features. Interest that accrues and increases the amount paid back to the investors, call features, and convertibility are some examples. There are other hybrid and very complex derivative structures.

Seven

Short-Term Markets:
The Money Market and the Foreign
Exchange Market

THE MONEY MARKET

The money market is a wholesale debt market composed of short-term debt instruments. These securities mature in less than one year. The instruments typically traded in the money market include Treasury bills, banker's acceptances, certificates of deposit, and commercial paper. The transactions are for large denominations of debt instruments. Most of the transactions are done electronically, over the telephone or the Internet.

Treasury bills are considered the most important money market instruments. Treasury bills, also known as T-bills, are issued in three-month, six-month, and one-year maturity terms. They do not directly pay periodic interest. Instead, the interest accumulates and is paid when the bill matures. T-bills are sold at a discount, because they are priced below their face value, or maturity value.

Certificates of deposit (CDs) were developed in 1961. When they were first issued, a physical certificate was given to the depositor as evidence of the deposit, which is how the product name was determined. These are issued by commercial banks and represent time deposits—deposits placed with a bank for a fixed period of time for a promised interest rate, which could be fixed or variable. Usually, though, the rates are fixed. The CDs are issued in very large denominations, often in $1 million increments. They are often purchased by brokerage firms, repackaged into smaller increments, and sold to their clients; they can be sold on the secondary market. Further, their market value may fluctuate based upon changes in the interest rate and the time remaining until maturity.

Commercial paper is a promissory note issued by financial and nonfinancial corporations, primarily commercial firms, with only the highest quality credit ratings. The proceeds from the commercial paper are used to satisfy their short-term borrowing needs. Because commercial paper is unsecured debt, the credit quality of the issuers is significant. Their high credit quality enables them to go directly to the market for financing rather than use a bank intermediary. Bank loans are more expensive than issuing commercial paper. Commercial paper can be issued for a maximum period of 270 days (nine months). This short time period avoids registration for the issue with the SEC and thus saves time and money. Most of the commercial paper issued matures in less than thirty days.

A banker's acceptance (BA) is a form of credit and debt financing. A BA is a bill of exchange that is drawn on a banking institution and acts as a guarantee to companies that are exporting goods to another country. It is used to assure that the exporter of the goods is paid by the importer to whom they are delivered. BAs are frequently used as a vehicle to facilitate international trade. They are time drafts issued by corporations that are smaller or by those who have neither the highest quality credit ratings nor are as strong as the companies that issue commercial paper. This time draft has a bank guarantee which assures payment of principal and interest. The guaranteeing bank is obligated to pay the draft when it is due. It receives a fee from the payor for guaranteeing payment. The credit quality of the draft is increased because of the bank's guarantee.

FOREIGN EXCHANGE

Foreign exchange is a concept that can be traced back to the early periods of human civilization. It began with trade and the need for a standard unit of value rather than using barter or exchanging commodities. In Babylon, receipts and paper notes were used to facilitate trade. They became a tool for economic exchange and trading. The term *forex* is used to describe foreign currency trading.

The forex market is the largest and most liquid financial market in the world. The industry is loosely regulated because of its international scale and scope. Technological advances, especially data transmissions and Internet capabilities, are a driving force behind the explosive growth of the forex market. Specifically, advances in electronic trading platforms, online, Internet-based currency trading, access to information, and the ability to transfer funds electronically are shaping the market's evolution. The response time needed to make a transaction is an amazing six milliseconds—yet many trading organizations feel that this is too long. Also, the barriers to entry are low for the trader. The use of leverage is another appealing factor.

Financial professionals segment their customers according to two fundamental classifications—retail and institutional. These terms can be likened to retail and wholesale. The retail customers are the general public. The institutional customers are primarily financial institutions but may also include corporate clientele. Studies indicate that electronic forex trading is increasing at the fastest pace among retail customers.

However, there is a considerable amount of fraud at the retail level because many new participants are inexperienced in the highly sophisticated forex market, and they are vulnerable and sometimes gullible to promises of riches. Nonetheless, there are many reputable and service-oriented dealers. Many offer training and support to novice investors.

A substantial amount of currency trading occurs in the interbank market, which is institutional. As the name implies, this refers to currency trading that is conducted between banks. Several bank consortia have attempted to develop electronic trading platforms for use by their members. Some of these groups have made considerable investments in these systems and tried to attract others into it in an attempt to establish their network as an industry standard. Relationships and reputation are important attributes in forex. Dealers exchange quotes and transact business between each other and their clientele.

The interbank market is loosely organized. There is not a formal regulated exchange that serves as a centralized forum. Transactions are often based on trust and confidence. Documentation, of course, is carefully constructed to comply with certain regulatory requirements. An institution may not want to develop a bad reputation because then it will not have any trading partners. Also, public trust is important to the financial services industry and, in general, the market participants act to uphold their collective integrity. Problems and fraud, however, do occur. Sometimes there are some very creative schemes.

The foreign exchange market is dominated by major banks and multinational corporations. The interbank market accounts for about 80 percent of the forex turnover. The retail market accounts for the rest, which amounts to $380 billion out of a total daily turnover of $1.9 trillion. Some of the reasons for participating in the forex market are listed below:

1. Direct foreign investment
2. Facilitation of trade
3. Investment in foreign financial assets
4. Investor speculation
5. Short-term deposit conversions

6. Transfer and management of risk through hedging

7. Central bank intervention

Central banks, in order to implement monetary policy, influence exchange rates. Their objective is not profit oriented; rather, it is based upon a political or economic agenda. They do not speculate in forex. They intervene in the market to correct imbalances, stabilize the market, and help maintain an orderly trading exchange market environment. In the United States, both the Federal Reserve and the Treasury are equally involved in forex intervention. The Federal Reserve conducts its intervention through the Federal Reserve Bank of New York. The objective for intervention can include adding liquidity, influencing or even reversing trends. Overall, though, central banks allow foreign exchange markets to determine their own rates and will intervene in cases of extreme disparity or fast-changing trends.

Hedging is a term often used by forex professionals. Do not confuse hedging, a strategy, with a hedge fund. Hedging describes investing to reduce risk. For example, if a U.S. company sold goods to a British company and was to be paid in pounds, the company would probably use the forex markets to lock in a current exchange rate rather than risk possible currency fluctuations.

The U.S. dollar is the benchmark currency in the global monetary system. Since the original Bretton Woods conference in 1944, most international trade and financial transactions have been denominated, at least in part, in the U.S. dollar. Approximately 63 percent of the reserves held by global central banks are in the dollar. Forex also provides a venue to facilitate trade in more than one currency, and companies involved in international trade rely on this market. Depending on the nature of their enterprise, they may use the spot market, futures, options forwards, or a combination of instruments.

The Bank for International Settlements (BIS) publishes a variety of economic information, including on the forex market. The BIS conducts a Triennial Central Bank Survey of Foreign Exchange and Derivative Markets. The volume in 2005 reflected a 57 percent increase from the previous survey conducted three years earlier. Recent data from the BIS indicate that the daily turnover in the forex market is about $2 trillion, which includes spot exchange and forward transactions as well as derivative products such as futures, options, and swaps.

More than half of the forex volume is from Europe. London is the world's leading forex financial center with 31 percent of the turnover value. Most experts attribute this to the country's favorable geographic location and time zone factors. North America accounts for about 21 percent of the turnover.

China is the largest holder of foreign exchange reserves in the world. China does not have a flexible floating currency exchange rate. Rather, the exchange rate is fixed to a basket of foreign currencies. The basket is a representative sample for a group of different national currencies. China has been criticized for keeping the value of its currency fixed at an artificially low rate to support its astronomical exports growth. A lower-valued yuan (their national currency) will translate into greater profits when exchanged for higher-value foreign currencies. It also makes the cost of Chinese goods artificially low in the global markets, especially when dealing with nations with strong currencies, like the United States. The world's industrialized nations are calling for the value of the yuan to be flexible. See Table 7.1 for the currencies of thirty-six nations.

THE SPOT MARKET

The spot market price is the cash price for a currency. Spot forex is a large over-the-counter marketplace. It deals with the rate at which a currency will be exchanged immediately or "on the spot." Transactions can take place virtually anywhere and can be both formal or informal. A formal, regulated, central exchange for spot forex is nonexistent. All transactions occur between the dealer and the customer. The dealer acts as a *principal* in the trade. A principal is a counterparty in a retail transaction and will buy or sell for their own account or act on behalf of the dealer's account.

The forex market is linked by a communications network, which is expanding and becoming increasingly efficient and accessible owing to technological advances, especially the Internet. Forex facilitates cross-border payments for goods and services when there is a currency mismatch. Spot transactions are used by market speculators and traders as well as companies engaged in cross-border commerce which need to settle commercial transactions.

There is also an active forex market in which both retail and institutional investors speculate on the movement of one currency versus another. There are two categories used to describe traders, and both relate to the amount of time between the purchase and sale transactions. The position trader's time horizon is greater than three days. The swing trader follows a shorter time span ranging from a few minutes to three days. Obviously, both approaches are short term. The spot forex market is a twenty-four-hour market during the week. The trading week begins on Monday in Sydney, Australia, when it is still Sunday in the United States. The forex week ultimately closes at the end of the trading day in New York City. There are three important trading segments in this rotation, and they are identified geographically. These are the Asian, European, and North American segments. Spot rates are used for an immediate transaction and are subject to frequent change.

TABLE 7.1
Currencies of Thirty-six Nations

Country	Currency
Australia	Dollar
Brazil	Real
China	Yuan
Czech Republic	Koruna
Denmark	Krone
Ethiopia	Birr
France	Euro (formerly French franc)
Germany	Euro (formerly Deutsche mark)
Ghana	Cedi
Greece	Euro (formerly drachma)
Haiti	Gourde
India	Rupee
Israel	Shekel
Italy	Euro (formerly lira)
Japan	Yen
Jordan	Dinar
Laos	Kip
Malaysia	Ringgit
Mexico	Peso
Mongolia	Tugrik
Morocco	Dirham
The Netherlands	Euro (formerly guilder)
Peru	Nuevo sol
Poland	Zloty
Portugal	Euro (formerly escudo)
Russia	Ruble
Saudi Arabia	Riyal
South Africa	Rand
South Korea	Won
Spain	Euro (formerly peseta)
Sweden	Krona
Thailand	Baht
United Kingdom	Pound sterling
United States	Dollar
Venezuela	Bolivar
Zambia	Kwacha

The primary forex banks are called market makers. These market makers are large international institutions and they buy and sell currencies on a continuous, twenty-four-hour-per-day basis. Most of the forex business ultimately becomes concentrated in the interbank market among a few major international banks. It is estimated that the twenty largest banks in the world handle about 70 percent of the global foreign exchange business, according to the BIS Triennial survey.

Most currency trading is concentrated on the seven major currencies of the world, which are listed below. The top five are often referred to as the "majors" by industry professionals.

- U.S. dollar
- Euro
- British pound (or sterling)
- Japanese yen
- Swiss franc
- Australian dollar
- Canadian dollar

Other national currencies that are actively traded are referred to as minor currencies. These currencies are completely convertible. They are liquid but the market for these currencies and currency pairs is not as large as that of the majors. "Exotic currencies" is the term used to describe the national currencies of emerging markets and transitioning economies. These markets exist in countries with developing economies, such as Russia and Mexico. Government policy and influence have an impact on exchange rates and stability, especially in emerging markets. Sometimes liquidity risk is present in these economies.

PRICE QUOTATIONS

The price of each currency is determined by market forces and they are permitted to float or fluctuate in value relative to other currencies. The market determines the parity rate. Forex prices are expressed in terms of one currency convertible into another. Forex transactions are priced according to whether one is buying or selling a currency. The price quote consists of two prices. The higher price is called the *ask* price and it represents the amount that a buyer must pay. The lower price is known as the *bid* price and this is the amount that a seller receives. The difference between the two is called the spread. This spread is the amount that the forex dealer will make through a transaction. The customer does not pay commission to make a transaction because the dealer's compensation is embedded in the spread.

The term *pip* is important to forex traders. A pip is the price interest point, also described as a price point spread. This is the minimum incremental price movement of a currency that is quoted in the forex market. Prices for currency pairs are listed with four decimal places.

Forex traders simultaneously buy one currency and sell another, which is why those used most widely and frequently are quoted as pairs. Certain matched pairs of currencies are becoming commoditized because transactions occur frequently and in high volumes. There are six major currency pairs. The first four represent a majority of the forex trading, the EUR/USD being the most heavily traded currency pair.

- EUR/USD: euro and the U.S. dollar
- GBP/USD: British pound sterling and the U.S. dollar
- USD/CHF: U.S. dollar and the Swiss franc
- USD/JPY: U.S. dollar and the Japanese yen
- USD/CAD: The U.S. dollar and the Canadian dollar
- AUD/USD: The Australian dollar and the U.S. dollar

Currencies from transitioning economies or emerging markets are less liquid and have wider spreads than the currencies referred to as the majors. There is greater risk (including political risk) with emerging markets. Also, these nations do not necessarily have a well-developed financial structure or the legal framework at the level of sophistication that is maintained in industrialized nations. The ability to enforce laws, even if they exist, is not necessarily reliable.

Arbitrage is an investment transacted to take advantage of price disparities between markets. Arbitrage provides the investor with the ability to lock in a risk-free profit. Speculators often seek triangular arbitrage opportunities. The ideal conditions exist when there is a pricing disparity in the cross-exchange rate relationship among three currencies.

Exchange rate behavior and fluctuations are based upon relative strength, which is determined by economic conditions, the GDP and economic growth rates, trade and the balance of payments, political factors, inflation, historical trends, and monetary policy. The number and complexity of these factors make it difficult to forecast exchange rates. The trading advantages go to those who have the best access to financial information and are able to respond in the quickest manner possible. Participants in the forex are exposed to market risk, which is an adverse change in prices. The same forces that represent risk also represent opportunity. Price fluctuations, or volatility, create opportunities for traders to sell at a profit, as well as present situations in which prices move adversely.

THE FORWARD MARKET

A forward contract is a customized legal agreement entered for the purpose of buying or selling a foreign currency at a point in the future. The forward market has its roots in the Middle Ages. Merchants often traveled long distances, from all parts of Europe, to participate in the sale of goods at large trade fairs. It was common for merchants to make commitments and agree to forward contracts for the next fair. Effectively, a forward contract is a futures contract. It is not exchange traded. Rather, it is a negotiated private agreement with a banking institution. There is no secondary market for forward contracts, so they cannot be resold. There is a liquid secondary market for exchange-traded futures contracts, and they can be resold.

There are a number of reasons that a party would enter a forward contract. Basically, the customer is contracting for a certain exchange rate today for delivery and settlement at some future date. Consider this example to better understand the forward contract.

A U.S. manufacturing company enters a contract with a German supplier to purchase two large custom-made factory machines. Then the company would probably pay for the product upon delivery. Assume that the machines will be delivered in four months at a cost of 2 million euros. Since the supplier is German, they want to be paid in their home currency, the euro. The value of the dollar versus the euro will fluctuate. There is no assurance that the U.S. company will be able to convert dollars into euros at today's rate. So, if the dollar becomes stronger relative to the euro, the purchase will actually cost less in four months because the exchange rate is more favorable for the United States. If the euro becomes stronger versus the dollar, it will require more dollars to convert into the 2 million euros.

The U.S. company may not want to accept the currency risk related to the uncertainty of currency exchange rates. It cannot be sure of the actual dollar cost of the transaction in four months. A forward contract could be used to arrange a fixed cost today for a transaction that will take place in the future. The forward contract is a commitment binding to both parties to purchase or deliver a fixed amount of a currency at a predetermined price by a specified date. The size of a currency conversion for commercial, cross-border trade does not always correspond to the fixed contract size and future delivery dates offered by a standard futures contract. The forward market satisfies this need when a custom set of terms is needed.

The forward market involves a bank and is an agreement with a customer concerning the exchange of two currencies at a future date with a predetermined fixed exchange rate. It is often used when there is a payment due or need for a foreign currency rather than one's domestic currency. Forward exchange rate quotes can be found in the interbank market.

A forward contract is a legally binding agreement negotiated in the over-the-counter market. The agreement stipulates the terms, which will call for the delivery of a quantity of a currency at a fixed price by some future date. The forward and futures markets appear similar. However, there is an important difference. The difference is so significant that it accounts for the reason many forwards are more desirable for many market participants. Futures expire on fixed dates and are for fixed amounts. Forwards are custom created. The amount of a currency involved and the delivery date are flexible and structured according to the needs of the client. Both parties are obligated to the terms of the agreement. Banks are the primary issuers of forwards.

Hedging is implementing a strategy to shift or minimize selected risk exposure. Using a forward contract to mitigate this risk is an example of hedging. Forward contracts are available for various financial instruments, not just currencies. This discussion is limited to currency forward contracts.

FUTURES CONTRACT

A futures contract is a standardized forward contract. These contracts trade on formal, regulated financial exchanges. The primary economic function of futures markets is price discovery. A forex futures contract is an agreement to buy or sell a standardized amount of a currency at a fixed price under the terms and conditions of the contract established by the exchange on which it is traded. The contract can be closed by reversing the position. For example, if you purchased a contract, you can try to sell it on the exchange through a broker. Commissions are charged for forex futures, unlike the spot market.

The buyer of a futures contract is obligated to purchase a fixed quantity of a currency at a set price on a certain future date and accept delivery. The seller of a futures contract is obligated to sell and deliver a fixed quantity of a currency at a set price on a certain future date. Like other forex transactions, the use of leverage is permitted and often used. The exchange traded futures market, though, is highly regulated.

Currency futures were introduced by the Chicago Mercantile Exchange (CME) in 1972. These were the first exchange traded financial futures instruments to be developed. The CME opened the International Monetary Market (IMM) as a formal forum for financial currency futures trading. The initial currencies included were the Swiss franc, the British pound, the German deutsche mark, the Canadian dollar, the Mexican peso, the French franc, and the Japanese yen. Later, options on futures contracts were introduced. Options give the buyer the right to purchase or sell the underlying

The Japanese yen is among the world's strongest currencies, along with the U.S. dollar, euro, British pound, Swiss franc, Australian dollar, and Canadian dollar dominating foreign exchange. Getty Images/PhotoLink.

instruments at a fixed price by a certain date. The value of exchange currency derivatives, including futures and options, represents only 1 percent of the forex market value.

REGULATORY OVERSIGHT

Trading in currencies at the retail level is growing at a seemingly exponential pace throughout the world with very little regulatory oversight. The forex market includes tourists, who visit a foreign country and need to exchange currencies, those who must pay for a purchase in a different currency; and speculators who trade currencies, often using borrowed funds or margin credit for leverage; as well as central banks, international financial institutions, and commercial enterprises. Also, the transaction can be in the spot, forward, or futures market.

The National Futures Association (NFA) is a U.S. regulatory agency created to oversee the registered dealers participating in the market, especially those involved with futures, including unregistered entities that conduct their business through an NFA member organization. The regulators advise businesses and individuals to only use firms for forex trading that are registered with the NFA and/or the Commodity Futures Trading Commission (CFTC) to avoid taking unnecessary risks. Despite the fraud prevention activities of the regulators the industry is still largely unregulated, and investors must exercise caution and stay informed to avoid fraudulent schemes, especially from trading entities, often online, located outside of the United States.

The CFTC is an independent regulatory agency, with the key role of protecting investors from fraud. The Commodity Futures Modernization Act of 2000 formalized the CFTC's authority to oversee the forex market in the United States. The CFTC investigates fraud complaints related to nonfutures forex trading jurisdiction. The NFA addresses futures-related fraud. In spite of occasional jurisdictional questions, the two organizations effectively coexist.

There is some confusion about the CFTC's authority because of the three components of forex trading, which are spot, forward, and currency futures trading. The CFTC continues to investigate fraud complaints in all these areas. To support this effort, the CFTC recently established a Forex Public Outreach and Education Task Force. In the five-year period from April through March 2006, eighty-seven forex cases were filed by the CFTC. These cases involved about 24,000 forex customers from various companies, some real and some fraudulent, and $380 million in customer losses.

TRADING ACCESS AND PORTALS

Automation and online electronic trading are driving factors behind the growth in forex. They also facilitate international trade by reducing currency-risk exposure, increasing the efficiency, and improving liquidity. More competition has also led to more transparent pricing.

There are two dominant interbank trading systems. The first is the Electronic Broking System (EBS), a forex trading system established exclusively for the interbank market. The EBS was established in 1993 and created electronically linked bank forex trading departments. The system is closed to nonfinancial organizations. The accessibility provided by the system and the ability to link with dealers throughout the world led to the explosive growth experienced since its launch. Prior to the introduction of EBS, the average daily turnover was $100 billion. Presently, the average daily turnover is about $2 trillion and even more. This phenomenal growth is attributed to the online portals and electronic interdealer networks that streamlined the marketplace. The other primary interbank trading system is Reuters Matching.

There are other systems that provide electronic market access to both financial institutions and corporate users. Currenex is another electronic bank trading system that is also used by corporate entities in the United States. FXall is another. These systems give the bankers and corporations more control and influence in the market. They also concentrate liquidity and provide a reliable and efficient trading mechanism. New electronic online access offered by dealers for retail customers is the fastest growing segment of the forex market. The number of new trading platforms is under development and the choices are likely to expand before any consolidation occurs.

There is a plethora of Web sites offering forex trading to individual investors. Retail investors can establish an online account and trade currencies with as little as $250. The amount of leverage available to unsophisticated retail customers creates systemic risk and the opportunity for fraud and defaults. Leverage increases the potential for gains as well as losses. Leverage in the spot forex market allows 100:1. Therefore, a deposit of $1,000 can control $100,000 of a currency.

In the 1990s, the stock market attracted a large group of day traders. They were named so because they had a short-term focus and made multiple buy and sell orders during the course of a single day. The profits were usually small, but successful day traders were able to consistently make profits. The strong stock market provided considerable assistance and encouragement to these traders. In 2000, the market was trading at near record-high levels and many considered it to be overvalued. It was, and much of the overvaluation was concentrated in technology stocks. Investors were overly optimistic and did not want to miss the next hot technology opportunity. The steep market decline created an adverse environment for day traders. Ultimately, the day traders found a new forum, the forex market. The forex market is volatile and allows the use of borrowing through credit as a strategy to possibly enhance returns.

The spot forex market provided an appropriate venue for the equity day traders who needed a trading forum in the post–Internet bubble environment. The barriers to entry are low and it is relatively easy to establish an account and begin trading forex. It is difficult, however, for novice forex traders to make profit. The market is complex and moves quickly. Leverage is often used, which can multiply profits. There are legendary stories of individuals who started trading with modest sums and became rich. Unfortunately, many novices fail to fully understand that leverage also multiplies losses. Most new retail forex traders, about 95 percent, fail in their first attempt. The newcomers do not understand the risks, complexity, or dynamics of the market. It appears easy, but this superficial facade is misleading.

Before choosing to trade forex, newcomers should research the availability of training programs and online trading simulations. Simulated trading is a useful tool because the student experiences real trading conditions but works with hypothetical gains and losses because real money is not used. It is a valuable method for learning the dynamics of the forex market and the dynamics of trading. Some of the training available online is free and others have a modest cost. Though this is not a trading and investment guide, a cautionary advisory concerning forex trading is appropriate.

A prudent investor should consider the most established and reputable forex Web sites rather than those making enticing claims. A prospective investor should also do some research to determine whether the online dealer is registered with the NFA or the CFTC, as well as check for past regulatory violation before opening a trading account.

SUMMARY

The forex market is largely informal, which is amazing considering the volume of currencies being exchanged on a daily basis. It is a network of banks, brokers, and dealers who are linked for the purpose of buying and selling currencies. The links among them are increasingly becoming more automated. Electronic trading platforms are making the market more liquid because transactions are consolidated and efficient. Pricing spreads are decreasing as competition increases.

Globalization is especially visible in the forex trading growth as international financial markets are becoming more integrated. Forex markets are essential to facilitate international trade and they provide a method for making cross-border payments. They also represent a market-based means to determine or discover currency values. Trading accessibility is becoming more portable. Wireless mobile devices can be used to make transactions and access financial information. Wireless remote trading availability provides convenience.

Eight

Financial Derivatives: A Revolution
in Finance

As we saw in Chapter Five, derivative markets became a major component of mainstream financial transactions beginning in the 1970s, but they have actually existed in some form throughout much of the world's financial history. This chapter defines the concept of derivatives, explains their role and function, and identifies their unique characteristics to give a better understanding of their significance and influence in global economies. In addition, we place financial derivatives in an historical context.

Any discussion of the types, role, and importance of derivatives can become extremely technical and complex. That is not our intention in this introduction. Rather, we want to provide a broad practical treatment of the subject, with the ultimate aim of emphasizing the crucial role derivatives play in global financial markets today, and what the implications of this role are and will be in the future.

DERIVATIVES DEFINED

A derivative, or a derivative security, is a financial instrument whose value depends upon the value of other, more basic, underlying variables. Derivatives are often referred to as contingent claims, but for the sake of simplicity we stick to the term *derivatives*.

The term *derivatives* developed negative connotations and images of extreme risk, which continue to exist today. Public opinion and the herd mentality created an erroneous impression that derivatives (i.e., the stock index futures) caused the U.S. stock markets to collapse in 1987. The numerous derivative debacles of the 1990s and the early 2000s, which were triggered by greed and fraud, failed controls, or lack of understanding, obviously did nothing to enhance the reputation or improve the public's perception of derivatives. Considering some of the financial disasters that have been attributed almost exclusively to derivatives, it is not difficult to understand why.

The use of derivatives is a controversial subject. Derivatives are often identified as the root cause of serious business financial losses. Proper understanding and appropriate use of derivative instruments are core issues. However, the real problem with derivatives ultimately lies with the people who use them. The derivatives are not inherently the cause of the problems attributed to them. Rather, it is the manner in which they are used, the motives of the parties, and the proper decisions concerning their use that are the actual causes. Derivatives can be overwhelming or at the least confusing for many people. Sometimes, large financial losses resulted more from the use of derivatives because people did not understand the risks or mechanics of derivatives rather than because of fraud or malfeasance. Problems are often magnified because of the use of margin or leverage. This concept involves the ability to control a large quantity of an underlying asset or instrument by providing collateral worth much less than 100 percent of the underlying value.

Let us consider the definition of *derivatives*. Even experts are likely to provide inconsistent definitions. Comparing three of the most widely accepted definitions will help to demystify and eliminate some of the confusion surrounding the use of derivatives. The first definition, provided by the U.S. Government Accountability Office (GAO), is a "financial contract whose value depends on the values of one or more underlying assets or indices of asset values."

The standardized de facto official definition is a globally accepted version, which was published by the G-30 Working Group in their influential derivatives report prepared in 1993, *Derivatives: Practices and Principles*. It is highly recommended reading for anyone involved with financial derivatives. The G-30 study defines a derivatives transaction as "a bilateral contract or payments exchange whose value derives from the value of an underlying asset, reference rate, or index."[1] The underlying asset, reference rate, or index is referred to as the underlying in practice. The G-30 identifies and differentiates between exchange-traded standard contracts and over-the-counter (OTC) derivatives, which are customized and privately negotiated contracts between a dealer and the end user.

The International Swaps and Derivatives Association (ISDA) is the source of the third standard definition for derivatives, which is widely used: "A derivative is a risk shifting agreement, the value of which is derived from the value of an underlying asset. This underlying asset could be a physical commodity, an interest rate, a company's stock, a stock index, a currency, or virtually any other tradable instrument upon which two parties can agree." Also, according to the ISDA, a notional principal (or the notional amount) of a derivative contract is the hypothetical underlying quantity upon which interest rates or other payment obligations are computed.

The primary users of derivatives are commercial banks, hedge funds, insurance companies, and multinational businesses. Their use, however, is not limited to these groups. There have been well-publicized cases involving use by government entities and domestic companies. Exchange-traded derivatives are those traded on a formal securities exchange. They do not eliminate risk. They are also a tool for managing risk by shifting the risk burdens or transferring an element of risk to another entity or individual.

Derivatives are traded in two primary venues. The first is known as the OTC market. The second is a formal, regulated securities exchange. Standard exchange-traded derivative contracts provide important benefits to market participants. The contracts are traded in standard-size quantities with standard terms. Also, the exchange assumes counterparty risk, so when you buy or sell a contract, the exchange becomes a third party to every transaction. The exchange becomes the counterparty to both the buyer and the seller to assure that the transaction takes place as intended. Exchange-traded derivatives are standardized and the risks are minimized. Nonetheless, risks still exist, especially concerning the use of leverage by trading on margin. Sometimes the quantities required for an exchange-traded security do not match the need or requirement of a client. So, the OTC market is the place to find a suitable counterparty with whom a contract can be negotiated.

The acronym OTC refers to the nonstandard customized or negotiated derivative contracts that take place outside of a regulated securities exchange. All foreign exchange forward contracts are OTC. The OTC derivatives involve specific counterparties. The performance is based on the ability and willingness of each party to satisfy their obligations. Exchange-traded contracts eliminate this risk. However, the standard sizes and other requirements for exchange-traded options are sometimes incompatible with the requirements of a potential participant, or the particular need cannot be satisfied because there is no comparable listed derivative. The advantage of OTC derivatives is that they are customized and negotiable. Large institutions often find that OTC derivatives can be more economical than exchange-traded derivatives. Required collateral can also be negotiated.

OTC derivatives are frequently used in emerging markets. All currencies are universally accepted in foreign exchange trading markets and standardized exchanges. For example, consider the Russian ruble. The currency is volatile and the government has already defaulted on its debt. There is a considerable amount of swap activity supporting the financing of international operations and trade and it is almost exclusively OTC. Swaps have been used for both legitimate and illegitimate purposes (e.g., money laundering).

The most important difference between the two categories is that OTC derivatives are customized, while exchange-traded versions are standardized. The OTC market exists primarily among banks. It is difficult to determine the total amount of OTC derivatives outstanding at any given point in time. This is a frightening reality.

Leo Melamed is one of the most highly respected pioneers and innovators in derivative trading, exchanges, and markets. He was the former CEO of the Chicago Mercantile Exchange and the inspiration behind the establishment of Globex, the first electronic derivative securities exchange. According to Mr. Melamed, the use of derivatives provides three key economic functions. The first is risk management, which is focused on protecting protects and assets, not creating more. Chapter Nine is devoted to the risk management function. The second is price discovery, which is more representative of exchange-traded securities than OTC. Price discovery allows values to be assigned or obtained from the market. It is also necessary that these prices be transparent and can be disseminated to all interested parties. The third primary function is transactional efficiency. Liquidity is available on exchanges-based transactions but often not available with OTC transactions. In order to terminate an exchange transaction all one must do is engage in the transaction necessary to close the position. Liquidity is often a problem for counterparties in OTC transactions, many of which are complex and involve many subparties and illiquid collateral. To close an OTC derivative contract one party usually needs the permission of the other. If permission cannot be obtained, then a contrary OTC derivative contract needs to be created with another party to synthetically close the position. It does not sound easy, and it is not.

Derivatives involve purchasing a right in return for a cash payment or are structured where participating parties will exchange obligations. The fundamental building blocks of derivatives are spot positions, forwards or futures, and options. Derivatives are variations of one or more of these elements. Swaps and futures are based on a forward, which is settled by cash. Examples of derivative contracts and instruments are identified and categorized in Table 8.1.

FORWARD CONTRACTS

Forward contracts or forwards are funds that are relatively easy to understand. The elements must include an obligation of one party to buy and the

TABLE 8.1
Derivative Contracts and Derivative Securities

Privately Negotiated (OTC) Forwards	Privately Negotiated (OTC) Options	Exchange-Traded Futures	Exchange-Traded Options
Forward commodity contracts	Commodity options Currency options	Eurodollar (CME) U.S. treasury bond (CBT)	S&P futures options (Merc)
Forward foreign exchange con-tracts	Equity options	9% British gilt (LIFFE)	Bond futures options (LIFFE)
Forward rate agreements (FRAs)	FRA options Caps, floors, collars	CAC-40 (MATIF) DM/$ (IMM)	Corn futures options (CBT) Yen/$ futures options (IMM)
Currency swaps	Swap options	German Bund (DTB)	
Interest rate swaps	Bond options	Gold (COMEX)	
Commodity swaps			
Equity swaps			
Derivative securities			
Structured securities and deposits	Stripped securities	Securities with option characteristics	
Dual currency bonds	Treasury strips	Callable bonds	
Commodity-linked bonds	IOs and POs	Putable bonds	
Yield curve notes		Convertible securities	
Equity-linked bank deposits		Warrants	

Source: The Group of Thirty. *Derivatives: Practices and Principles*, July 1993.

obligation of a counterparty to sell a specified underlying element. The con-tract also states the quantity, price, and future date for performing or meeting the terms. The value changes in proportion to the underlying element.

The most basic type of derivative is a forward contract, which is simply an agreement to buy or sell an asset at a certain time for a certain price. Forwards are usually part of the transactions between financial institutions and are not traded. One party assumes a long position and the other a short position. The former agrees to buy the asset at a certain price and the latter to sell the asset for the same price. The specified price is the delivery price.

FUTURES CONTRACTS

Futures contracts are like forward contracts, except that they are generally traded on an exchange. Both futures and forwards are contracts made between parties that require action at a later date. Futures contracts can be perceived as a finite series of one-day forward contracts. Parties in an option contract have the right to a future action. An important difference is that futures contract has an obligation required for future performance. Another important distinction is that an exact delivery date is not required in the case of forward contracts. Most futures contracts are exchange traded. The contracts are standardized and liquid. Price discovery and transparency are also important features limiting risks which are provided by exchange-traded futures contracts. It is easy to use leverage by using margin collateral when using exchange-traded futures. The Chicago Board of Trade (CBOT) and the Chicago Mercantile Exchange (CME) are the two largest exchanges but there are also others.

There is a trend toward automation and electronic trading on derivative exchanges throughout the world. Further, deregulation is expanding globally and competition is becoming fierce among exchanges. Further mergers among exchanges are likely. The competition and technological advances are reducing transaction costs to investors and increasing efficiency.

OPTIONS

Exchange-traded standard options were introduced in 1973 when CBOT established the Chicago Board Options Exchange (CBOE). Later the same year, Myron Scholes and Fischer Black published an options pricing model. The logic of their model was expanded to the pricing of other derivative securities. Myron Scholes received a Nobel Prize in 1997 for his continued work in this area, which he shared with a colleague and fellow contributor, Robert Merton, who was an associate since 1970. Fischer Black passed away before that and was not permitted to share in the Nobel Prize because of the restriction on posthumous awards. More contemporary models have been introduced, such as that of Cox, Ross, and Rubenstein, along with various incremental modifications that overcome some of the shortcomings and limitations discovered within the Black-Scholes model. For example, the more recent model works better with European-style options than with the American style. Regardless of the later improvements, the Black-Scholes model is a milestone in financial progress. It solved a problem that confounded researchers for more than a century.

Derivatives based upon options can be standardized or OTC. Option contracts provide the right to the options holder to buy (call option) or sell (put option) an underlying asset at a specified price. The underlying assets include stocks, stock indices, foreign currencies or baskets of foreign currencies (for instance, some combination of euros and dollars, or euros and pounds, or more complex transactions), debt instruments, commodities, and, returning to our earlier derivative instrument, futures contracts. This predetermined price referenced herein is called the strike price. The options contract also specifies the specific settlement date or identifies a time period. Options owners have the right but not the obligation to buy or sell an underlying asset. The owner can choose not to exercise the option if there is a negative change in value and only incur the loss of the premium associated with the purchase of the option.

At this point, it is most useful to elaborate on the two basic types of options, call and put. Call options give the holder the right, but not the obligation, to buy the underlying asset by a certain date for a specified price. A put option gives the holder the right, but again, not the obligation, to sell at a

A trading board, the iconic image of financial markets. Corbis.

certain date for a specified price. The price in the contract is the stock price; the date in the contract is the maturity (or expiration or exercise date).

Options have been in the news lately because of the controversy over the role of stock options in compensating employees of some companies. Options were often granted by corporations as incentive to employees. Granting stock options was a technique frequently used by cash-strapped upstart technology growth companies during the technology boom of the 1990s. Often, start-up companies that could not afford a prevailing market salary package paid their employees in stock options. Once the stock reached a certain price (the strike price), employees could sell their options and take the value of the stock. Of course, they could also hold the options with the hope that the stock would go still higher. Some options had clauses restricting the sale of an underlying stock for a fixed period of time. Unfortunately, many employees and "millionaires on paper" suffered when technology and other start-up firms went bankrupt following the dramatic technology collapse in 2000–2001. The practice of providing stock options to employees is less popular now because of proposed accounting treatments and the controversy surrounding whether they should be considered a current expense of the company.

Corporate scandals such as those of Enron and the American International Group have contributed to a public sentiment favoring more conservative accounting treatment of the stock options granted by corporations. Many companies have been expensing options in anticipation of impending rule changes. Stock options for employees, and particularly for higher-level executives, have also been criticized. They are thought to encourage the company to act on the basis of what is in its short-term interest, bidding up the stock price, rather than taking a longer-term perspective that might reflect a greater long-run potential for the company but at the expense of more immediate success— which translates into what critics would contend as an inflated, artificial stock price. Accordingly, there has been considerable concern expressed that the very heavy usage of such options could lead to distorted resource allocations for an entire industry. For instance, if Internet companies use options as a lure for attracting employees, and if inflated stock values lead to a massive shift of venture and institutional capital, it would lead to other industries being relatively starved of investment. Whatever the merits, pros or cons, options are likely to be a significant incentive in attracting valued employees.

SWAPS

A swap transaction involves two parties who enter a contract that obligates them to exchange specified cash flows. The exchanges are made on a specific predetermined date called a settlement date (or a payment date). The cash flows may be fixed or variable depending upon the terms of the contract. Varieties of swaps include currency, commodity, equity, or interest rate. The underlying asset or its value (i.e., the notional value) is typically not exchanged in a swaps transaction. It is essential to understand the terms of derivative contracts. The basis of problems can usually be traced to fraud and greed or, more frequently, one party not fully understanding the terms and conditions contained in the derivative contract. This leads to misconceptions concerning the potential consequences and underestimation of the risks involved.

The origin of swaps transactions can be traced to conditions that emerged during the 1970s. A law was enacted in Great Britain that imposed a restrictive tax on the British pound and foreign currency exchange transactions when the proceeds were invested overseas. The British government imposed the tax to promote domestic investment. In an effort to avoid this tax, several British firms and U.S. companies swapped equivalent sums in their respective home currencies at the outset of their agreement and promised to return the amounts upon its conclusion.

The swap transaction that is credited with being the original currency swap was arranged by Salomon Brothers and involved IBM and the World Bank as counterparties. The World Bank had an interest in borrowing funds at the lowest possible rate available. It needed to borrow money to lend for projects in developing countries. At the time, the amount that the World Bank could borrow in West Germany and Switzerland was legally restricted and it had reached this limit. As a result of its international business operations, IBM accumulated a large quantity of debt denominated in Swiss francs and West German deutsche marks. Accordingly, this debt was being repaid in these currencies.

To further understand the incentive and motive for this transaction it is relevant to consider the context of the economic environment. In 1981, interest rates were high and the prime lending rate was in the upper teens (i.e., approximately 17 percent). The rates in West Germany and Switzerland at the time were 12 percent and 8 percent respectively. IBM and the World Bank entered a discussion through Salomon Brothers to discuss the disparity and their interests. The outcome was a negotiated contract. The World Bank then issued debt denominated in U.S. dollars. The U.S. dollar proceeds were swapped for an equivalent sum of Swiss francs and West German deutsche marks. Both parties agreed to make periodic payments to cover the interest expenses of the other in the respective currency. When the debt matured, the World Bank received its original dollars back and IBM received deutsche marks and francs so that both could repay the debt principal. This transaction is considered to be the official birth of the OTC interest rate swap, which has become the most popular type of swap based upon notional value.

Significant functional, operational, and regulatory differences exist between the swaps and futures derivatives industry. There is also an ongoing issue concerning regulatory jurisdiction. In 1989, the swaps industry was exempted from Commodity Futures Trading Commission (CFTC) regulation. The CFTC issued the "Policy Statement Concerning Swap Transactions," in which it agreed not to be responsible for the oversight of any OTC swaps transactions as long as they did copy or imitate listed exchange-traded futures contracts. These standards established a safe harbor from direct CFTC oversight for the swaps industry. The standards established in the CFTC's 1989 policy statement are noteworthy and useful because they identify five key characteristics of OTC swaps that distinguish swaps from futures:

- Individually tailored terms
- Absence of exchange-style offset
- Absence of clearing organization and margin system
- Undertaking transactions in conjunction with a line of business
- A prohibition against marketing to the public

The ISDA defines a swap as a privately negotiated agreement between two parties to exchange cash flows at specified intervals (i.e., payment dates) during the agreed-upon life of the contract (maturity or tenor). The parties then substitute or trade their future obligations.

TRADERS AND TRADING

Before we move into a discussion of the recent history of derivatives trading, the reader should understand that there are three types of traders. Traders can be defined as hedgers, speculators, or arbitrageurs. A hedger reduces the risk that would arise from the normal course of business. Examples include currency price fluctuation and commodity (raw material input) prices needed for the production process. Hedgers seek, in a sense, an insurance policy. Southwest Airlines remained profitable during periods of rising fuel prices because it hedged its market price risk with futures contracts. The airline was able to lock in its cost in advance. The market price risk was assumed by another party.

Some investment firms use hedge funds as part of their portfolios. Pension plans, who are institutional investors, often place a part of their assets with multiple hedge funds to diversify and increase their returns. Some firms operate hedge funds to the exclusion of everything else. We will discuss this later, and observe how difficulties can sometimes arise with the use of hedge funds.

Speculators want to actually take a position in the market. They are betting that the price of the asset (whatever that asset is, as we discussed earlier) will go up or come down. In the argot of the market, speculators who are betting that a stock option will go up are said to be long in the market; if they are betting it will come down, they are short. Speculation involving forward markets does not require an initial cash payment, and thus gives the speculator greater leverage. However, it introduces credit risk. The counterparties in a forward transaction must be concerned about their creditworthiness and ability to satisfy the terms of the forward agreement. Counterparty and credit risk are minimized when using a formal regulated securities exchange as the exchange assumes this risk.

Arbitrageurs are the third and, in many respects, the most interesting set of traders. Arbitrage involves locking in a riskless profit by engaging in transactions in two or more markets. Many arbitrage strategies rely heavily upon the ability to replicate, often artificially, a target security. The combination of instruments used to replicate a target security is known as a synthetic security.

Arbitrage opportunities can be used with any asset, although the time period in which the arbitrage has to take advantage of the opportunities may vary. The more sensitive markets are to the forces of supply and demand the less time they have to execute the trades and reap their profit. Arbitrage can only exist because there are often tiny, temporary lapses between the time trades are made and their eventual impact on the market. Arbitrage is used to capture a profit by recognizing and quickly, often spontaneously, taking advantage of pricing disparities among financial instruments and markets. Let us consider an example for illustrative purposes. During the early 1990s stock traders based in Mexico took advantage of temporary price disparities on Telmex (Telefonos de Mexico), a security that traded as a stock on the Mexican Bolsa (exchange) and as an American Depository Receipt (ADR) on the NYSE. Traders would simultaneously buy and sell one side of the position on the separate exchanges to lock in a profit. Once the orders are placed to take advantage of the price differential, the window of opportunity closes quickly.

So, there are some very basic types of derivatives, and there are three basic types of securities trader. But there is virtually no limit to the kind of derivatives that can be developed. While the underlying asset behind a derivative is typically a stock price or an index, interest rate or commodity prices, spot currency price or fixed income instrument, many other variables are often used.

LEVERAGE

An overview of derivatives trading would be incomplete without a brief summary of the use of leverage and the concept of margin. Options provide a good example to demonstrate the use of both leverage and margin. Exchange-traded options provide speculators with leverage in two ways. The first is that an options contract allows the purchaser to control a standardized and specified amount of an underlying asset. Usually, the quantity of underlying assets under control is quite large in proportion to the actual cost of the option. Margin is the collateral deposited by an investor to satisfy the requirement for purchasing or selling an option, futures contract, or other derivative. Margin also applies to the difference between the face value of a loan and the market value of pledged collateral. It can also be used to trade stocks and bonds. It provides an investor with additional leverage. When you purchase an option or future, you do not need to fully collateralize the full face value of the transaction. Instead, you deposit a portion and effectively borrow the balance. An example will help to illustrate the concept and the potential benefits and risks.

If an option investor decided to purchase a call option on the ZZZ Corporation, certain information is needed. The minimum information required is the price of the underlying stock, the price of the call option, its strike price, and the expiration date. Options have an intrinsic value based upon the strike price and the price of the underlying stock, and a time value that decays as the option approaches expiration.

If ZZZ stock is trading at $36 per share and an investor wants to purchase a call option, he wants the price of ZZZ stock to increase. Remember, a call option gives the investor the right (but not the obligation) to buy the underlying ZZZ stock. Assume that the investor selects a call option with a strike price of $40, which expires in three months. The price is currently quoted at $1 per call option contract. Based on this information the investor decides to purchase 200 contracts.

Each standard exchange-traded call option's contract represents the right to buy 100 shares of stock. So, 200 contracts multiplied by 100 shares means that the investor acquires the right to buy 20,000 shares of ZZZ at a future date at $40 per share. The investor pays $20,000 (200 contracts × 100 shares per contract × $1 price per contract) for this position, not including a commission. Today, the cost to purchase 20,000 shares of XYZ stock at $36 is $720,000 (not including any commission). So, for $20,000, a speculator is able to control $720,000 worth of XYZ stock. In addition, the speculator may be eligible to trade using margin, in which some collateral (cash or marketable securities) is pledged to a brokerage firm. Trading on margin (according to U.S. regulations) allows the speculator to purchase the 200 XYZ call options valued at $20,000, by placing collateral valued at 50 percent of the cost of the options ($10,000). So now, the speculator can control $720,000 worth of stock for $10,000. In effect, the speculator borrows the extra $10,000 from his brokerage firm and pays a low interest rate to the firm, called the broker call rate.

If the investor chooses to trade on margin, collateral can be deposited, which is only a percentage of the cost of the position. This is how leverage works. It enables the investor to enhance gains as well as expand losses. Not all securities have the same margin collateral requirements. The amount required to be deposited for futures transactions is less than for stocks or options, providing more leverage (and more risk) to the futures investor. Currency trading requires only a 1 percent margin. So, an investor can control $1,000,000 of a currency with a $10,000 deposit.

There is a substantial risk associated with using collateral and gaining an additional 50 percent level of leverage, as in the above example. An important requirement for margin trading is to maintain the collateral at a certain fixed percentage of market value. If the value of the position moves adversely against an investor, additional collateral will be requested (actually demanded). The market value of the collateral may also fluctuate and could trigger a margin call, too. This demand issued for additional cash or securities collateral is referred to as a margin call. If a margin call is issued, additional collateral must be deposited immediately or the position will be liquidated. If liquidation occurs, the speculator is responsible for all losses. Using too much leverage and not having the ability to meet margin calls has also contributed to high-profile derivatives disasters. The use of leverage is the most compelling reason for greater derivatives disclosure, scrutiny, and regulation.

HISTORICAL SUMMARY AND MILESTONES

Having provided a broad overview of derivatives markets, let us take a somewhat closer look at their history.

Recall that the downfall of Bretton Woods sent shockwaves throughout the world of money and finance. The stable, cozy system of a gold standard tied to the U.S. dollar was gone. In its place developed a "cowboy" culture in which currency trading by the late 1970s was among the most powerful and influential professions on earth. Some traders, such as George Soros, were to later demonstrate an ability to bring down entire financial systems, as was proven during the Asian currency crisis of 1998, which is referenced later in this chapter.

Derivatives are not a new concept, but they have been granted notoriety because of their connection to recent financial debacles. Early options derivatives trading can be traced back to ancient Greek folklore. Aristotle told a story about Thales, a philosopher. Thales was often criticized for not being wealthy. He was told repeatedly by a group that if he were really a smart person, he would be rich. The constant criticism ultimately inspired him to take action. Being an avid astronomer, he studied the skies and determined that the weather would create a strong olive crop in the upcoming growing season. Based upon this belief, he steadfastly proceeded to purchase the "option" to be the first to use the olive presses when the crops were harvested, which was in nine months. The olive harvest was strong, as Thales had predicted. He proceeded to sell the rights he obtained to use the olive presses first, and to the chagrin of his pundits, became rich.

Farmers have been using derivatives to presell crops at a certain price and shift a part of the harvest risk to the purchaser. Farmers typically were in debt from financing their operation until the harvest and sale of products. Low prices were bad for farmers and, conversely, high prices were bad for businesses that required agricultural products for their production needs. Both sides wanted to gain an advantage, limit or manage risks, and increase predictability. Pests and weather conditions can easily and unexpectedly devastate a crop. Accordingly, prices for agricultural products were highly volatile.

Demand for derivative-type instruments has been in existence for centuries. Forward contracts and options, among other trading variants, can be traced to the Amsterdam Bourse in the 1600s. The markets never formally developed, but there was an interest in derivatives. The government enacted legislation to eliminate these derivatives from the financial markets. Options trading proliferated in Europe during the 1600s and 1700s in the financial centers. Much later, options, forward contracts, and other financial instruments were exchanged on the Amsterdam exchange before the Dutch government eventually made the contracts unenforceable.

Derivatives played only a minor and unnoticeable role in the global economy until 1973. As we saw in Chapter Two, this landmark year marked the creation of exchange listed options contracts in the United States. The CBOT established the CBOE. The introduction of stock index futures is another important financial milestone. They were first traded on the Kansas City Board of Trade in 1982.

DERIVATIVES AND RISK MANAGEMENT

Derivatives are, basically, a conduit for managing and redistributing risks. The use of derivatives can be compared to purchasing an insurance policy to reduce the risk of financial loss. Derivatives can be viewed as a twenty-first-century equivalent of a customized insurance policy for investors. Complex derivatives might be based on an index, say the Dow-Jones index or the Nikkei 225, or even some basket of equities in the two markets, or, for that matter, other equities that are publicly traded. One example of a relatively complex derivative play took place in the early 1990s, when Bankers Trust, recognizing that Japanese insurance executives were unable to enter the Nikkei market, which was soaring due to legal rules prohibiting such transactions, worked out a deal whereby Canadian bonds would borrow Japanese yen, and, instead of paying interest, would give the lender an option in the Nikkei stock index. The lenders, of course, were the Japanese insurance companies. To complicate matters, in a complex trade, Bankers Trust agreed to exchange the yen held by the Canadians for Canadian dollars. This left the Canadians perfectly hedged since there was no way they could lose, given the interest-rate terms. To protect Bankers Trust, or to hedge their own investment, European investors were brought into the deal. These investors were eager to bet against the Japanese stocks, provided they had a hedge against stocks increasing in value.[2]

Several key factors contributed to derivatives becoming a dominant and influential force in modern finance. The collapse of Bretton Woods, discussed earlier, created a market for currency trading. Currency derivatives became an obvious way in which to hedge one's investments. Equity-based derivatives, credit derivatives, and insurance derivatives later followed. Second, the intellectual breakthrough of Black and Scholes in 1973 provided a means of actually pricing an option. Their great achievement, published in their seminal paper "The Pricing of Options and Corporate Liabilities," which was first published in the *Journal of Political Economy*, provided a means of fairly determining the risk involved in purchasing an option, and hence also determining what a fair price would be. Relatedly, advances in computing actually provided a means of doing the kind of high-speed complex computations necessary to determine prices. Without the computer, finance would still be relegated to the most basic of financial instruments since the means of readily computing its value would not be available. Today, this computational advantage can be seen in the evolution of purely electronic trading systems such as NASDAQ, Globex, Instinet, Arca-ex, and Eurex.

In addition to the above explanation for the emergence of derivatives markets, we could also suggest a confluence of a financial rationale for derivative contracts, a la the emergence of a market in currencies, and the growing intellectual force of free-market intellectuals plus the rise to power of free-market conservatives such as Jack Kemp and Ronald Reagan within the Republican Party. The selection of the great free-market economists Fredrick Hayek and Milton Friedman and the dominance of the free-market Chicago school of economics provided an amazingly fertile climate for the fostering of financial innovations.

Moreover, the political agenda of conservative Republicans with their support for deregulation of the financial and other sectors of the economy offered a supportive environment, particularly with the reelection victory of Ronald Reagan in 1980. Reagan's victory set the stage for the greatest bull market in U.S. history and the Reagan administration's free-market, laissez faire philosophy provided a favorable context for derivatives trading to gain a foothold. Among financial elites, derivatives were increasingly accepted, to the point that a Democratic-appointed chair of the Securities and Exchange Commission (SEC), Arthur Levitt, made numerous favorable comments about the use of derivatives.[3]

Finally, derivatives markets developed as a result of the increasing complexity of, and participation in, global financial markets. Derivative trading helps to grease the wheels of an increasingly integrated global financial system. Derivatives play an enormous role in hedging the risks that global investors take on a daily basis. A U.S. semiconductor firm wishing to build a manufacturing facility in Singapore may purchase a derivatives-based contract to hedge, in Singapore currency, on the cost of constructing the facility.

Hedging has become so prevalent that the financial services industry has developed a category of funds known as hedge funds. They are a fast-growing segment in the financial services industry. In 2004, 8,000 hedge funds were registered, reporting holdings of more than $1 trillion in assets in the United States. This does not include hedge funds based offshore and registered in other jurisdictions. Many pension plans invest portions of their assets in hedge funds to diversify among other professional money managers in their portfolio of advisors. Many hedge funds rely on leverage to enhance their returns. Leverage also provides the reverse opportunity to substantially increase losses, adding to substantial risks.

Hedge funds are unique and somewhat secretive about their operations. Much of their reporting is voluntary and they are not required to publish their returns. They often engage in sophisticated high-risk strategies. Hedge funds are not intended for the general public. They have marketing restrictions, and high net worth standards must be met to be eligible as an investor. It is difficult to obtain accurate data concerning fraud and misrepresentations because of the loose reporting standards. Most hedge funds are largely unregulated.

The hedge fund industry must have greater transparency, oversight, and stability. Hedge funds, like many multinational corporations and financial firms (banks, brokers, and investment banks), are involved in activity that has the potential to threaten the entire financial system with instability or collapse. These funds use synthetic positions and derivatives as part of their normal operation. Their primary objective is to make profits. Although the method or model may be different, the objective is the same. The unique appeal of certain hedge fund managers is based upon the track records and a unique trading style or modeling method. Long Term Capital Management (LTCM) is a hedge fund. The discussion that follows demonstrates why hedge funds and their operations need additional regulatory oversight.

DERIVATIVES AND MARKET SHOCKS: BLUNDERS, FRAUD, AND DEBACLES

Although derivatives are clearly an important financial innovation, they can be used improperly. The last few years have witnessed several scandals involving derivatives that are worth noting. Some of the most publicized and important incidents are described below.

LONG TERM CAPITAL MANAGEMENT

Perhaps the most significant instance to date of an institutional derivatives use leading to disaster was the case of LTCM. LTCM had made an extraordinary name for itself in financial circles during much of the 1990s through its ability to use complex derivatives trades in the currency markets to amass a fortune not only for the firm but also for the senior officials in the firm. The firm had developed a reputation as a highly "quantoid" group, being dominated by mathematicians who had, over the years, used their not inconsiderable skills to develop highly complex mathematical models of financial market behavior. As noted by Lowenstein in *When Genius Failed*, they tended to ignore the old trading rules of thumb used by traditional traders. The mathematical models served them well until 1998, when they were caught in a vise born of the Asian currency crisis. A series of trades that were essentially betting on the continued values of currency baskets produced a catastrophic decline in the firm's position, ultimately leading to the need for the top banking institutions in the United States and elsewhere to step in and provide enough liquidity to avoid financial meltdown.

The legacy of LTCM demonstrated a frightening insight into the manifestation of the problems that can occur when derivatives trading becomes reckless. While a detailed analysis of LTCM problems would take an entire book, the essence of the problem, as viewed by Lowenstein, began when LTCM began trading large amounts of equity volatility, or "Equity Vol." The essential strategy was to assume that the volatility of stocks is, over time, consistent. Stock prices will typically vary by 15 to 20 percent a year; on occasion, volatility may increase, but it will quickly revert to historical form. The leadership of LTCM essentially "bet the firm," in Lowenstein's words, on the assumption that volatility could be predicted using the Black-Scholes theorem, which assumed a world of normal (bell-shaped) distributions of volatility.[4] This proved to be a catastrophic error in judgment.

Unless one believes that the past behavior of markets is a reliable guide to the future, and unless one believes that the volatility of markets over time follows reliable patterns, what LTCM did was incredibly irresponsible. LTCM decided to short options. In other words, their models of market behavior concluded that the option market expected volatility in the stock market of 20 percent, while their own model, based on the Black-Scholes equation, called for volatility of only 15 percent. As Lowenstein put it, the crux of the strategy was that "if long-term was right—if the price of options was too high—then in effect it was charging a premium price for insurance, and over the life of its option contracts, which was five years, it should expect to come out ahead." If they were wrong, particularly if they were seriously wrong about market volatility, then LTCM could lose everything. And, of course, that is precisely what happened, when the South Asian currency crisis led to a dramatic decline in stocks.[5]

ENRON

LTCM was foolhardy, but was nonetheless acting within the acceptable parameters of market behavior. The near disaster brought on by the LTCM problem and the potential consequences is an example of the real possibility of systemic risks. Enron, however, proved to be a paradigmatic example of a firm using financial products in a self-conscious way to prop up a pyramid of highly questionable operations that were so misleading to investors and others that they resulted in the criminal conviction of Enron's top executives.

In certain respects, the rise of Enron to financial glory, and its subsequent fall, could be traced to its decision in 1989 to become involved in financial trading in order to complement its physical trading in oil and gas. The company's partnerships with Bankers Trust, a New York–based investment bank with experience in derivatives trading, allowed Enron to establish a derivatives trading office. Much of what Enron did was perfectly legal. For instance, the relationship with Bankers Trust allowed Enron to identify options embedded in Enron contracts, which increased the value of the contract. As described by Loren Fox, "Enron could . . . sell this flexibility in the form of a 'call' option, which enables the holders to buy an asset. . . . Enron could use the money from the option sale to help pay for the gas purchase contract."[6]

This kind of trade was absolutely legitimate and illustrated the power of derivatives. It actually represented a prudent business strategy. Effectively, Enron presold natural gas while it was still in the ground. But other uses were not as appropriate.

Enron had worries about debt and its credit rating. This credit rating was critical to the ability to maintain and attract customers to their energy trading exchange. These concerns led Enron to create energy derivatives designed to hedge credit risk. In February 2000, "Enron's EnronOnline initiative allowed customers to hedge their credit exposure instantly using tradable credit derivatives. . . . The launch of Enroncredit.com carried immense irony because the source was a corporation with such a precarious credit situation. Adding to the irony, Enron soon developed bankruptcy swaps, a new product, as part of Enroncredit.com."[7]

By the mid-1990s, Enron had become more of a derivatives trading financial services entity than an energy trader (or producer). But, as Fox presciently notes, although Enron saw its dramatic expansion into derivatives, particularly credit derivatives, as a way of hedging risk, it was actually creating more risks, as Enron had to keep generating returns in order to avoid the house of cards from unraveling. Importantly, there was little limit as to how much credit could be hedged away by Enron, since the usual capital reserve requirements that banks had to obey did not apply to Enron. The real risk confronting Enron, which ultimately led to its demise, was the fraudulent use of derivatives to conceal multibillion dollar losses created by incompetence and poor business decisions. Derivatives were used to help create the illusion of legitimate cash flow.[8]

One of the main reasons that Enron imploded was incompetence. Within Enron, it existed on a group level and created a negative synergy. It began at the senior management level and became pervasive throughout the organization. How do you measure the ethics, greed, and competence level of people in positions to make decisions concerning derivatives? Critical flaws in Enron's strategy can be linked to the aggressive use of derivatives and liberal interpretation of accounting regulations. Their exploitation of special purpose entities is a highly visible example. Special purpose entities are permitted under current accounting rules. A company can establish an off balance sheet special purpose entity but it cannot have more than a 3 percent ownership stake. Andrew Fastow seized the opportunity and took advantage of the situation. Somehow the top management at Enron, including the board of directors, approved the use of special purpose vehicles, which were financed by Enron and owned by Fastow, his family, or his handpicked designates. Enron usually provided all of the funds, authorized by Fastow, to capitalize and establish these entities. The entities were used to hide losses, embezzle money, and create the illusion of revenue to Enron. Enron executives used derivatives to hedge the capital in these entities by selling a floor on how low the value of its Enron equity could fall, while simultaneously selling a ceiling on how much the value of the equity could increase. The position was essentially a bet on the stability of the share price within a certain range. While not controversial in and of itself, it later proved critical in the accounting scandal by which Price Waterhouse Coopers determined the value of the stock, because Enron was bound by the accounting concept of conservatism in reporting. EDS encountered a dilemma in August 2002 using a similar derivative-based hedging strategy, which did not involve any special purpose entities.

Enron may have been an extreme case, but countless other examples of inappropriate or illegal behavior can be found. Prior to its collapse, Enron was the seventh largest company in the United States and the largest energy trader in the world. Frank Partroy's *Infectious Greed* describes what can happen when the accumulation of wealth is unrestricted by ethics and morality. The fallout can affect a full range—from investment banks selling derivatives packages to customers who have no idea of the true value of the deals, to Enron-type fiascos and institutions as diverse as Barings Bank, Worldcom, or Global Crossing.

China Aviation Oil

In December 2004, China Aviation Oil (CAO) declared losses of more than $550 million (U.S.). The enormous losses accumulated by the company somehow went undetected by auditors and apparently by the independent board of directors, and grew to a multiple of approximately three times the net worth of the entire company. The disclosure essentially eliminated all shareholder value. The Singapore Securities Investors Association (SIAS) promptly intervened and appointed Price Waterhouse as a special investigator to determine the cause of the problem, which was reportedly linked to derivatives. The quick intervention by the SIAS helped to protect Singapore's reputation as a center of commerce in the international community and demonstrated its concern and commitment to corporate governance, full and fair disclosure, and regulatory compliance.

Orange County

In Orange County, California, Robert Citron, the county treasurer, attained some degree of notoriety because of his ability to obtain investment returns about 2 percent higher than other alternatives. He managed a $7.5 billion portfolio of public funds. Citron's strategy for achieving superior results involved investing in derivatives securities and leveraging the portfolios to the maximum level (it was leveraged to a value of $20.5 billion!), which obviously adds risk. In 1994, parties outside of the county were asking Citron to manage their portfolios. He refused agencies outside of Orange County, and they were quite fortunate that he refused. The Federal Reserve initiated a series of successive interest rate increases in 1994 and altered investment conditions. The floating rate notes, reverse floating rate notes, and other structured notes were adversely affected.

The Orange County investment portfolio began incurring losses because the investments were highly sensitive to interest rate increases and were fully leveraged. When the losses mounted, the county liquidated the portfolio and filed for bankruptcy. The loss attributable to Citron's ill-fated high-risk strategy was $1.6 billion of public funds.

Metallgesellschaft

In 1994, Metallgesellschaft (MGRM) was the fourteenth largest commercial company in Germany. The MGRM business model was based on a marketing program that promised customers price guarantees on the purchase of petroleum products. MGRM would hedge their exposure, primarily market risk, with derivatives. In 1993, oil prices fell, and some losses from hedging appeared to exceed offsetting gains from forward delivery commitments. When rumors of the possible problem reached the markets, their ability to obtain credit was impaired.

Metallgesellschaft's supervisory board observed huge unrealized losses from the companies hedging positions and became immediately concerned. In response, the board liquidated all of the companies hedging positions and created substantial realized losses. They did not recognize the offsetting unrealized gains from the positions having physical delivery. The result was a loss of $1.5 billion. In the aftermath, the problem was attributed to lax operational controls by senior management.

Accounting rules must recognize the symmetric link between derivatives and hedged positions. This is a matter of knowledge and understanding. Derivatives and associated strategies are complex and can be confusing.

Barings Bank

Barings bank was founded in 1762. Barings maintained a reputation of being a conservative financial institution. Nick Leeson, a Barings employee since 1992, was about to change that perception in early 1995. He worked as a trader in the Singapore branch of Barings Futures.

Leeson was directed to engage in arbitrage trading, and initially he did. At some point, he began a different, more risky trading strategy. He began to speculate on the direction of price movements on the Tokyo Stock Exchange by selling options on the Nikkei 225 index, which was traded on SIMEX, the Singapore exchange. To his superiors, Leeson's performance appeared to be spectacular, but he was actually hiding his losses. It was later discovered that he had been concealing losses since 1992.

By January 1995, Leeson had accumulated enormous losses. He began the year with a huge and highly risky options position that would be profitable if the Japanese Stock Market Index increased. Unfortunately, the Kobe earthquake, which struck on January 17, doomed the position. The Japanese market declined precipitously. As the market dropped, he started buying more options in an effort to average down his cost and hoped for a positive spike in the market. Initially, it appeared that his desperate strategy might work. Then, suddenly, the market began to fall again. So, Leeson increased his positions again along with the corresponding risk exposure. As the losses escalated, Baring began receiving large margin calls from SIMEX. Barings ultimately collapsed because the bank did not have the collateral to meet the calls. The ING Bank took over Barings in March 2005. Derivatives, leverage, poor internal controls, bad judgment, and improbable circumstances were the cause of the crisis.

The losses attributable to Leeson exceeded $1.4 billion, well above Baring's total equity capitalization. Nick Leeson was labeled as a rogue trader for causing the collapse of the venerable Barings bank. After serving four years in a Singapore jail and writing a book called *Rogue Trader*, Leeson was appointed to a new role as the commercial manager of the Galway United Football Club, a professional soccer team.

BANK OF AMERICA

In October 1998, Bank of America revealed that it had lost $372 million. The loss resulted from a joint venture with David E. Shaw, the hedge fund operator. Shaw, the fund's principal and founder, was a former professor at Columbia University. He developed a sophisticated computer trading system designed to take advantage of arbitrage opportunities. After the Asian financial crisis and then the Russian government bond default, the computer trading system short circuited, and the outcome was a huge loss. Bank of America compounded the problem by not properly accounting for the losses and the valuation of its $20 billion U.S. bond portfolio acquired through the joint venture relationship. The Final Accounting Standards Board (FASB) requirements for reporting market values is underscored and reinforced by this example.

ALLIED IRISH BANKS

In February 2002, Allied Irish Banks (AIB) discovered that its U.S. subsidiary had lost approximately $691.2 million (U.S.) through losses resulting from trading Japanese yen and spot, options, and forward contracts versus the U.S. dollar. An internal criminal investigation by the Federal Bureau of Investigation (FBI) determined that a single currency trader, John Rusnak, who worked at AIB's Allfirst subsidiary, was the cause of the loss. The loss was attributed to lax controls and poor judgment rather than an elaborate fraud scheme, which was initially suspected. The Japanese yen weakened substantially against the U.S. dollar in the year before the problem was made public. This created huge losses in Rusnak's position and holdings. Rusnak entered option trades that appeared to offset the other losses. However, the option transactions were never executed (fictitious) and created only the illusion that the losses were offset. Further, AIB's internal controls failed to spot the inconsistencies. Rusnak did not obtain proper authorization for the size of his cumulative transactions and tried to hide his trail. Trading limits and controls, which are the essence of internal operational risk management for trader oversight, somehow failed. Ultimately, like Nick Leeson, who brought down Barings, John Rusnak was determined to be a rogue trader, which seems to be a rather polite way of describing an employee whose misdeeds lost $700 million.

Derivatives, in part but not exclusively, also played a role in the problems incurred by Gibson Greetings, Proctor and Gamble, Parmalat, K-Mart, Worldcom, Tyco, Global Crossing, AIG, Argentina, and still counting. Some of the problems with derivatives were compounded by off-balance-sheet financing, outright fraud, and loopholes in accounting reporting requirements. Given the fact that the derivatives market can be abused, there are organizations that exist in part to establish the rules of the game.

DERIVATIVES-RELATED FINANCIAL ORGANIZATIONS

There are several industry organizations that work to protect the integrity of the markets and address derivatives issues. Examples of key international institutions supporting derivatives and sources of reliable research and historical data are included in this section with brief descriptions. An expanded group of organizations with Web site listings is included at the end of this chapter.

The Bank for International Settlements (BIS) was established in Basel, Switzerland, in 1930 and considers itself to be the world's oldest international financial institution. The BIS is a bank for central banks. It is a global organization committed to promoting financial and monetary cooperation. Its functions include providing a forum to promote discussion and facilitate decision-making processes among central banks and within the international financial community, maintaining a central venue for economic and monetary research, acting as a prime counterparty for central banks in their financial transactions, and providing service as an agent or trustee in connection with international financial operations of central bank participants. The BIS does not provide services (including accepting deposits) to private and corporate entities. It collects, maintains, and regularly publishes aggregated data or statistics for derivatives, securities, banking, and foreign exchange and is an excellent resource.

The ISDA, established in 1985, is an international trade industry association. It represents participants involved with over-the-counter or privately negotiated derivatives across all asset classes. The ISDA has 625 institutional members from forty-seven different countries. Its stated purpose is to facilitate the use of derivatives by identifying and reducing the sources of risk in the derivatives and risk management business. The ISDA publishes master agreements for derivative contracts, related documentation, and legal opinions, and promotes the use of sound risk management practices throughout the world.

The Group of Thirty (G-30) is an influential organization created to further the understanding of international issues related to economics and finance as well as examining decisions that are made in both the private and public sectors. It was established in 1978 as a private nonprofit international organization. Its members are senior-level executives from both the private and public sectors as well as highly regarded academics. The G-30 commissioned the Group of Thirty Derivatives Project in 1993 and appointed a study group to prepare a comprehensive report that included a description and analysis of derivative instruments, activity, and markets. The final report also included case studies and recommendations for derivatives policy, use, and management. The final result or conclusions from the study were published as a three-volume report. It immediately became influential and frequently referenced. It was also used for benchmarking, establishing standards, and setting policies. The study was unique because it primarily involved a broad cross-section of actual market participants separate from work being conducted by central banks and regulators.

The International Association of Financial Engineers (IAFE) is an industry group dedicated to promoting financial innovation and addressing financial services issues. Members of the IAFE include academics, industry participants (banks, pension funds, broker-dealers, hedge funds, and asset managers), law firms, technology companies, industry regulators, and accountants. Both institutional entities and individuals can be members.

Most financial professionals concede that the term *financial engineering* was coined in London during the 1980s. Many London banks began to develop risk management services and formal departments. During the same time period, Wall Street firms began to hire analysts from the academic ranks for their quantitative expertise. These individuals were respectfully referred to as "quants." Computers and technology supported the quants and, as a result, new financial products and more sophisticated trading strategies emerged. Financial engineering involves the design, development, and implementation of innovative financial instruments and processes, and the formulation of creative solutions to problems in finance.

The organization has been instrumental in the establishment of financial engineering as a legitimized profession. The IAFE worked with top-tier universities to develop programs and curricula in financial engineering. It is based in New York.

ACCOUNTING AND REGULATION

Financial accounting standards are continually being upgraded. Recently, derivatives accounting and reporting has attracted considerable debate. A regulation requiring the expense of employee stock options (FAS 123r) was temporarily postponed, but its implementation is inevitable. Companies are required to treat employee stock options as an expense, effective from the first quarter of their next fiscal year after June 15, 2005. Many companies decided not to wait and have already adopted the practice.

Choosing a model for use to properly value the options is an important decision related to FAS 123r. Most companies have indicated that they will select the Black-Scholes model or binomial lattice models. Companies are likely to analyze models to determine which will provide the most favorable outcome.

FAS 133 is a noteworthy accounting statement intended to establish accounting and reporting standards for derivative instruments. It was issued in June 1998. The objective of FAS 133 is to measure all the financial assets and liabilities at their fair value. The statement became effective in 2000 and includes hedging activities. The designation and valuation depend upon the intended use of that derivative contract, including any embedded components. The OTC derivative instruments are often complex and difficult to value. FAS 133 was implemented in response to derivative debacles resulting from derivatives used improperly, fraudulently, or for speculation, or to enhance earnings. Corporate hedging activity should be directed at risk management rather than increasing earnings. Statement 133 is very complex but is necessary to increase the oversight and improve the disclosure of derivatives activity.

The Sarbanes-Oxley Act (SARBOX) is a law enacted in 2002 in response to high-profile corporate fraud cases, some of which were directly related to derivatives use. The act effectively made top-level management in organizations accountable and responsible for compliance. Also, internal controls were mandated and were required to meet standards and be audited. Companies are finding SARBOX compliance to be time consuming and a tremendous financial burden. Many public companies are investigating the advantages of becoming private. Ultimately, increased regulation of derivatives dealers and derivatives users is necessary to protect the integrity of the financial system.

Some dealers fall into a gap in which they are unregulated. Bank OTC derivative dealers are more regulated than those affiliated with securities firms and insurance companies. Hedge funds must register as Registered Investment Advisors under the Investment Company Act of 1940. Registration helps to filter criminals or known hucksters from hanging out a sign and opening a U.S. hedge fund. Registration requires periodic filing updates and allows periodic physical inspections. Unfortunately, the SEC lacks adequate resources for all the inspections needed to be performed.

In America, there is a short-term myopic attitude toward business. There is tremendous pressure for companies to meet or exceed quarterly earnings expectations when results are publicly reported and filed with the SEC. These pressures often push companies to use derivatives to enhance their revenues and take unnecessary risks. Financial deregulation contributed to a revolution and to the accelerated growth of derivatives. It is difficult, if not impossible, for a government regulator to maintain the regulatory expertise and resources necessary to monitor and enforce regulations. An even greater concern is the fact that some derivatives are not well regulated or just unregulated. Vigilance rather than complacency is needed to assure that derivatives use does not result in a disaster.

WHAT NEXT?

Financial deregulation in the United States was supported by a strong economy during the 1990s, and it stimulated financial innovation. The 1990s also provided a glimpse of the potential for catastrophe from the improper use of complex derivatives. Derivatives helped to improve the understanding, measurement, and management of various types of risks. Basically, the use of derivatives is positive for managing the exposure to risk limits. The system, however, is susceptible to rogue traders; inept corporate managers; regulators lacking laws or jurisdiction; self-regulatory organizations confronted with a perceived conflict of interest; inadequately trained auditors; and regulators lacking an understanding of the full scope and potential risks, counterparty quality, and integrity. A single major default, though, can initiate a series of correlated short-term, cascading defaults creating a major systemic crisis. Considering the size of the markets, being concerned about proper regulation and systemic risk is imperative.

Financial derivatives provide tools necessary to implement business plans, promote trade and enable international business, and manage risks. Further, they enable participation in multiple markets. They enhance economic efficiency when they work as intended. When they do not, whether because of human error or an improbable event, they have the potential to destroy the world's financial infrastructure. An economic catastrophe is improbable but not impossible. The risk exists. Should we stop or restrict derivatives trading? No, of course not. Derivatives are integral to the facilitation of international trade, promotion of economic stability, and enhancement of growth. The risk of a disaster in a nuclear power plant does not necessarily mean that we should close all the nuclear power plants. Actually, we have encountered nuclear power plant disasters. The outcome was the recognition of risks and understanding that more regulatory oversight and risk management were necessary. Are derivatives contracts like nuclear fissile materials? Volatility is hard to accurately predict, especially if the source, duration, or intensity is potentially unknown.

Consider JP Morgan Chase, with the largest derivatives portfolio on the planet. According to the U.S. Office of the Comptroller of Currency, JP Morgan Chase had more dollars at risk than it had in capital. JP Morgan's derivatives portfolio is approximately one-and-a-half times the entire global economy! Concentration of risk among the largest U.S. banks is also a red flag. Approximately one-third of the derivatives market is controlled by just three banks: JP Morgan Chase, Bank of America, and Citigroup. A substantial percentage of them are OTC, with embedded options, special clauses, cross-collateralization, and interrelated parties. Further, many have an off-balance-sheet status, and reporting requirements are limited (i.e., weak) and sometimes voluntary. This situation has the potential to trigger a financial disaster.

In general, derivatives are controversial, are poorly understood, and have a poor public image. The amount of derivatives being used indicates that these markets are important and growing. According to the ISDA, there was a combined $165 trillion notional value of interest rate and currency OTC derivatives at the end of the 2004 calendar year. The National Futures Association estimated that the number of listed exchange-traded futures contracts entered in 2004 was approximately $1.3 billion. This figure only counts the contract once, not the counterparty.

The daily average global turnover in currency markets is $1.9 trillion ($1,900,000,000,000). This amount includes the intervention of central banks to influence exchange rates. It also includes business exchanges, tourists

Useful Financial Web Sites

Association of Investment Management and Research (AIMR)
www.aimr.net

Federal Reserve
www.federalreserve.gov

Financial Accounting Standards Board (FASB)
www.fasb.org

Futures Industry Association (FIA)
www.futuresindustry.org

Global Association of Risk Professionals (GARP)
www.garp.com

Government Accountability Office (GAO)
www.gao.gov

Government Finance Officers Association (GFOA)
www.gfoa.org

Group of Thirty (G-30)
www.group30.org

International Accounting Standards Board (IASB)
www.iasb.org

International Association of Financial Engineers (IAFE)
www.iafe.org

International Swaps and Derivatives Association (ISDA)
www.isda.org

National Association of Securities Dealers (NASD)
www.nasd.com

Office of the Comptroller of Currency (OCC)
www.occ.gov

Public Company Accounting Oversight Board (PCAOB)
www.pcaob.com

Securities and Exchange Commission (SEC)
www.sec.gov

Securities Industry Association (SIA)
www.sia.com

spending money, investors in foreign securities (not currencies but requiring settlement in a foreign currency), hedging, and speculation. It appears that more risk management directed toward systemic risk is necessary. Large multinational financial institutions wield a considerable amount of political influence and oppose further regulation. Derivatives are an extremely important financial tool, but the moral is that they have to be used carefully and responsibly.

The summary in Table 8.1 is a representative sample, not an exhaustive list, of derivative products. Since financial engineering is ongoing, the pace of innovation constantly introduces new products and instrument concepts. Customized derivatives from the OTC market are constantly being created in response to demand.

NOTES

1. Global Derivatives Study Group, *Derivatives: Practices and Principles* (Washington, DC: Group of Thirty, 1993): 28.

2. See Frank Partnoy, *Infectious Greed* (New York: New York Times Books, 2003): 40–41.

3. Ibid., 145–46.

4. Roger Lowenstein, *When Genius Failed* (New York: Random House, 2000): 123–26.

5. Ibid.; see especially chapter 7.

6. Loren Fox, *Enron: The Rise and Fall* (New York: John Wiley, 2003): 27–28.

7. Ibid., 167–68, 187.

8. Ibid., chapters 11 and 12.

Nine

Risk Management, Regulation, and Politics

RISK MANAGEMENT: TYPES OF RISK

Risk management can be broadly defined because there are so many different types of risk that can be identified. Risk is the uncertainty about an outcome. Risk is not inherently negative although the term typically has negative connotations. Our focus will be on financial risk management. The amount of risk that an individual or an organization can accept varies according to the tolerance for risk. If an organization is completely opposed to risk, it is said to be risk averse. Trade and other forms of commerce involve risks. Uncertainty related to risks can also present opportunities. If an organization takes action to eliminate all risks, it also eliminates all the opportunities for profits. In fact, it will likely lose money because there is often a cost involved in managing risks.

An organization is faced with four different alternatives when making decisions about risk tolerance. Expected losses and risk impacts are usually measured in monetary terms. An organization should prioritize the risks it faces and attempt to prioritize the most important concerns. This will help the organization to create a risk profile, which contains risks that must be managed by regulation and risks that require discretionary management. An organizational risk policy can then be developed and implemented as a risk management plan. The four alternatives for managing risks are risk avoidance, risk transfer, risk reduction, and risk acceptance.

Risk avoidance means avoiding the conditions or business activities that involve a particular type of risk. Risk transfer involves sharing risk with another party or shifting the burden of risk to another party. When an organization purchases insurance, it either transfers or shares certain risks with the insurance company. Insurance provides an important tool for managing risks. Various types of insurance allow risks to be shifted to or shared with the insurance company. The insurance company charges a fee for this service. The insurance company then shifts or shares its risks with wholesale insurance companies called reinsurers, who insure the insurance companies. There is a cost, however, for this service. A premium is paid to the insurance company according to the contractual terms. Risk reduction involves taking steps to minimize or mitigate the amount of risk that is undertaken. Many organizations use financial derivatives to reduce risk. And the final alternative, risk acceptance, is basically a conscious decision made to accept the risk and its potential consequences.

There is a multitude of risk types that can be identified. There are entire texts devoted to the subject, especially risks related to physical security, disaster recovery, and contingency planning. Physical and property risks are the traditional forms of risks addressed by organizations. This section focuses specifically on the risks that are directly related to financial risk management rather than those related to physical security, though they are very important. Governments have been much more focused on physical security and risks related to national security since the September 11, 2001, terrorist attacks. Protecting its citizens is the single most important responsibility of the government.

SYSTEMIC RISK

Systemic risk describes risks that can cause severe adverse affects. It involves a breakdown of a system. These problems are usually severe and difficult to protect against. An example is the 1929 stock market crash and its aftermath, the resulting bank crisis, and subsequent Great Depression. A system usually has multiple points of failure. As systems become more complex and sophisticated, the number of possible points of failure increases.

CREDIT RISK

Credit risk is also referred to as default risk. Banks and lending institutions are particularly attentive to this type of risk. Credit risk is the possibility of a borrower being unable to pay interest and repay principal on schedule. Investors of bonds and other fixed-income securities often use the credit ratings issued by the major agencies to evaluate the creditworthiness of an issuer. Lending institutions consider the financial strength, credit history, and credit rating to evaluate a potential borrower.

PREPAYMENT RISK

Prepayment risk is the possibility that a lender may receive the principal and interest due back sooner than expected. This condition occurs frequently with mortgage backed securities. When interest rates decline, consumers often refinance their mortgages. As they do, their existing mortgages are paid off with the proceeds from the new replacement mortgage with the lower interest rate. The holder of the mortgage backed security will have principal and interest paid back sooner than expected. The investor will then have cash to reinvest. Since interest rates have declined, it would be difficult or impossible to reinvest the returned funds at the previous interest rate without taking additional credit risk. The inability to invest the returned money at the previous interest rate is an example of reinvestment risk.

COUNTRY RISK

Country risk is the possibility that a nation will be unable to repay its debts. In 1998, Russia defaulted on its government debt because of domestic financial problems and fallout from the earlier Asian financial crisis. If a country defaults on its financial obligations, it creates a negative business environment for corporations operating in the region. Country risk can include any type of financial instrument issued within a nation. Emerging markets and transitioning economies are most likely to be subjected to country risk.

POLITICAL RISK

Political risk is the possibility that a government will abruptly change policies. Companies are sometimes reluctant to establish operations or engage in direct investment in Third World nations if a government is unstable or prone to frequent policy changes. Suppose a U.S.-integrated oil company enters a partnership with a company in a Third World country to extract and ship oil. If the partnership becomes very profitable and the government imposes a special tax on the foreign (U.S.) company, it would be an adverse policy change and an example of a possible political risk.

FOREIGN EXCHANGE RISK

Foreign exchange risk concerns the volatility or fluctuation in the value of one currency versus another. The value or rate at which one currency can be converted into another is always changing. Some currencies experience greater volatility than others. The possibility of an adverse move in the exchange rate affecting you is the foreign exchange currency risk.

Interest Rate Risk

Interest rate risk refers to the possibility that interest rates may increase or decrease in a way that will adversely affect your investments. If you are holding a fixed-rate bond and interest rates rise, the price value of your bond will likely decline.

Market Risk

Market risk is the possibility that an investment will lose money value because of a general decline in the financial markets. A declining market, characterized by falling prices, is called a bear market. Conversely, an advancing market, characterized by rising prices, is called a bull market. Stock prices rise and fall daily throughout a trading session. These price fluctuations, again, are referred to as volatility. The prices of some stocks will have wider ranges and more frequent price changes, which means that these securities are more volatile. Volatility refers to the behavior of the price of a security and is often considered to be a measure of risk. The volatility of a security is often compared to benchmark, such as an index. Price volatility represents the possibility of a loss. However, it also represents the possibility of a profit.

Liquidity Risk

Liquidity risk is the possibility that you will not be able to sell your asset(s) at a desired price or possibly not be able to sell at all. Liquidity refers to the ability of a person to convert an asset to cash. Liquidity risk is typically present in real estate investments but can appear in varying degrees in other investments, too. If you owned a piece of land, you may want to sell the property at what you believe is a fair market price. In order to complete a sale, you need a buyer. The possibility that you may not find a buyer is an example of liquidity risk.

Inflation Risk

Inflation risk is also called purchasing power risk. During periods of high inflation, prices increase. As prices rise, it will require more money to purchase items that previously were priced lower. The price of gasoline is a good example. Increases in gas prices affect the cost to produce and transport many goods. In order to reflect higher production costs, companies will raise their prices. When prices increase, the purchasing power of a dollar will decline. In 2004, a person could purchase a gallon of gas for $2. In 2006, the price of 1 gallon of gasoline was $3. So, the $2 that could purchase a full gallon of gas in 2004 can only purchase two-thirds of a gallon in 2006. Hence, the purchasing power of your $2 has declined.

COUNTERPARTY RISK

Counterparty risk refers to the possibility of a loss from the default of a trade counterparty. Counterparty is the term used to describe the other party in a securities transaction. This risk is more of a concern in the over-the-counter (OTC) market than in exchange-regulated securities exchanges. The securities exchange acts as a third party (counterparty) for every transaction to prevent an investor from being exposed to this type of risk. This creates greater transparency and improves investor trust and confidence in the regulated exchanges.

OPERATIONAL RISK

Identifying, understanding, and measuring risk exposures are important activities, but they do not necessarily protect an organization from these risks. A practice called risk management is necessary to determine which risks are acceptable, as well as the level or amount of risk to assume.

Controlling and understanding operational risk is important for modern financial institutions. Operational risks are often related to the presence, enforcement, and adequacy of internal controls. The effectiveness of overall corporate governance is another potential source of operational risks. Internal controls and corporate governance must be measured and monitored to validate their viability. Breaches in internal controls and weak governance can lead to fraud, careless mistakes, risky behavior, or other types of malfeasance. Another aspect of operational risk is management failure. If an organization loses focus, the possibility of problems in technical or information system and financial loss increases. The efficient, optimized, and ethical performance of an organization is a function of a financial institution's formal principles of governance and organized system of internal controls.

BASEL II AND OPERATIONAL RISK

During the 1990s, a series of financial debacles brought considerable attention to operational risk issues. Several of these financial debacles are identified in Chapter Eight. Many of the problems encountered were the result of fraud or corruption, which existing internal controls failed to prevent. Some of the problems were related to decisions involving financial derivatives, the impact of which was not fully understood.

The Basel Committee on Bank Supervision was created in 1974. Since its inception, the organization has been involved in establishing and standardizing bank regulations internationally. This standing committee was established with the support of the Bank for International Settlements (BIS). The headquarters of the BIS is in Basel, Switzerland. Basel is where the committee meets. The committee is composed of representatives from twelve of the world's industrialized nations. The representatives are from regulatory agencies and the central banks of the participating nations. Participation is voluntary and the Basel Committee is self-governing. All of the participants agree to be bound by the committee's recommendations. The organization assures that banking institutions are governed by a regulatory authority in their home country. It also recommends standards such as uniform capital requirements for banks and helps to establish the roles of regulators when cross-jurisdictional issues arise.

In 1988, the Basel Committee held an important meeting. The outcome was a recommendation for the establishment of minimum capital requirements for banks. These minimum capital requirements became known as the Basel Accord or Basel I. Each of the Basel Committee's member countries subsequently established laws in their home countries setting provisions for adoption and implementation. The Basel Accord recommendations were intended specifically for banks. Banking restrictions in the United States that had been in effect since the 1930s were becoming incrementally liberalized. The traditional boundaries between banks and securities brokerage firms were beginning to erode. The Basel I Accord was difficult to apply to both banking and brokerage firms because of regulatory and operational differences. The Basel Committee began making changes to Basel I during the early 1990s. The committee agreed to adopt the revisions in 1996 as an amendment, which appropriately became known as the 1996 Amendment. Essentially, it was a provision to address market risk. It was updated under Basel II in 2004.

Throughout the 1990s, the Basel Committee observed and monitored an increasing number of financial calamities. It became concerned about the financial strength and integrity of the banking system, especially with the emergence of many new, complex derivative instruments. Many of these derivatives were credit derivatives. Also, many financial institutions were increasing the practice of securitizing assets to create liquidity. These securitizations were often credit-based debt instruments. It also became apparent to the committee that operational risks represented serious potential risks for financial institutions. A new accord was proposed by the committee in 1999. The recommendations were drafted during the year in which most banks were trying to understand the risks that could affect their operations with the turn of the millennium. There were many prognosticators who predicted a catastrophic global financial collapse because computer systems' internal clocks and old programs lacking documentation would crash at the turn of the century. There were also predictions of massive power failures that did not materialize. The Basel Committee allowed a long period of review and consultation before adopting the new accord. In 2004, the committee reached an agreement and adopted what is known as Basel II.

The foundation for Basel II has three main components, which are referred to as pillars. The first is the establishment of minimum capital requirements. The second applies to supervisory review. The third pillar is market discipline and disclosure. Basel II was scheduled to take effect from December 2006. Some countries, especially the United States, were encountering implementation issues and concerns. As a result, in March 2006, the Federal Reserve announced that the date for the United States to comply would be delayed until 2008. This announcement was controversial and some of the committee members, especially Europeans, were upset with the decision.

Historically, there have been many different interpretations of operational risk in the banking and financial industry sector. Some defined the risk very narrowly while others had a broad or vague interpretation. In order to facilitate a consensus, the Basel Committee developed a formal, standard definition. In 2004, Basel II defined operational risk as "the risk of loss resulting from inadequate or failed internal processes, people and systems, or from external events." The committee purposely excluded systemic risk, legal risk, and reputation risk from the definition of operational risk. The nations included in the Basel Committee on Bank Supervision are referred to as the G-10. There are actually eleven countries in the G-10 because Luxembourg is included. The participating nations are listed below, in alphabetical order:

1. Belgium
2. Canada
3. France
4. Germany
5. Italy
6. Japan
7. Luxembourg

8. Netherlands
9. Sweden
10. United Kingdom
11. United States

Basel II provides a framework for operational risk management and capital adequacy. It is formally called "International Convergence of Capital Measurement and Capital Standards: A Revised Framework." Basel II compels banks to upgrade their risk management practices and revise organizational risk policies.

Basel II requires banks to establish capital to cover the contingencies related to operational risk. Banks are required to identify, collect, aggregate, analyze, and report financial activity with greater detail under Basel II. Identifying, measuring, and managing risks is a dynamic process. The environment is constantly evolving, and managing risks requires vigilance, often a tolerance for ambiguity, strong ethical principles, and strategic thinking. Present capital rules for banks in the United States are outdated and need to be revised. Basel II compliance will improve internal controls as well as the integrity of the banking system on a global scale.

THE MARKETS IN FINANCIAL INSTRUMENTS DIRECTIVE

The Markets in Financial Instruments Directive or MiFiD is issued by the European Union (EU). The MiFiD directive is comprehensive and seeks to improve investor protection and transparency among the European states. The purpose of the directive is financial markets reform. The implementation will take place between 2007 and 2009. According to the European Commission, the objectives include increasing financial market efficiency, increasing market transparency, providing access to best executions, and, overall, increasing investor protection. The directive will also help financial forms to expand by allowing them to provide services within any of the EU members as long as they have permission from the home nation. Consistency and fairness related to the sale of a financial product is a key objective.

Suitability is an area addressed by MiFiD. Suitability means financial firms must make sure that the investments of the client are appropriate and consistent with their objectives and resources. Firms must assure that their technical systems are auditable and in compliance with requirements. As a result, financial firms will place a greater emphasis on client relationships, risk management, and regulatory compliance.

These regulations are supposed to be phased in beginning in 2007. The reforms are broad and encompass all of the financial markets, including derivatives. Most of the reforms are focused on equity-related markets, but they will also affect elements of forex trading. The impact in the spot forex market is minimal compared to other financial markets. The initiative is to make the markets more transparent and fair.

THE FALL OF COMMUNISM AND FINANCIAL CHANGE

The collapse of Communism in Eastern Europe is an important milestone in modern history. The scope of change during the subsequent transformation of the former Communist nations to democracy and free-market economies was enormous. It involved economic reforms and political restructuring, both of which represent transformational change. It was also a peaceful transition.

The development of capital markets in these nations during this period has been, as a complement, followed by a privatization process involving formerly state-owned businesses. The development of a regulatory structure accompanied privatization and the growth of financial exchanges, but the legal role of this structure is beyond the scope of this work.

Russia's transformation was difficult because the requisite financial and legal infrastructure was underdeveloped. It also required behavioral adjustment and a shift in mindset because of the radical ideological changes. The sale of state-owned enterprises in Russia in the 1990s was a reversal of public policy from the previous Communist governance regime. Privatization is an important element of financial reforms in many nations. Often it is part of an overall global strategy. Integrating domestic capital markets with global markets can result in positive economic benefits.

Transitional Economic Change

As a result of the collapse of command economy and Gosplan, the Soviet-era body that regulated every aspect of planning and distribution, factories had to deal with their goods by themselves; there was no state body that would provide supplies and take their inventory, and they did not have sales or marketing departments. Also, after the breakup of the Soviet Union, some former suppliers and wholesalers became separated by state borders, and the distribution channels were destroyed. The acceleration of import created competition that did not exist before, and Soviet-era enterprises with their high prices, notorious low quality, and lack of new distribution channels were left with huge inventory and debts. In the 1990s, it was typical for enterprises

St. Basil's Cathedral in Moscow, a symbol of a Russia undergoing dramatic changes as it reinvents its financial and economic systems after Communism. Getty Images/Emma Lee/Life File.

that had no money and huge debts to pay their employees' salaries in goods produced by the enterprise. This was a wide-spread phenomenon that affected every part of Russia.

Goods received as salary were sold by common people everywhere, from open markets in Moscow, to freeway shoulders, bus stops, and train stations throughout the country. When a train stopped at a station, an incessant flow of people would walk through the train, trying to peddle whatever was produced in the area, from toys, crystal, and utensils, to bras and condoms. One could create a map of manufacturing facilities by taking a train or driving. In the Kola Peninsula, north of Murmansk, the sides of the roads were decorated with racks of furs swaying in the wind, such as raccoon, fox, mink, and sable.

The collapse of Communism and the transition to a free-market economy was difficult. There was no precedent or blueprint outlining the process. Russia, under Communism, did not have the type of economic or business infrastructure needed to support a new democracy with free markets. Many institutions as well as rules and regulations simply did not exist.

One of the first steps undertaken by the government during the transition was to convert state-owned enterprises into privately owned companies, a process called privatization. Some government enterprises were sold to the highest bidders. Some organizations distributed stock to their workers. Stock represents equity or ownership. Distributing stock and sharing ownership with the employees was a practical concept. Unfortunately, many employees did not understand what a share of stock was. In addition, there was no way to determine an accurate value. It was also difficult for an employee to sell the shares of stock that they received since a regulated stock market did not yet exist.

In the early 1990s, during the beginning of the privatization period (1992–1993), some enterprising businesspeople bought large amounts of shares from employees, sometimes even controlling interest in a company. The businesspeople realized that the employees did not fully understand the value of their stock and, further, found no use for the paper ownership vouchers/stock shares. They often paid cash for the shares. It was not uncommon for shares to be traded for goods. Some shares were even traded for bottles of vodka. There were no laws preventing such exchanges. To the average worker, something tangible was more useful and practical than a piece of paper. Besides, there was considerable uncertainty during the transition and often distrust of the government. There was no real assurance that a conversion to democratic rule and a free-market economy would be successful.

Some of these businesspeople were able to leverage their share purchases into controlling interest in companies and used this wealth and power to acquire more companies. In 1992, the Russian government established an interbank currency market called the Moscow InterBank Currency Exchange (MICEX). It began as a conduit for the Central Bank of Russia's daily currency fix and an incremental step in creating functional and legitimate financial markets. MICEX was successful following its introduction.

Prior to MICEX, there was an underground black market in which the U.S. dollar was the primary currency. There were government restrictions in effect concerning the use and exchange of dollars. However, the Russian ruble was experiencing a loss of purchasing power because the country was experiencing high inflation and rapid price increases. The U.S. dollar was more stable. MICEX provided an official forum for banks to engage in forex operations legally.

Another significant economic reform was marked by the Russian Ministry of Finance, the Central Bank, and MICEX cooperating to develop and create an open market for the issuance and secondary trading of the Russian Federation's government bonds. When a security is first issued, it has an initial public offering (IPO) that occurs in the primary market. The security is sold through an intermediary, directly to the buyer. When securities are bought and sold after the initial issue, the trading is said to take place in the secondary market. MICEX created a securities exchange division for the secondary trading of government bonds. It was successful. Creating the exchange was difficult because Russia did not have an existing banking and regulatory infrastructure. These institutions had to be developed, which was difficult. Another constraint was that the judicial system needed reform. Many securities laws did not exist, since previously under Communism, all of the companies were state owned. The Russian legislature had to pass a series of laws to support the development of a new economic system. This, too, was a difficult process, since not all of the elected officials were supportive of the economic and political reforms.

MICEX's history is very short relative to most regulated securities exchanges. However, the development and growth of MICEX demonstrates how the exchange as an economic and political institution was an integral part of the transition of Russia from a Communist-planned economy to a free market–based system. MICEX was formally established and registered as a legal entity in the Russian Federation on January 9, 1992. The exchange relied upon expert consultants, internal competence and commitment, and leading-edge technology to rapidly ascend the learning curve anddevelop a world-class securities exchange.

Examining the political and economic conditions during the period before MICEX's formal registration will help us understand the motives and events that led to its creation. The organization probably began in 1989, during the perestroika of the former Soviet regime. An informal and spontaneous effort to establish a market exchange rate for hard currency emerged. This period was marked by social unrest and political turmoil. The government of the USSR had encountered systemic financial problems. During the late 1980s, the exchange rate for the Russian ruble was set by the State Bank of the USSR. The State Bank's official exchange rate was typically higher than a market rate that began to develop in the informal underlying market. This artificial rate caused an OTC, intermarket currency trade to proliferate because market participants believed that the official rate did not accurately reflect the ruble's relative purchasing power. Also, prevailing sentiment, including public communication of their disagreement by major businesses and trade enterprises, confirmed that the rate did not effectively support external trade needs of the decentralized USSR. This problem inhibited the development and expansion of foreign economic relationships.

The increased visibility of the exchange-rate issue pressured the government to respond by establishing the Department of Currency Auctions at the Bank for Foreign Economic Affairs of the USSR. This ultimately became the central forum for almost all of the currency settlements among industrial and trade entities in the USSR. The currency auctions at the Bank for Foreign Affairs officially began on November 3, 1989, and they determined a single dollar-ruble exchange rate. This form of currency market auctions lasted for about one-and-a-half years and included nineteen auctions. State organizations and enterprises were the primary participants in the first auctions. Over time, the number of participants expanded, and eventually all persons who were legal residents of the USSR were permitted to be part of the free currency market. The market expansion applied to newly privatized companies and corporations, too.

During the period from 1989 through 1991, a network of new, independent commercial banks developed rapidly. The proliferation of these banks paralleled the June 1990 declaration of independence by the Russian Federation and the ultimate formal breakup of the Soviet Union in December 1991. Most of these banks acquired licenses to transact international currency operations. The proliferation of independent banks led to further demand for a true market-based forum for hard-currency exchange. In response, the State Bank of the USSR established a new division in April 1991, appropriately named the Center for Carrying out Interbank Currency Transactions. This division was informally referred to as the Currency Exchange, and formal currency auctions were conducted weekly. By the end of 1991, the rate established by the Currency Exchange became recognized as the official ruble rate. The Currency Exchange continued to be a state-controlled entity. It remained under the direct supervision of the State Bank of the USSR. This relationship and governance structure created problems for the Currency Exchange because its scope of operation and potential for development were severely limited.

The economic pressures that accompanied the collapse and breakup of the Soviet Union in 1991 placed additional burdens on the Currency Exchange, and its role needed to be expanded to help stabilize the economy of the Russian Federation. The State Bank of the USSR ceased to exist and was directly replaced by the state-controlled Central Bank of the Russian Federation. As the internal banking market in Russia continued its accelerated pace of growth, increased capacity and a more reliable market-based mechanism were needed for banks to conduct hard-currency operations. In response, the Central Bank collaborated with leading Russian banks to find a solution. The result was the conception of a new organization to accommodate existing market demand along with the authority and flexibility to expand trading operations in the future. The name of this new organization is the Moscow Interbank Currency Exchange or MICEX. It became a legal entity on January 9, 1992, registered as a closed joint-stock company intended to replace the existing Currency Exchange. There were thirty-four founding owners of MICEX. The founders included thirty of the leading banks in Russia (including the Central Bank of Russia), the Association of Russian Banks, the Moscow City Government, and two financial companies. This ownership structure remained stable through MICEX's history, although the ownership shares from Russian banks that failed during the 1998 national economic crisis were acquired by the Central Bank, increasing its influence and power.

The Currency Exchange thus eventually became MICEX. The transition took from January 1992 until April 1992 to complete. The rules developed for the Currency Exchange auctions became the basis for the currency law of the country. Following the formal transition, MICEX declared that, like its predecessor, it did not have a profit motive. Following this announcement in April 1992, MICEX reduced fees and commission rates. According to the organization's charter, it was established to harmonize the interests of enterprises and banks, state bodies, and the pursuit of monetary and financial policy. The charter also enabled it to pursue and secure opportunities in other sectors of financial markets and exchange trading.

MICEX has been well received by the banking and business community. Within its first year of operation, MICEX attracted ninety-three registered participants for exchange trading. Transaction volumes rapidly increased. By 1993, MICEX was recognized by the Central Bank as the most liquid and reliable securities market in Russia. The Central Bank logically selected the exchange as the forum for trading government bonds, both in the primary (initial issue) and secondary trading markets. This declaration and recognition led to further concentration of trading activity and liquidity at MICEX. The introduction of government bond trading (GKO, OFZ) in 1993 represented a major milestone in the process of transforming MICEX from a currency exchange into a universal exchange for trading multiple types of financial instruments.

MICEX implemented a new trading and depository system in 1994 to accommodate the trading of government bonds and to prepare for future growth and expansion. The exchange upgraded and expanded its internal infrastructure with state-of-the-art computer and telecommunications hardware and software. MICEX, along with the Central Bank of Russia, determined that the exchange would use a fully electronic system rather than the more widely used traditional open-outcry auction model. It proved to be a successful strategic decision. In addition, the preliminary task was to organize exchange trading in new financial instruments for both stock and derivatives markets. This development focus continued through the next two years. MICEX also began the creation of a modern depository system for securities. Its volume of transactions continually increased, and the number of registered bank and financial company members of the exchange continued to grow.

In 1996, MICEX established a forum for trading in corporate bonds and continued to develop the policies and procedures necessary to trade equities of the leading Russian companies (i.e., blue chip equities). MICEX also established a derivatives exchange market. The first derivative instruments developed were the U.S. dollar futures contract and the GKO (short-term Russian government bond) futures contract. This market was developed in response to heavy member demand. It was recognized as one of MICEX's premier accomplishments.

The pattern of accelerated growth and development dramatically changed in the summer of 1998, and was abruptly halted by a nationwide banking and financial crisis in Russia that crested in August. The Russian government defaulted on its debt obligations because of liquidity issues created by systemic problems. Many banks failed and defaulted on their obligations to depositors. Russia did not have any form of deposit insurance and there was no government backing to rescue failed banks. The population, in general, lost trust in Russian banks, and the economy was forced to become a cash-based (hard-currency) market for about the next six months.

The MICEX leadership pledged to cooperate with the Russian government and its market participants throughout the crisis and worked to make the exchange as stable, productive, and well managed as possible. Its risk management systems and safeguards worked as intended during the crisis. The exchange was not only able to survive but also played a key role in the recovery of the financial system. Its electronic system remained reliable and was able to maintain liquidity for the equity shares of the key issuers. It was the only liquid trading forum for the interbank currency operations during the crisis. MICEX cooperated with the Central Bank and Ministry of Finance to guide the nation out of the financial crisis. The exchange survived and in the process increased public trust and confidence in its institutional role.

Fortunately, the crisis was short-lived and the recovery was rapid. The financial markets and Russian economy began a recovery in early 1999.

Frozen funds were released, and the IMF brokered a syndicated loan deal to provide assistance and support the recovery. The volume of transactions at MICEX sharply declined during the crisis but gradually returned to precrisis levels when the situation stabilized. By the summer of 1999, the Russian financial markets displayed clear signs of recovery. The recovery was aided by both international and domestic economic factors. The stability of MICEX, as a forum for currency operations and securities trading, was essential to the recovery and the restoration of the confidence of member banks, trade partners, and investors. MICEX continued its recovery and gradually added new stock and bond listings. It refined listing requirements and created indices for both stock and bond trading. In 2003, the exchange adopted and agreed to comply with a national code of conduct along with new, more stringent listing rules. MICEX is still the primary forum for currency trading. Its initial role expanded and it now supports markets for trading stocks, options, corporate bonds, government bonds, and derivative instruments. These operations exist for both the primary and secondary markets. Further growth is planned.

MICEX is a key institution in the Russian Federation and an integral part of economic reform. It provides a stable basis for banks to perform market operations. The history of Moscow Interbank Currency Exchange is synonymous with the development of financial markets in the Russian Federation.

Banking Sector Concerns

The development of the Russian banking system faces sizeable challenges. Much of the strong initial economic growth has been influenced by extraneous factors such as the business environment. High oil prices have netted huge benefits for Russia's energy sector. Profits in other natural-resource-based exports have also been strong. The biggest challenge confronting banks, however, is their ability to finance the upgrades and modernization of the manufacturing and production infrastructures. Many of the plants and factories are operating with obsolete equipment, some of which has not been upgraded for decades. The Russian transition to a free-market economy was constrained by the legacy of the former Communist-planned economy. The structure of the economy was not readily available to transition because it lacked the appropriate infrastructure. Furthermore, much of the production and manufacturing capacity was military related. In order to compete, Russian businesses must improve production and technology capabilities.

The Russian banks have had only a modest role in financing business investments over the past few years. This is partly attributable to the Russian banking system's relatively low level of overall capitalization. While stable, the banking system requires further development to support the growth and financing necessary to improve Russia's decaying business infrastructure. The financing problem could be compounded if global interest rates rise significantly. If the ability to obtain financing from foreign entities is impacted, companies will be more inclined to consider domestic sources, with their limited capacity. Improvements in the banking infrastructure will help the capital markets to develop, improve the competitiveness of Russian companies, and increase the gross domestic product (GDP), all of which will lead to an increased standard of living. It will be a forward step toward improving social conditions.

Russia experienced a rapid economic transformation from the state-controlled Communist government. The transformation is manifested in the dramatic transfer of national wealth from state ownership to private ownership. In 1991, nonstate enterprises produced 5 percent of the per capita GDP. In 2002, the amount was more than 70 percent. In slightly more than ten years, the economy transformed from one of state control to one in which the private sector was dominant. A strong securities exchange and financial architecture is critical to continued economic development and growth. Russia's economy remains fragile as privatization initiatives continue. A nation's economic growth requires a healthy financial sector. The fairness and objectivity associated with MICEX as an institution has facilitated, and should continue to facilitate, the development of Russia's capital markets. MICEX has become an institution in the Russian economy and is supporting the nation's economic development for the benefit of the Russian people.

Economic Issues

The products introduced by MICEX, especially the recent dollar and euro exchange rate currency, will help to increase international trade and minimize payments risks. This will help Russia advance toward a national goal of establishing an open economy and a fully convertible currency (ruble). The transition to currency convertibility is a process. The removal of the barriers to full convertibility will likely involve incremental changes in restrictions, efforts to stabilize the economy, and increases in international trade and legal reforms. This goal will not be achieved within the next few years but opportunities exist for considerable progress. MICEX, by providing a trading forum based upon trust and integrity, serves a public good.

Russia has achieved an investment grade rating from the major rating institutions for its sovereign debt, which is largely attributable to the stability of the financial system. Improving the banking system and financial markets infrastructure will help position Russia for consideration and possible acceptance in the World Trade Organization. If Russia is accepted, the benefits of membership include improved access to global trade markets, multilateral trade, and an improved international reputation.

Ten

Beyond Money

PHYSICAL TRANSPORTATION OF MONEY

Transporting precious metals, high-value items, and money has always been a challenging task. Their physical nature and value present obstacles. Physically transporting cash has been a difficult, sometimes risky, and time-consuming endeavor. It requires manual intervention, is labor intensive, and requires considerable security precautions. Recent technological advances are revolutionizing the way money is transferred and transported. They have enabled new channels of commerce using the Internet. Many companies involved with money have developed new methods that have incrementally changed the way money is handled. This chapter provides a summary of how the actual money is handled by merchants and banks.

Wells Fargo was officially founded in 1852 in San Francisco as a bank, hoping to capitalize on the riches of the 1849 California gold rush. Wells Fargo became a pioneer in shipping money and goods across the country. The bank earned a reputation for reliable and fast delivery of goods. It used stagecoaches, steamships, and the railroad for transportation. The bank was even granted the contract to carry mail across the country to California via stagecoach. Wells Fargo established the dominant stagecoach system and, true to its plan, was successful in banking as well as gold and money transport during the booming economy that accompanied the California gold rush.

The railroad ultimately displaced the stagecoach for cross-country transportation, leading to radical changes in transportation. Transporting money and gold was a dangerous business, robbery being an operational peril. In

1905, Wells Fargo separated its banking business from the express (transport) business. The automobile ultimately replaced the railroad as a mechanism for transporting cash locally and air transportation replaced the train for cross-country transportation. Wells Fargo continues to be an innovative organization. In 1995, they became the first major bank to introduce Internet banking.

Brinks had modest beginnings in Chicago as a simple baggage transport company. The organization was incorporated in 1873, following the death of its founder. The company became involved with the transportation of money in 1897, when it signed contracts to deliver local payrolls. This marked the company's shift toward becoming a money courier and vaulting service. After the turn of the twentieth century, Brinks Express expanded their Chicago-based money transport business by entering contracts with local banks, merchants, and the commodities exchanges. Brinks made a substantial investment in horses and wagons to accommodate the needs of their growing business. The employees were bonded. The couriers established a reputation for being "strongmen," and some of their feats demonstrating strength became legendary.

Brinks recognized the commercial potential of the automobile, which was unpopular at the time because the noise scared the horses on the street and people did not like the exhaust fumes. The company purchased motorized transport vehicles and began to expand its operation with branch offices in other major cities. By the 1920s, Brinks had an entire fleet of armored transport vehicles. Banks, that had been using their own vehicles, started outsourcing the business of moving money to Brinks, which also helped them avoid the risk of making the deposits themselves. The regional Federal Reserve Banks entered contracts to have Brinks physically move money. Many companies hired Brinks because of the security they offered in transactions. Brinks revolutionized money transport and helped to create a special industry niche. The transportation process still involves risk and is time consuming, and it is manual and labor intensive. Nevertheless, armored vehicles, manned with crews of trained, armed, and bonded personnel are indeed a substantial achievement compared to the couriers on horseback or wagon train at the turn of the twentieth century.

Western Union was established in 1851, shortly after the introduction of the telegraph. The company was first named the New York and Mississippi Valley Printing Telegraph Company. Five years later the name was changed to Western Union and it became a pioneer in data communications, financial messaging, and money transfer. Western Union first introduced money transfers in 1871. In 1989, they began international money transfers. The company transmitted telegrams for more than 144 years. The last telegram was transmitted in January 2006. The telegraph, considered a revolutionary technological advance, was replaced by faster, less expensive methods of communication. Western Union continues to provide money transfer services and has global capabilities.

Today, armored cars are used extensively, but the volume of electronic, paperless transaction is increasing. The main reasons for this trend are technological advances, which enable new financial products and services to be created. Financial transactions are being conducted electronically using credit and debit cards, which eliminate the need for paper checks. Many bank customers are beginning to take advantage of other automated preauthorized services such as electronic bill payments and electronic direct deposit of paychecks. These new changes reduce the handling of paper money, which is dematerialization.

The number of electronic transactions continues to increase. The new systems and services are earning customer trust because they are more reliable and efficient. Consequently, the electronic financial services industry will continue to expand. Many countries, which do not have a mature, well-established, and bureaucratic financial infrastructure, are making use of highly advanced electronic innovations. But it is more difficult for countries such as the United States, which have well-developed financial systems, to displace an existing system and adopt a new one. Furthermore, some developments have been resisted by businesses that control and dominate the existing industry structure. Technology, however, is impacting and changing financial services throughout the world.

Loomis Fargo and Co. is the second largest armored car company in the United States. According to them, the cost of processing and transporting cash amounts to more than $100 billion a year. Banks and merchants are aware that the rising cost of gasoline is increasing the cost of physically transporting money and checks for processing. Electronic processing is thus certainly a more efficient and less expensive alternative. Check 21 (a federal law that enables banks to handle more checks electronically), though, requires a bank to accept a negotiable image of a check as a legal equivalent of the original paper check. The number of electronic payments has been increasing at an almost exponential pace. Predictions of a cashless society, though, are premature. According to the Federal Reserve, the amount of U.S. currency in circulation has increased by 45 percent in the last ten years. It is unlikely that anyone visualized electronic commerce and the Internet when the nation's currency was being adopted.

DEMATERIALIZATION OF MONEY

As discussed above, cash management and transport are becoming more computerized and automated. The use of paper is being displaced by electronic record keeping and automated transactions. Physical stock and bond certificates are being replaced by electronic ownership records. Many experts forecast that paper money will likely be used less because of the convenience provided by credit cards and debit cards in electronic consumer transactions.

Another example of dematerialization is online statements rather than paper statements. Banks and other institutions save a considerable amount of money by sending electronic statements and notices. The savings are substantial when one considers the cost of paper, envelopes, postage, and labor. Also, an electronic online statement will arrive faster than a mailed statement.

PLASTIC CARDS

Clearly, banks play an important role as intermediaries in the economic system. Banks, though, are not the only financial institutions that provide credit. They are confronted with competition from nonbank financial institutions (NBFIs), which are nondepository financial firms such as insurance companies, investment banks, finance companies, pension funds, and mortgage companies. Bank lending represents less than 20 percent of the credit market in the United States. The introduction of the plastic credit card is a milestone in the history of money.

Credit cards and debit cards offer a means to pay for goods and services electronically. The debit card takes funds directly from the user's checking account to pay the merchant. The transaction typically is completed in a matter of seconds. A credit card provides the holder with a revolving line of credit, up to a set limit. It is hard for many people to believe that the credit card business is a young industry and the systems have existed for just fifty years. Prior to the issuance of credit cards and the proliferation of consumers' credit, people saved their money to make purchases, especially those involving large expenditures.

Most large department stores offered their own proprietary credit cards to customers as far back as the 1930s. The department store did not actually extend credit, a bank did. The department store guaranteed payment and acted as an intermediary to transactions. Basically, the bank was financing the store's receivables. In the 1950s, credit cards were issued to consumers to purchase gasoline only. These gasoline cards were restricted to the company's brand. Sears was developing a successful credit card enterprise and J.C. Penney provided credit to its catalog customers.

The first credit card that could be used at a range of merchants was the Diner's Club card, which was launched in 1950. It was developed to be a charge card for use at restaurants. The card program was structured so that the restaurant paid the fees. In return, the payment was guaranteed directly by Diner's Club. Record keeping and processing were manual during this period. As a result, these cards were not profitable for the first five years of existence.

Reportedly, a businessman named Frank McNamara had dinner with Alfred Bloomingdale, the founder of Bloomingdale's Department Store, to discuss customer credit collection problems. McNamara had planned to pay for the meal until he discovered that he had forgotten his wallet and did not have enough cash to cover the check. He was quite embarrassed. After this incident, he conceived the concept for the Diner's Club card. He discussed the matter with Bloomingdale and an attorney. The three men created a partnership and introduced the Diner's Club. McNamara sold his share of the company to his partners because he thought that the initial success of the company represented a passing fad.

In 1958, American Express issued a competing card, which was intended for businesspeople who would charge their travel and entertainment expenditures. In 1958, Bank of America also began testing its BankAmericard in California. The concept was structured differently than the previous plastic card pioneers. The concept included three sources of revenue to the bank. The first was a charge that would be imposed on the merchant accepting the card. Next, a monthly charge that would be imposed upon the consumer for unpaid balances. The third, an annual fee that would be charged to the cardholder.

Bank of America, based in San Francisco, California, was established in 1904 as the Bank of Italy. It gained a reputation for reliability after the 1906 San Francisco earthquake and fire by providing loans for reconstruction. In 1929, the Bank of Italy merged with the Los Angeles Bank of America, becoming the largest bank in California. The following year, the name Bank of America was adopted. The bank, however, was in a different time zone than New York, and that was a disadvantage.

Bank of America responded to this challenge with innovation and became more efficient and competitive. Since reporting and reconciliation needed to take place in California at odd hours, the bank developed automated check processing, magnetic ink character recognition for checking account numbers, and other innovations to reduce administrative costs. From humble beginnings, it developed into one of the largest banks in the world. Since its inception, it has been one of the most technologically innovative banks. Competition and technological capabilities continue to drive innovation in the nation's financial services industry.

The experiments in California demonstrated that using cards for credit would be profitable. However, banks realized that there was a problem with consumer awareness and acceptance. The cards represented a change from the manner in which customers made purchase transactions. Change is often accompanied by uncertainty and people were predisposed to ignore the cards. The banks also had to determine how to get the cards into the hands of the public to achieve profitability. Initially, the banks sent invitations to apply for cards. The response rate was negligible. Next the banks sent mass mailings of unsolicited credit cards to customers and even potential customers in an attempt to quickly saturate the market and to encourage the use of the cards. This, however, worked. When the cards were sent, people tried them often out of curiosity. Throughout the early 1960s, banks adopted this mass mailing, hit-or-miss approach to gain consumer acceptance and get the cards distrtibuted to the public. Looking back, almost fifty years, this approach obviously succeeded, but not without problems.

Banks lost a considerable amount of money through their aggressive marketing style. These early cards did not have any security features, like those issued today. Cards were often stolen, or found after they were discarded and then used for purchases. Customers were billed for purchases they did not make. Since the cards were relatively new, the laws had not yet been developed to address such issues. Commercial businesses, too, were alleged to have over-billed customers for merchandise that was never purchased.

In 1968, the Fed appointed a task force to investigate and prepare a report analyzing this emerging industry. The report identified many of the new problems that accompanied the credit card business. Congress was urged to enact legislation to limit consumer liability for improper card use and fraud. The liability limit was $50, and it remains in effect today. Card issuers also imposed credit limits above which merchants would not be paid if they accepted a card for purchases.

The BankAmericard dominated the industry during the 1960s. However, the cards had limitations based upon the states in which they were issued. The Glass-Steagall Act placed restrictions on interstate banking, limiting the BankAmericard to use in California, where it was originally launched. In order to compete, several smaller banks organized partnerships whereby they would honor each other's cards. In California, the major competitors formed a group and issued a Mastercharge credit card. They also entered agreements with bank groups outside of California to accept the cards in other states. In response, Bank of America began franchising its BankAmericard throughout the country in 1967, thus creating the National BankAmericard.

An official National BankAmericard corporate entity was established in 1970 and the BankAmericard was spun off from the parent, Bank of America. Six years later, the company announced that the name of the franchise would be changed to Visa, to remove the Bank of America brand name connection. Processing receipts for credit card transactions was a cumbersome, manual, time-consuming process. As a result, there were many mistakes and frequent time delays in both billings and merchant payments. After the name Visa was adopted, the organization spent considerable time and money adopting automated computer processing technology in order to provide more efficient and profitable service. Prior to this technology, every credit card transaction required that the merchant receive charge authorization by physically making a telephone call to the credit card issuer. Next, a handwritten charge slip was created. An imprint of the card was then made of the slip, which contained carbon paper and multiple duplicate copies. This process was messy and inefficient.

Later, Sears introduced a general purpose credit card in addition to the store charge card. This new card venture was called Discover. In 1990, AT&T launched a national credit card called the Universal card. The financial innovation surrounding card use was one of the most significant developments of the twentieth century. It affected the economy, permanently changed consumer shopping and spending, and created a multibillion dollar industry. A credit card provides a mechanism for purchasing, but it is important to note that these expenditures are made based upon borrowing. You do not need to have money before making a transaction using a credit card or a charge card. You are obligated, however, to repay the credit or cash advance at some point in the future.

As computer and data communication technologies advanced, the credit card industry became more efficient and expanded globally. Record keeping and processing for credit purchases became fully automated. Merchants still pay a fee for being part of a credit card system but these are paid quickly and efficiently. They also reap the benefits of additional purchase customers make on credit. Entire industries emerged as a result of credit cards. Credit card issuers such as MBNA and Capital One are now multibillion dollar enterprises. Another industry emerged to provide support and outsourced processing services for banks and other credit card issuers. This allowed companies to focus on their primary business and attract new customers rather than focus on building a card processing and settlement infrastructure, which would be expensive. Companies like Electronic Data Systems (EDS), FiServ, First Data, CardSystems, and IBM are willing to provide outsourced support services at reasonable prices because the back office processing business is highly competitive and dominated by large companies. In addition, large banks often provide processing services to smaller banks.

AUTOMATED TELLER MACHINES

Another important financial innovation of the twentieth century is the automated teller machine or, as it is ubiquitously known, the ATM. Our

Twenty-four-hour banking—everywhere, all the time. Getty Images/PhotoLink.

society is becoming increasingly automated because of technological advances. ATMs were initially developed to dispense cash as a convenience for the bank's customers. Customers were able to withdraw cash after regular banking hours. The first ATM machines restricted use to the customer's bank. Gradually, networks of banks were established. In 1984, the Supreme Court determined that ATMs were not considered bank branches. This decision meant that ATMs were not governed by laws restricting the establishment of branches across state lines. This led to national expansion of ATM networks. Consumer acceptance and increased demand for ATM services were the result. The decision also led to intense competition among banks.

The first ATM machine was introduced in 1969. It was owned by Chemical Bank and opened at its branch located in Rockville Center, New York. Within a year, many individual banks were installing their own machines. It did not take long for the bankers to realize that the power of the ATM could be leveraged by sharing resources and establishing networks to accept all of their cards. The costs and risks could be spread among the members, and capabilities for customer services could be expanded.

Initially, however, banks would not accept ATM cards issued by other banks until they realized how much money could be made by charging transaction fees. Then banks rushed to put machines in areas with high consumer traffic, where customers would likely need to access cash. As ATMs became more accepted by consumers, groups of banks organized networks through which they would reciprocally accept each other's cards. Examples of these networks include Pulse, MAC, Cirrus, Money Station, and Cash Station. These networks were accused of engaging in anticompetitive practices that eventually resulted in mergers and consolidations. The machines were owned by banks and often merchants. Banks now have nationwide and international cooperative agreements that allow customers of one bank to use the ATMs owned by others to access cash.

In the middle 1990s banks began to use ATMs more strategically. Banks tried to encourage ATM use by introducing a disincentive for dealing with a human bank teller. Banks began charging customers a fee for the privilege of making a transaction with a teller. It was not a popular move but it did increase teller use. Over time, many, but not all, banks eliminated these fees and provided free ATM access for its own customers. They realized that it was much more economical to install multiple ATM machines in convenient locations than building and staffing expensive bank branches. Banks began to close down unprofitable branches and replace them with cost-effective ATMs. Soon, large companies, the same as those processing credit card transactions, began servicing the ATM networks for banks.

An ATM card is a plastic card with an embedded magnetic strip. The strip contains encoded identification information about the account. This information is transmitted to the bank's computer to initiate an ATM transaction. In order to prevent unauthorized access, a unique personal identifier, called a PIN (personal identification number), must also be used to access an account. ATMs provide twenty-four-hour service to customers, eliminating the need to wait in a line inside a bank branch to make a transaction or get cash. Banks charge a nominal transaction fee for this convenience. The fee is a significant revenue source for banks, especially if the customer using the network is a customer from a competitor bank.

ATMs are now widely accepted and are available internationally. A U.S. bank customer is able to use his ATM card in foreign countries and even make withdrawals in a desired currency. The ATM machine essentially performs a spot forex transaction.

DEBIT CARDS

The next step in the evolution of cards is the use of debit cards. Instead of writing a paper check for a purchase, customers can use a bank card that deducts the amount of the purchase directly from the customer's checking account. The funds are taken from the account immediately as the processing is done electronically. Point-of-sale (POS) terminals are card readers that streamline the payment operation. They are connected to a larger network to authorize and process the transaction. Credit and debit cards removed the boundary between credit and money/cash. The credit card is a readily accepted cash surrogate. Debit cards are often issued by banks to serve as ATM cards, too.

Many merchants allow their customers to make cash withdrawals at the time of sales. The withdrawals are also deducted directly and immediately from the customers' accounts. Debit and credit card processing machines are being installed at the checkout counters of most retail businesses. Some retail establishments, grocery stores in particular, are experimenting replacing the checkout cashier with automated bar code scanners and credit/debit card machines. The initial feedback from customers is negative, but many innovations are slow to gain acceptance because they represent change to established routines. Now, even fast-food restaurants are accepting credit and debit card payments in lieu of cash. The transaction acceptable to a merchant once had a minimum purchase requirement. This is no longer the case.

Debit cards and payment cards are not money. They can be used to make transactions, but they do not fit the traditional definition of money. Rather, they are a mechanism that allows access to money.

MORE INNOVATION

The growing practice of electronic bill paying had an unlikely beginning. The concept was conceived in 1981 in Columbus, Ohio, by Peter Knight, a former college athlete and philosophy major. Knight was the manager of a health club. He recognized that there were fundamental problems with the way health clubs approached business development by building membership bases. Most of the new health club members lost interest in the clubs within a year. They also lost interest in paying for the memberships. The industry recognized this trend and it became a common practice to prepay memberships so that the club would receive its fees in advance and avoid expensive delinquency payment collection procedures.

Knight recognized an opportunity to improve the efficiency of this system. He contacted local banks in Columbus about having health club membership fees deducted from bank accounts. A group of banks agreed to cooperate. Next, he contacted area health clubs, who also showed interest in the program. Knight then hired a software programmer to develop a system to automate the process. Knight's company, the CheckFree Corporation, signaled the start of the online billing and electronic payments industry. The technological advances in the personal computer industry, along with new data communications links, like the Internet, helped the concept expand to include major banks, insurance companies, and technology vendors. Electronic payments are efficient and reduce transaction costs. The business infrastructure is still in the process of development, and so the regulatory authority is unclear.

Prepaid merchant cards represent another form of automated payment and are a cash substitute, once they are purchased. A person prepays to purchase a certain value which is redeemable with that particular merchant. Several years ago fast-food restaurant chains only accepted cash. Prepaid gift cards helped the retail industry and the restaurant industry boost revenues.

Smart cards, which can store a large amount of information, are widely used outside of the United States. Data is stored on a computer chip embedded in the card.

TECHNOLOGY AND ELECTRONIC MONEY

As we saw in the foregoing sections, money is incrementally being displaced by electronic substitutes. Information technology advances have enabled the creation of a new industry for electronic payment systems and cash alternatives. Electronic money and related transfers help settle Internet purchases. Business-to-business (B2B) transactions are evolving and gaining acceptance. Some of these developments were introduced in the late 1990s but encountered a setback during the market correction in the technology stock sector that began in 2000. Most of the digital currency companies established in the 1990s have failed. This section identifies selected examples of popular payment networks and emerging electronic cash alternatives.

The Japanese are the source of many electronic communications and financial services technological advances. The culture is also embracing and encouraging development. Investors in the Japanese securities markets are able to place orders remotely using their cellular telephones. In Japan, it is often more economical to use Web-enabled cellular phones for Internet access than landlines. The financial services industry responded by providing services directed at the cell phone users with Internet access. The value of mobile phone orders to buy or sell securities on the Tokyo Stock Exchange increased by 90 percent in 2005 over the previous year.

The term *electronic money* is used rather loosely and can be used to describe many payment services enacted on the Internet or by other means such as electronic funds transfer. Electronic money is also called digital money. It can be considered, in a broad sense, as a substitute for currency. Checks, credit cards, debit cards, and traveler's checks are not considered electronic money. Computer network systems such as Paypal, which help to transfer funds or effect cash payments, can be considered electronic money.

Digital gold currency (DGC) is a general term for a private currency that uses gold reserves as collateral to provide greater security. It is a form of electronic money and is denominated in a standard gold weight. A number of different networks are established that provide digital gold currency. Examples are E-gold, GoldMoney, and e-Bullion. E-gold, established in 1996, is the oldest. GoldMoney and e-Bullion were established in 2001 and 2000, respectively. Each of these networks is proprietary and independent. E-gold and e-Bullion are the most popular networks. GoldMoney, though, has the most gold being stored in reserves. The DGCs hold all of their clients' funds in reserves. Since the DGC currency is based upon weight, the value will fluctuate with the market value of gold bullion. Many DGC account holders are not interested in making transactions. They are holding gold in storage as investment, to hedge against inflation.

Paypal is a new service that was created because the Internet introduced the capabilities and platform from which to launch the business. Paypal has been acquired by E-bay. Amazon and E-bay are also examples of new businesses that emerged because of the Internet. The use of credit cards also expanded because the cards are the payment method of choice when using online merchants. The credit card business was firmly established when the Internet became mainstream in the mid-1990s. The capabilities of the Internet and the ability of credit cards (and debit cards) to function as a paperless payment mechanism were mutually beneficial and helped trigger the 1990s technology stock boom.

GoldMoney.com was established in 2001. The company intended to create a payment system using a digital currency backed by gold reserves. GoldMoney, unlike some of its competitors, has procedures and policies to verify the identity of account holders in order to help prevent fraud and money laundering. As the market price of gold began to increase beyond its current trading range, GoldMoney attracted attention as an alternative method to invest in gold. The company allows investors to purchase small amounts of gold, denominated as "goldgrams." The gold backing the accounts is stored in the UK and is insured by Lloyds. GoldMoney can be converted to cash and wired to any bank. Also, using GoldMoney directly is cheaper for investors than purchasing small amounts of gold through brokers. Many people still consider gold a hedge against inflation and financial disaster because of its intrinsic value.

There are more than 3 million E-gold accounts established as of May 2006, according to E-gold, although not all of them are active. E-gold claims to have more than 3,784 grams of gold in storage. The number of daily transactions averages about 66,000, and the value will vary based upon the market price for gold. At its price level in May 2006, value of the daily transactions was about $10.5 million (U.S.). There are more than three tons in reserve. The system has experienced tremendous growth since 2005, because the price of gold has been rising.

E-gold makes money from storage and transaction fees. All transactions are completely electronic. E-gold transactions cannot be reversed. So, even if there were a mistake, there is no recourse. By comparison, there is recourse with Paypal transactions; they are more like credit card transactions. Fraud accusations, regulatory challenges, and security are a concern. In 2005, a Trojan horse was launched in the E-gold system that recorded log-in and password information of some of the users and then emptied their accounts. The value from the victims' accounts was transferred to the hackers. The hackers attack was stopped but many accounts were compromised by this targeted hacker attack.

E-gold has attracted controversy. The value and existence of its physical reserves are verified by the company itself. Critics raise concerns about the lack of an independent auditor for this purpose and are skeptical about the existence of the reserves. E-gold does, however, publish up-to-date statistics about their reserves.

ELECTRONIC CRIME AND ITS REGULATION

U.S. law enforcement agencies, especially the Secret Service and the Federal Bureau of Investigation (FBI), indicate that they suspect that some of the online digital currency and electronic money networks are being used by criminals as a payment system. The U.S. offices of E-gold were raided by law enforcement officials executing a warrant. Files and computers were confiscated as part of an ongoing investigation. The funds in two of E-gold's bank accounts were also targeted.

Gold and Silver Reserve, which operates under the name OmniPay, uses gold or silver reserves to back the private digital currency that it issues. International criminals are suspected of using OmniPay as a conduit to convert money into E-gold currency units. Both E-gold and OmniPay are controlled by the same individual and are challenging the authority of the government to regulate their business.

Both these companies have reportedly been used by fraudsters and con artists for laundering money and as a forum for engaging in scams such as pyramid schemes. The founders of digital currency companies envisioned them as one day being ubiquitous and global, without political ties to a particular currency. E-gold customers are not required to provide their real names to open an account and there is no way to verify the voluntary information that a customer provides. E-gold units can be purchased by wire transfer of a credit card. Stolen credit cards and identity theft are growing problems. The anonymity, convenient access, and, especially, the irreversible nature of transactions make E-gold an attractive target for online criminals.

New technologies bring opportunities for criminals as well as for legitimate businesses. This is a challenge for law enforcement and regulatory agencies. Criminal activities are similar to a game in which the criminal activity emerges, is shut down, and then reappears. Criminal activity is frontrunning law enforcement efforts and regulatory initiatives. Illegal money laundering is a major concern, and there are more than ten services that provide digital currency payment systems similar to E-gold and OmniPay.

The financial system is the backbone of the economy. This fact makes critical support systems and important financial institutions attractive targets to terrorists. Many experts are predicting that a terrorist attack on the financial system's vulnerabilities is likely. This attack is expected to be a nontraditional terrorist attack. It will likely be a cyber-attack targeting communications networks or key financial institutions in order to disrupt and disable their operations. This type of attack would likely create fear and panic and could lead to a run on the banking system. Historically, these conditions have had catastrophic economic consequences. The system is heavily reliant on technology, computers, electronic record keeping, and data communications networks and, if the system becomes unstable or unusable, there could be a global disruption of trade and commerce. It is difficult for law enforcement agencies to remain prepared and stay ahead of potential cyberterrorists. The law enforcement community must become partners with the financial services industry to foster cooperation and mutual support.

The business of electronic money is addressed in the Money Laundering Suppression Act of 1994. Businesses involved in money transmitting must register with the U.S. Treasury Department. The business of transmitting money is difficult to precisely define, especially as new technology and service offerings are developed. The law is primarily focused on companies that transmit currency or are denominated with a currency. The currency can be either U.S. or foreign. Businesses covered under the law include only those that both transmit and receive cash.

Electronic crimes are also referred to as e-crimes or cybercrimes. Digital currency networks are not directly covered by the U.S. Patriot Act and the Bank Secrecy Act. They are not defined as financial institutions and are not covered by the current legislation. Digital currency networks use terms that are different than banking jargon to avoid being subject to certain laws. The terms deposit and withdrawal are substituted with other words (e.g., inexchange and out-exchange). The Financial Crimes Enforcement Network (FinCen) is an agency of the U.S. Treasury Department that focuses on these types of crimes, and is trying to identify the legal loopholes and ways to close them. In addition, sponsored terrorist groups are continually trying to exploit the vulnerabilities of computer and communications networks.

In February 2006, the Department of Homeland Security conducted a training operation dubbed Cyber-Storm. It was a simulated war game. In the exercise, hackers took control of the power grid in ten states and caused the banking system to fail. They exploited security holes in popular Internet browsers and other widely used computer programs. The participants included software companies and the law enforcement agencies under the Department of Homeland Security. The simulation was considered a success but raised serious concerns about a cyber-attack and its potential consequences. More public and private cooperation is necessary to promote mutual support. Regulation and oversight remain an unresolved challenge, although, it is rational for a legal and regulatory infrastructure to lag behind change.

There is no regulatory agency specifically organized to govern the digital currency industry. They do not have to follow banking regulations. The Global Digital Currency Association (GDCA) was established among industry members for self-regulation. Should the Fed be the only supplier of currency in the United States? It will be up to consumers and regulators. Bank deposits are FDIC insured and private electronic currency networks are not.

INTERNET BANKS

Some banks offer services exclusively online. These Internet-only banks have reduced overhead expenses because they avoid the costs of physical branches, which can be labor intensive. In a recent study, the consulting firm Booz, Allen and Hamilton determined that an average online bank transaction costs about a penny, while an ATM transaction costs about twenty-seven cents and a transaction using a branch teller costs about $1.07.

For consumers, there does not seem to be a compelling reason to establish a single financial relationship with an online-only bank. It is more likely that it will be used to diversify banking relationships. Most online bank customers have traditional bank accounts, too. Many ATM machines are capable of offering the same services that an online bank does. The ATM can dispense cash, accept deposits, sell postage stamps, and provide other customer conveniences. Internet banks are niche competitors, and their potential seems to be limited. Established banks seem better positioned to attract and retain customers than upstart Internet banks.

Internet banks are dependent on technology. Their growth and acceptance are expected to increase among consumers, especially if the overhead costs are shared with the customers in the form of higher returns. Internet banks, however, have not met optimistic projections concerning profitability because of their high fixed cost base related to large technology expenses. Marketing and advertising expenses are also high relative to the physical competitors. The biggest criticism of Internet banks is that they are impersonal and disconnected from their customers, which makes it difficult to establish long-term relationships. The most successful bank business model combines a traditional branch-banking network with enhanced and convenient online, value-added services. Examples are electronic bill payment, securities investment services, account management capabilities, and twenty-four-hour access.

CONCLUSION

Money is a social construct. Paper money will not disappear soon, but it does face competition. Technological advances have streamlined and essentially revolutionized the way we make payment for goods and services. For good reasons, credit is the first choice of payment method. There is a record of the transaction. Some credit cards provide extra services for their clients and aggregate and even categorize expenditures to help them when filing expense reports and taxes. The liability of the cardholder is limited to $50 if the card is lost. Many cards offer incentive features like insurance or extending a manufacturer's warranty on purchases, and they provide an opportunity to contest vendor charges when warranted. Credit cards facilitate online payments as well as telephone purchases. They can also provide record keeping and expense control assistance to businesses.

The use of paper checks has been declining as card-based and other electronic payment methods are gaining acceptance. According to research and forecasts published by Celent, 53 percent of consumer bill payments in the United States were made using checks in 2004. The amount paid by check could be 29 percent because electronic payments are becoming more mainstream.

Electronic methods are changing the traditional ways in which business and commerce are connected. Change is constantly occurring. Challenging change is positive, but resisting change should be done with an open mind. Initially, people objected to the automobile because it scared the horses, which were the primary mode of transportation. Most people were against change, especially those who had substantial investment wrapped up in horses and wagons. The telegraph disrupted the way business was conducted. The American pioneers who traveled across the country by stagecoach spent seventy to ninety days traveling one way. They probably could not imagine making the same trip by jetting through the air in a matter of hours. Change and innovation are tributes to our human spirit, vision, and dynamic nature. We encourage change tempered by social responsibility.

Financial conglomerates are increasing their power and influence throughout the world. Online banks and brokerages provide up-to-the-minute account access, remote access, and new services. The physical elements of banking and brokerage relationships are being removed. Customers are being provided with greater control over their accounts. Once an account is opened, you may not ever need to speak with a human to access account capabilities. National boundaries are also eroding as more banks establish an international presence. Cost structures for banks are being reduced.

Electronic funds transfer systems allow banking transactions to be made anytime. Payroll checks can be directly deposited into a person's checking account. Payments can be made through automatic bill paying systems, and the amount of purchases made via the Internet is enormous. Credit cards can be used to achieve all of the legal objectives of the digital cash networks except directly investing in gold. Alternative digital forms of currency exist but their future and growth rate are difficult to forecast. They may remain part of the underground currency network.

The Internet has changed many of the traditional ways that business was conducted, and financial services are no exception. New business sectors, distribution channels, and product and service developments are being created. It is possible to open a stock brokerage account and engage in trading completely online. Online brokers are more economical and offer discounted commissions.

Banking services are developing at a rapid pace. Balances and transactions can be made in an account through the Internet. Customers no longer have to physically travel to a bank branch during the restricted hours during which they are open. ATM services are expanding and they are available seven days a week for twenty-four hours a day. There are new ways to access purchasing power. Purchasing power is a combination of cash and credit accounts. Smart card technologies are becoming more refined. Innovative access to financial information and purchasing power are presently under development. Financial exchanges are speculating that the role of intermediaries such as banks and brokers will be reduced because of electronic capabilities for investors to place orders directly on an exchange. The role of a physical open outcry exchange can be accomplished online. Exchanges are increasing their capabilities and will eventually be able to provide direct access.

Society is becoming less dependent upon cash, at least from a physical perspective. The Internet and electronic data communications are changing many of the business processes that we have come to accept as routine. The pace of development and innovation is accelerating. It is being driven by technological change and intense business competition. Dematerialization is removing much of the paper that has become a fixture in daily life. Plastic cards are acting as a substitute for paper checks and money. Transportation costs and time delays are eliminated. New methods of remotely accessing securities and currency markets exist. This is an exciting time to be part of an electronic and communications revolution that is challenging the utility of paper money and traditional methods of commerce.

Glossary

agency bonds. Bonds issued by government-sponsored, quasi-independent entities, such as the Federal Home Loan.

Allied Irish Banks. A major Irish banking establishment—in 2002 they declared its U.S. subsidiary had lost nearly $700 million through trading of currency derivatives.

arbitrage. An investment transacted to take advantage of price disparities between markets.

ASEAN. Association of South East Asian Nations, or trade pact between a number of South Asian nations.

auction exchange. A financial exchange in which bids are made face to face or in "open outcry" environments. Such exchanges, the key example being the New York Stock Exchange, are gradually being replaced by automated markets.

Automated Clearinghouse Network. A national electronic funds transfer system, established as an electronic alternative to the previous manual paper-based collection system.

banker's acceptance. A bill of exchange drawn on a banking institution. It acts as a guarantee to companies that are exporting goods to another country.

Bank for International Settlements (BIS). An international banking forum based in Basel, Switzerland, that sets standards in bank capital and risk management. The membership in BIS is one means of achieving cooperation between central banks.

Banking Act of 1933. Act of Congress establishing the Federal Deposit Insurance Corporation, designed to prevent the kind of depositor losses experienced during the Great Depression and to bolster depositor confidence.

Bank of America. A major U.S. bank, Bank of America revealed in 1998 that it had suffered losses of hundreds of millions of dollars due to its association with D.E. Shares, a hedge funds operator heavily involved in derivatives.

Bank of England. Central banking authority for the United Kingdom, it has operated continuously for 300 years.

Bank of Sweden. The oldest central bank, established in 1668.

Bank of the United States. A federally chartered national bank that was the source of much contention in the early decades of the Republic. The First Bank was chartered in 1791, with Treasury Secretary Alexander Hamilton its most ardent supporter, but later expired at the end of its charter. A second national bank also expired in 1837 (1817–1837) due to bitter conflicts between the bank and President Jackson.

Barings Bank. One of the leading lights of the British banking establishment. Barings collapsed due to the activities of a rouge trader Nicholas Leeson, whose reckless trading in currency derivatives was not uncovered until it was too late to save the firm.

Basel I and Basel II. Agreements established by the International Basel Committee on Bank Supervision, first established in 1974, to regulate the amount of risk to which financial institutions are exposed.

basket. A representative sample for a group of different national currencies.

benchmark currency. Any currency that is used to denominate trades used in international transactions. The U.S. dollar is a benchmark currency.

bill of exchange. A written order from one party to another to pay a sum of money on a given date. It is essentially a check.

bills of credit. Paper currency used in the American colonies in the eighteenth century.

Black, Fischer, and Myron Scholes. The authors of the famous Black-Scholes equation that provides a means of determining the future value of an option. This intellectual breakthrough provided impetus for today's thriving options market.

bond. A debt instrument representing a process to repay those who hold the bond with interest. Governments and corporations issue bonds to finance activities.

Bond Market Association. A New York–based industry trade association that promotes public policies favorable to bond traders.

Bretton Woods Agreement. The critical agreement reached in July 1944 between the United States and its allies to establish a new post–World War II international economic order. A major element of the agreement called for the United States to have other countries peg their currencies to the dollar, with the United States agreeing to convert dollars to gold at a set $35 per ounce.

brokered certificate of deposit. Marketable CD that allows for transfer of ownership.

Bryan, William Jennings. Democratic presidential candidate in 1896 who lost to Republican William McKinley. Bryan was a staunch opponent of the gold standard.

Bureau of Engraving and Printing. A division of the Treasury Department responsible for printing U.S. paper currency.

CAFTA. The Central American Free Trade Agreement, a trade agreement reached in 2005 between the United States and Central American nations.

capital markets. The trade in those markets that mature in more than one year.

central bank. A nation's principal monetary authority such as the U.S. Federal Reserve or the Bank of England.

certificate of deposit (CD). A financial instrument in which a customer deposits money for a fixed period of time in order to receive an agreed-upon rate of interest.

check. A written financial instrument that allows for the transfer of funds from one account, or depositor, to another.

Check 21. A standard term for legislation that Congress adopted into law in 2003, and formally known as the Check Clearing for the Twenty-first Century Act. It is intended to reduce the time delay between when a check is written and when it is settled among banks.

Chicago Board Options Exchange. The CBOE is the largest options exchange in the United States. Founded in 1973, it trades foreign-currency options, index options, and interest-rate options.

Chicago Mercantile Exchange. The world's leading exchange for trading futures contracts and options on futures. Products include currency and short-term interest-rate options.

China Aviation Oil. A Singaporean company that incurred enormous losses through derivatives trading that went undetected by auditors until December 2004.

clearing function. A service provided by the Federal Reserve System; it allows banks to reconcile checking account activity.

commercial bank. A bank whose principal functions are to receive deposits, make short-term loans, and provide other services to the public. Such banks range from small commercial banks to very large highly capitalized banks.

commercial paper. A promissory note issued by corporations with high-quality credit ratings. It is a means by which corporations finance their debts.

Commodity Futures Trading Commission. A federal regulatory agency that oversees commodity trading.

community bank. Typically defined as a relatively small local bank with assets of less than 1 billion dollars.

corporate bond. A debt instrument issued by corporations to finance economic activities.

credit union. Mutual or member-owned organization, including public employee credit unions, company credit unions, and the like.

currency debasement. Reducing the value of gold- or silver-based currency system by reducing the amount of precious metal in the coin. Monarchs of the sixteenth to eighteenth centuries were known for such actions as a means of financing additional spending.

currency devaluation. The reduction in the value of a nation's currency relative to another currency or other currencies.

decimalization. Refers to the decimal character of the U.S. monetary system.

dematerialization. The use of electronic record keeping in financial exchanges as opposed to the maintenance of paper documents.

depository institutions. Financial institutions including banks, credit unions, savings and loans (S&Ls), and savings associations.

derivative. A financial instrument whose value depends upon the value of other, more basic variables.

dollar. A U.S.-denominated currency. Its name has its origins in the use of the term by the Scots in the sixteenth century.

electronic broking system (EBS). An electronic foreign-exchange trading system established for the interbank trading market.

electronic exchange. A financial exchange in which bids are made via electronic, that is, computerized systems. Such exchanges are gradually replacing the traditional auction or open outcry exchange.

ENRON. An energy-trading giant of the 1990s whose reckless and sometimes fraudulent derivatives trading led to the company's collapse in 2002.

equities. Shares of stock—common stock or preferred stock.

European Exchange Rate Mechanism. A system introduced in 1979 as part of the European Monetary System to reduce exchange-rate fluctuations.

European Union. The economic and political union between Western nations and, since the collapse of communism, several East European nations including Poland and the Czech Republic.

Federal Deposit Insurance Corporation (FDIC). A federally chartered corporation that insures deposits at commercial banks up to $100,000. The FDIC seeks to prevent individuals from withdrawing funds from an institution even if it is failing, in order to prevent systemwide panic.

Federal Reserve Act. Legislation passed in 1913, also known as the Currency Act (and the Owens-Glass Act) that established the Federal Reserve Board.

Federal Reserve Bank. Any of twelve regional banks of the Federal Reserve System that serves as a depository institution and carries out federal reserve policy.

Federal Reserve Board (FRB). Established in 1914, the FRB is the U.S. central bank officially known as the Board of Governors of the Federal Reserve System. It is comprised of seven members appointed by the president. The board establishes policies including setting of federal funds rate and directs monetary policy through the buying and selling of government securities.

Federal Reserve Note. Paper currency issued in various denominations and serves as legal tender in the U.S. monetary system.

fiat currency or fiat money. Legal tender, authorized by government but not based on some underlying equivalent of gold or silver.

filthylucre. A derogatory term, dating from the Middle Ages, used to describe money.

financial markets. A forum for trading various financial instruments, including stocks, bonds, derivatives, and other instruments.

foreign exchange market (forex). The market for transactions in foreign currencies, with transactions over computerized communications networks where sellers and buyers can quickly carry out any currency exchange.

forward contract. A customized legal document that obligates one party to buy and another party to sell a good or currency, at some point in the future.

Franklin, Benjamin. An American patriot and diplomat of the late eighteenth century, and a leading advocate of paper currency in the U.S. republic.

Free Banking Era. An era from 1837 to 1862 that was characterized by the spread of state-chartered banks.

Friedman, Milton. University of Chicago economist and Nobel Prize winner. Friedman is a leading advocate of free-market economics and a critic of Keynesian economic policy. He was a leading advocate of letting currencies float after 1971.

Friedman, Thomas. A *New York Times* reporter and author who, in many articles and books, has explored the process of globalization.

futures. A standardized forward contract.

futures contract. Essentially a forward contract except that it is traded on an exchange.

Garn-St. Germain Depository Institutions Act of 1982. Congressional legislation that, among other things, substantially deregulated the savings and loan industry. It is blamed by many for the later S&L collapse in the late 1980s.

Glass-Steagall Act. Legislation adopted in 1934 separating the commercial and investment banking sectors. Depression legislation passed in 1932 that addressed several reforms of the banking and monetary system.

globalization. A term used to describe the increasing integration of the world's economies and financial markets.

gold standard. A monetary standard under which the basic count of currency is equal to and exchangeable for a specified amount of gold.

Gold Standard Act. Legislation adopted by Congress in 1900 that placed the U.S. currency on a gold standard.

Gramm-Leach-Bliley Act (GLBA). Legislation that was adopted in 1999 that removed many of the previous New Deal–era restrictions on bank expansion, including the ability for banks to enter the securities and insurance business.

greenback. A term used to describe U.S. paper currency, it first came into use during the Civil War. The precursor to Federal Reserve Notes originating with the Legal Tender Act of 1862.

hedge fund. Any investment fund that uses hedging techniques such as options funds using futures contracts on stock market indexes and short sales with stock options. Hedge funds are exempt from many of the rules and regulations governing mutual funds.

hedging. An investment strategy designed to reduce risk.

individual loan corporations. Special purpose entities that represent a combination of banking and commercial enterprises.

interbank market. Currency trading that is conducted between banks.

International Association of Financial Engineers. An industry trade group dedicated to promoting financial innovation and addressing financial service issues.

International Monetary Fund. An international organization, whose main functions include lending to member nations in order to finance short-term balance of payment problems.

International Securities and Derivatives Association. An international trade industry association established in 1985.

International Swaps and Derivatives Association. A trade association that promotes derivatives trading and financial organizations that deal in derivatives.

investment bank. A financial institution that is concerned primarily with raising capital, securities trades, funding corporate mergers and acquisitions, and the like.

Islamic banking. System that avoids lending on interest as it is prohibited by Islam. Islamic banking also prohibits investment in certain activities such as gambling, alcohol, and other commercial activities.

JPMorgan Chase. One of the largest U.S. banks, it has an enormous exposure in the derivatives market; at one time the exposure was more than the entire global economy.

Keynes, John Maynard. The twentieth-century economist who developed the theory of Keynesian economics with its activist role for government in seeking to ameliorate market failure. Keynes was also a leading figure in promoting the post–World War II international economic order.

Knights Templar. A secretive group of knights during the Renaissance who helped create a system of finance allowing for cross-national financial transactions. These Christian crusaders of the twelfth and thirteenth centuries grew to become a powerful political force, and their commercial activities provided the foundation for modern commerce. The knights were abolished in 1307 by the order of the pope and the king of France.

Legal Tender Act of 1862. Legislation authorizing the United States to print U.S. Notes or greenbacks to help finance the Civil War.

London Stock Exchange. The leading exchange for equities in Europe, it is the counterpart of the New York Stock Exchange.

long-term capital management. An investment firm whose speculation in currency and related derivatives nearly created an economic crisis in 1998 when the firm failed due to a series of disastrous trades.

margin. The collateral deposited by an investor to satisfy the requirements for purchasing or selling an option, future contract, or other derivatives.

Markets in Financial Instruments Directive (MiFiD). Directive issued by the European Union (EU) that seeks to improve investor protection and transparency among EU member states.

Medici family. A leading family of fifteenth-century Florence, they were extensively involved in patronage of the arts as well as important bankers and leaders of commerce. One of the most important figures was Lorenzo de Medici, 1449–1492.

Melamed, Leo. Former CEO of the Chicago Mercantile Exchange and the founder of GLOBEX, the first electronic derivative securities exchange. Melamed is famous for establishing exchange-traded currency options in 1973.

merchant banks. Businesses that grant credit, serving a function very similar to a regular banking enterprise.

MGRM (Metullgesellschaft). A large commercial company in Germany. Their use of hedging with derivatives in an effort to reduce expansion in the petroleum market led to huge losses for the firm.

MICEX. The Moscow Inter-Currency Exchange, the primary Russian stock market.

money. Any medium that can be exchanged for goods or services, and which is used to measure the value of those goods and services. Gold, silver, and officially issued notes all can serve as money. Anything used as a unit of account and means of exchange.

money market. A debt market composed of short-term (one year) debt instruments.

mortgage-backed securities. A term encompassing securities backed by a pool of mortgages, both residential and commercial.

municipal bonds. Bonds issued by various local government entities to finance debts and economic activities.

NAFTA. The North American Free Trade Agreement, an economic pact negotiated in the early 1990s between Canada, Mexico, and the United States.

NASDAQ. A financial exchange, first established in 1971.

National Bank Act of 1863. Legislation adopted by the nation's Congress placing a tax on notes issued by state banks.

National Bank Act of 1908. Also known as the Aldrich-Vreelard Act, which created the National Monetary Commission (NMC). The NMC led to the passage of the Federal Reserve Act in 1913, establishing the Federal Reserve Board.

National Banking Acts of 1804 and 1863. Federal legislation intended to increase federal control over the state banking system and the free banking movement.

National Futures Association. A trade association that promotes financial industry position related to futures markets.

New Deal. The plan by President Franklin Roosevelt designed to provide relief from the Great Depression. The New Deal ushered in a new kind of government activism and regulation of the economy.

nondepository institutions. Those institutions including credit card companies, finance companies, insurance companies, and pension funds.

NOW account. A negotiable order of withdrawal. It is a demand account that includes a check-writing privilege.

Office of the Comptroller of the Currency (OCC). An office established within the U.S. Treasury that provided for regulatory control over federally chartered banks.

Office of the Treasurer. The oldest finance-related office in the U.S. government, the Office of the Treasurer is older than the U.S. Treasury Department itself. Its role has varied dramatically over the years. Today the treasurer advises the Director of the Mint, the Director of the Bureau of Engraving and Printing, and the Deputy Director of Treasury on matters related to coinage and currency and the production of other instruments by the United States. The treasurer also serves as one of the Treasury Department's principal advisors in the areas of financial literacy and education.

Open Market Committee. The committee that sets short-term policies for the Federal Reserve. It consists of twelve members: the seven members of the Federal Reserve Board and five of the twelve Federal Reserve Bank presidents. The New York Bank president is a permanent member; others serve on a rotating basis.

option. The right to buy (a call option) or sell (a put option) an underlying asset at a specified price.

over-the-counter (OTC) market. A market in which stocks, foreign currencies, and other financial products are bought and sold by telephone and other means of communication.

Panic of 1837. Banking crisis brought on in part by the collapse of many small, poorly capitalized independent banks. The collapse led to a severe recession from which the nation did not recover until the 1840s.

Panic of 1857. A banking and financial crisis brought about by the overextensive and bad loans of many banks in the period leading up to 1857. When the bubble burst, many banks did not survive.

pip. The minimum incremental unit of price movement of a currency that is quoted in the forex (foreign exchange) market.

real estate mortgage investment conduits. A complex pool of mortgage securities created for the purpose of acquiring collateral. This base is then divided into different classes of securities backed by mortgages with different maturities and coupons.

reserves. The portion of commercial bank deposits that is not loaned out but is deposited with the central bank; also, gold in foreign exchange held by a central bank in order to settle international transactions.

Resolution Trust Corporation. An independent government corporation established in 1989 to handle the assets of failed savings and loans following the S&L debacle of the 1980s, and to attempt to ensure that depositors were compensated for losses incurred.

Reuters Matching. Along with the electronic broking system, one of the two electronic foreign exchange trading systems.

Riegle-Beal Interstate Banking and Branch Efficiency Act. Legislation adopted by Congress in 1994 that allowed for bank expansion beyond state geographical boundaries.

risk. The uncertainty that may exist regarding the value of asset values.

risk avoidance. Avoiding the conditions or business activities that involve particular types of risk.

risk management. A systematic effort by a corporation or other entity to determine the risks the organization faces and to develop means of dealing with those risks. The actions taken to reduce uncertainty about certain outcomes. There are many different types of risks, such as systematic risks, foreign exchange risks, and the like.

Sarbanes-Oxley Act. A law enacted in 2002 designed to address business-related accounting scandals, some of which dealt with the issue of determining the value of derivatives and expensing of options.

savings and loan (S&L). Depository financial institution that obtains most of its deposits from consumers and holds the majority of its assets as home mortgage loans. The collapse of many S&Ls in the late 1980s led to billions of dollars in losses, and ultimately required a taxpayer bailout.

Securities and Exchange Act of 1934. Legislation that empowered the Securities and Exchange Commission with broad regulatory powers designed to protect the investing public.

Soros, George. A leading currency trader of the late twentieth century. Soros is blamed by some for destabilizing certain Asian economies due to his currency dealings.

speculation. Taking risks in order to gain rewards; often used in the context of financial speculation.

spot market price. Cash price for a particular currency.

swap transaction. A contract between two parties that obligates them to exchange specified cash flows.

Thales. An ancient Greek philosopher and by some accounts the first person to use an early version of a derivatives contract.

Treasury Bill. Generally considered the most important money-market instrument, it is a primary means by which the federal government finances its debt. Issued by the U.S. government, it matures in a year or less.

U.S. Department of the Treasury. The U.S. cabinet department established in 1789 and charged with the task of managing the federal government's revenue.

U.S. government bond. Debt instrument issued by the U.S. Treasury Department.

usury. The lending of money at exorbitant rates of interest.

zero coupon bond. Debt instrument that matures at a fixed value. An example is the U.S. series E savings bond. Such instruments do not pay periodic interest, and mature at their so-called face value.

Bibliography

Allen, Franklin, and Douglas Gale. *Comparing Financial Systems.* Cambridge, MA: MIT Press, 2001.

American Bankers Association. *About ABA.* http://www.aba.com.

American Municipal Bond Assurance Corporation. *About AMBAC.* http://www.ambac.com.

American Securitization Forum. *About the ASF.* http://www.americansecuritization.com.

———. *Hearing on Protecting Homeowners: Preventing Abusive Lending While Preserving Access to Credit.* Statement of Cameron L. Cowan on behalf of the American Securitization Forum before the Subcommittee on Housing and Community Opportunity Subcommittee on Financial Institutions and Consumer Credit, United States House of Representatives. November 5, 2003, New York. http://www.americansecuritization.com.

Association of Financial Guaranty Insurers. *Financial Guarantors Insured Record Levels of Asset-Backed and Public Sector Securities in 2005.* New York: AFGI, May 16, 2006. http://www.afgi.org/fin-annualrept05.html.

———. *Who We Are.* http://www.afgi.org/whoweare.htm.

Athanasoulis, Stefano, Robert Shiller, and Eric Van Wincoop. "Federal Reserve Bank of New York," *Economic Policy Review* 5 (1999): 21–39.

Balcerowicz, Leszek. *Post-Communist Transitions: Some Lessons.* London: Institute of Economic Affairs, 2002.

Bank for International Settlements. *About BIS.* http://www.bis.org.

———. *Triennial Central Bank Survey: Foreign Exchange and Derivatives Market Activity in 2004.* Basel, Switzerland: Bank for International Settlements, 2005.

Benford, Gregory. "Zoomers." In *Year's Best SF:2*, edited by David G. Hartwell. New York: Harper Prism, 1997.

Black, Jes. "Futures vs. Cash—What's the Difference?" *Futures* (Fall Special Edition, 2005): 22–26.

Black, William K. *The Best Way to Rob a Bank Is to Own One: How Corporate Executives and Politicians Looted the S&L Industry.* Austin: University of Texas Press, 2005.

Bond Market Association. *About MBS/ABS. Asset-Backed Securities.* http://www.investingbonds.com.

———. *About MBS/ABS. CMOs.* http://www.investingbonds.com.

Bradley, Brendan. "For FX Sake!" *FOW* (November 2005): 22.

Buchan, James. *Frozen Desire.* New York: Farrar, Straus, Giroux, 1997.

Canadian Foundation for Economic Education. *Money: Its Functions and Characteristics.* Toronto: Canadian Foundation for Economic Education, 1994.

Cargill, Thomas F. "U.S. Financial Policy in the Post-Bretton Woods Period." In *Money and the Nation State*, edited by Kevin Dowd and Richard H. Timberlake, Jr., pp. 193–212. New Brunswick, NJ: Transaction, 1998.

Castronova, Edward. *Synthetic Worlds: The Business and Culture of Online Games.* Chicago: University of Chicago Press, 2005.

Chorafas, Dimitris N. *The Market Risk Amendment: Understanding the Marking-to-Model and Value-at-Risk.* New York: McGraw-Hill, 1998.

Cofnas, Abe. "A Beginner's Guide to Forex." *Futures* (Fall Special Edition, 2004): 34–40.

Cohen, Benjamin J. *The Geography of Money.* Ithaca: Cornell University Press, 1998.

Committee on Uniform Security Identification Procedure. *CUSIP Service Bureau.* http://www.cusip.com.

Commodity Futures Trading Commission. *About CFTC.* http://www.cftc.gov.

Cook, Scott. "The Financial Services Revolution." In *The Future of Money in the Information Age*, edited by James A. Dorn, pp. 51–58. Washington, DC: Cato Institute, 1997.

Cribb, Joe. *Money.* New York: Dorling Kindersley, 1990.

Critchfield, T., Tyler Davis, Lee Davison, Heather Gratton, George Hanc, and Katherine Samolyk. "The future of Banking in America: Community Banks: Their Recent Past, Current Performance, and Future Prospects." *FDIC Banking Review* 16, no. 3 (2004): 1–56.

Davidson, Andrew S., Thomas S. Y. Ho, and Yung C. Lim. *Collateralized Mortgage Obligations: Analysis, Valuation and Portfolio Strategy.* Chicago: Probus Publishing, 1994.

Davies, Glyn. *History of Money.* Cardiff: University of Wales Press, 2002.

Davies, Roy. *Who's Who in Bowie Bonds.* February 1, 2006. http://www.ex.ac.uk/~RDavies/arian/bowiebonds.html.

Dicken, Peter. *Global Shift: Reshaping the Global Economic Map in the 21st Century.* New York: Guilford, 2003.

Dowd, Kevin, and Richard H. Timberlake, Jr. "Introduction." In *Money and the Nation State*, edited by Kevin Dowd and Richard H. Timberlake, Jr., pp. 1–20. New Brunswick, NJ: Transaction, 1998.

Edmunds, John C. *The Wealthy World: The Growth and Implications of Global Prosperity*. New York: John Wiley and Sons, 2001.

Eichengreen, Barry. *Golden Fetters: The Gold Standard and the Great Depression, 1919–1939*. New York: Oxford University Press, 1995.

Fabozzi, Frank J. *Bond Markets, Analysis and Strategies* (2nd edition). Englewood Cliffs, NJ: Prentice Hall, 1993.

Fabozzi, Frank J., and Franco Modigliani. *Mortgage and Mortgage-Backed Securities Markets*. Boston, MA: Harvard Business School Press, 1992.

Farrell, Diana, Aneta Marcheva Key, and Tim Shavers. "Mapping the Global Capital Markets." *The McKinsey Quarterly*, 2005. http://www.mckinseyquarterly.com.

Federal Deposit Insurance Corporation. *About FDIC*. http://www.fdic.gov.

Federal Home Loan Bank. *The FHL Bank System*. http://www.fhlbanks.com.

Federal Home Loan Mortgage Corporation. *About Freddie Mac*. http://www.freddiemac.com.

Federal Housing Authority. http://www.federalhousingauthority.com.

Federal National Mortgage Association. *About Fannie Mae*. http://www.fanniemae.com.

Federal Reserve Bank of Chicago. *Modern Money Mechanics: A Workbook on Bank Reserves and Deposit Expansion*. Chicago: Federal Reserve Bank of Chicago.

Federal Reserve Board. *About the Fed*. March 27, 2006. http://www.federalreserve.gov.

———. *Monetary Policy*. January 2, 2006. http://www.federalreserve.gov/policy.htm.

———. *The Twelve Federal Reserve Districts*. December 13, 2005. http://www.federalreserve.gov/otherfrb.htm.

Fischer, David Hackett. *The Great Wave: Price Revolution and the Rhythm of History*. New York: Oxford University Press, 1996.

Fisher, Rosalind S. "New Payments Technology." In *The Future of Money in the Information Age*, edited by James A. Dorn, pp. 59–64. Washington, DC: Cato Institute, 1997.

Fligstein, Neil. *The Architecture of Markets: An Economic Sociology of Twenty-first Century Capitalist Societies*. Princeton, NJ: Princeton University Press, 2001.

Foust, Dean. "Chucking the Checkbook." *Business Week*, February 6, 2006, p. 22.

Fox, Loren. *Enron: The Rise and Fall*. New York: John Wiley and Sons, 2003.

Friedman, Thomas. *The Lexus and the Olive Tree*. New York: Anchor Books, 2000.

FXall. *Best Practice in Foreign Exchange Markets*. New York: FXall, 2006.

Galati, Gabriele, and Michael Melvin. "Why Has FX Trading Surged? Explaining the 2004 Triennial Survey." *BIS Quarterly Review*, December 2004, pp. 67–74.

Galbraith, John Kenneth. *Money: Whence It Came, Where It Went*. Boston, MA: Houghton Mifflin, 1975.

Gallarotti, Giulio. *The Anatomy of an International Monetary Regime: The Classical Gold Standard, 1880–1914*. New York: Oxford University Press, 1995.

Garsson, Robert M. "Hearings into Silverado May Help Even Political Score." *American Banker*, May 1990, p. 6.

Gordon, John Steele. *An Empire of Wealth*. New York: HarperCollins, 2004.

Government National Mortgage Association. *About Ginnie Mae*. http://www.ginniemae.gov.

Groner, Alex. *The History of American Business and Industry*. New York: American Heritage, 1972.

Grow, Brian. "Gold Rush: Online Payment Systems Like E-gold Ltd. Are Becoming the Currency of Choice for Cybercrooks." *Business Week*, January 6, 2006, pp. 69–76.

Hall, Kenji, and Ian Rowley. "Cell-Phone Stock Traders." *Business Week*, February 6, 2006, p. 14.

Hanc, George. "The Future of Banking in America: Summary and Conclusions." *FDIC Banking Review* 16, no. 1 (2004): 1–14.

Hayek, George. "Competition as a Discovery Procedure." In *New Studies in Philosophy, Politics, Economics, and the History of Ideas*. New York: Routledge, 1982.

Heilbroner, Robert L. *The Nature and Logic of Capitalism*. New York: W. W. Norton, 1985.

Hunter, Richard. "Ratings." *Credit*, September 2005, p. 69.

International Finance Corporation. *IFC at 50*. May 2006. http://www.ifc.org.

International Monetary Fund. *Globalization: Threat or Opportunity?* January 2002. http://www.imf.org/external/np/exr/ib/2000/041200.htm.

———. *What Is the International Monetary Fund?* July 30, 2004. http://www.imf.org.

Johnson, Earl. "Day Trading FX? Ignore the Fundamentals at Your Peril." *SFO*, July 2005, pp. 67–69.

Keynes, John Maynard. *The General Theory of Employment, Interest and Money*. New York: Harcourt, 1965.

Kindleberger, Charles P. *Manias, Panics and Crashes* (4th edition). New York: John Wiley and Sons, 2000.

Lowenstein, Roger. *When Genius Failed*. New York: Random House, 2000.

Luke, Rob. "Forex White Hats." *SFO*, March 2005, pp. 78–83.

Madura, Jeff. *International Financial Management* (3rd edition). St. Paul, MN: West, 1992.

Manning, Robert D. *Credit Card Nation: The Consequences of America's Addiction to Credit*. New York: Basic Books, 2000.

Mayer, Martin. *The Bankers: The Next Generation*. New York: Truman Talley Books/Dutton, 1997.

———. *The Greatest Ever Bank Robbery: The Collapse of the Savings and Loan Industry*. New York: Charles Scribner's Sons, 1990.

Meyer, Paul A. *Monetary Economics and Financial Markets*. Homewood, IL: Richard D. Irwin, 1982.

Millman, Gregory J. *The Vandal's Crown: How Rebel Currency Traders Overthrew the World's Central Banks*. New York: Free Press, 1995.

Moody, J. Carroll, and Gilbert C. Fite. *The Credit Union Movement: Origin and Development, 1850–1970*. Lincoln: University of Nebraska Press, 1971.

Moody's Investors Service. Global Credit Research. A Product of the Securitization Standing Committee. *Demystifying Securitization for Unsecured Investors*. New York, January 2003.

Moscow Interbank Currency Exchange. www.micex.com.

Murphy, David. "Virtual Currency." *PC Magazine*, June 28, 2005, p. 26.

NACHA Electronic Payments Association. *ACH network*. http://www.nacha.org.

National Association of Securities Dealers. *About NASD*. http://www.nasd.com.

National Futures Association. *About NFA*. http://www.nfa.futures.org.

Ng, Serena. "Web-Based Bonds for the Rest of Us." *Wall Street Journal*, February 11–12, 2006, p. B1.

Office of the Comptroller of the Currency. *About the OCC*. www.occ.gov.

Partnoy, Frank. *Infectious Greed*. New York: Henry Holt, 2003.

Pilzer, Paul Zane, and Robert Deitz. *Other People's Money: The Inside Story of the S&L Mess*. New York: Simon and Schuster, 1989.

Preston, Ralph D., III. "Gold Has Found New Life." *Futures*, November 2005, p. 34.

Professional Risk Managers' International Association. *The Euromoney Derivatives and Risk Management Handbook 2005/06*. Brighton, UK: Wyndeham Grange Limited, 2006.

Rauf, Feisal Abdul. "Bringing Muslim Nations into the Global Century." *CNN*, October 18, 2004. http://money.cnn.com/magazines/fortune/fortune_archive/2004/10/18/8188085/index.htm.

Ray, Christina I. *The Bond Market: Trading and Risk Management*. Homewood, IL: Business One Irwin, 1993.

Rose, Peter S. *The Changing Structure of American Banking*. New York: Columbia University Press, 1987.

Rosenstreich, Peter A. "The Evolution of the FX Markets." *SFO*, March 2006, pp. 65–69.

———. "Exotic Currencies: What to Know before Trading FX in Emerging Markets." *SFO*, March 2006, pp. 39–42.

———. *Forex Revolution: An Insider's Guide to the Real World of Foreign Exchange Trading*. Upper Saddle River, NJ: Prentice Hall, 2005.

Ross, Stephen A., Randolph W. Westerfield, and Bradford D. Jordan. *Fundamentals of Corporate Finance* (2nd edition). Burr Ridge, IL: Irwin, 1993.

Rothbard, Murray N. *A History of Money and Banking in the United States: The Colonial Era to World War II*. Auburn, AL: Lugwig von Mises Institute, 2005.

Schlossberg, Boris. "FX Education: Key to Success or Waste of Time?" *SFO*, September 2005, pp. 45–48.

———. "So, You Want to Day Trade Spot FX? Think Again." *SFO*, October 2005, pp. 31–34.

———. "What Makes Forex So Different?" *SFO*, March 2005, pp. 29–34.

Seng, R. A., and J. V. Gilmour. *Brink's, the Money Movers: The Story of a Century of Service*. Lakeside Press, 1959.

Shelton, Judy. *Money Meltdown: Restoring Order to the Global Currency System*. New York: The Free Press, 1994.

Shiller, Robert J. *Irrational Exuberance*. New York: Broadway Books, 2001.

———. *The New Financial Order: Risk in the 21st Century*. Princeton, NJ: Princeton University Press, 2003.

Smithson, Charles W., and Clifford W. Smith, Jr., with Dr. Sykes Wilford. *Managing Financial Risk*. Burr Ridge, IL: Irwin, 1995.

Solnik, Bruno. *International Investments* (2nd edition). Reading, MA: Addison-Wesley, 1993.

Spufford, Peter. *Power and Profit: The Merchant in Medieval Europe*. New York: Thomas and Hudson, 2002.

Stigum, Marcia. *The Money Market* (3rd edition). Homewood, IL: Business One Irwin, 1990.

Strange, Susan. *Mad Money: When Markets Outgrow Governments*. Ann Arbor: University of Michigan Press, 1998.

Student Loan Marketing Association. *About Sallie Mae*. http://www.salliemae.com.

Tabarrok, A. "Trumpting the Genetic Tort Card: Insurance against Bad Genes." *Contingences* 9 (1997): 20–23.

Taylor, Francesca. *Mastering Foreign Exchange and Currency Options*. London: Pitman, 1997.

Taylor, Mark C. *Confidence Games: Money and Markets in a World without Redemption*. Chicago: University of Chicago Press, 2005.

TreasuryDirect. *About TreasuryDirect*. http://www.treasurydirect.gov.

Turner, Frederick. *Shakespeare's Twenty-first Century Economics: The Mortality of Love and Money*. New York: Oxford University Press, 1999.

U.S. Bureau of Engraving and Printing. *New Money*. http://www.moneyfactory.gov/newmoney/print.cfm/currency/history.

U.S. Department of Housing and Urban Development. http://www.hud.gov.

U.S. Department of the Treasury. *Policies and Notices*. http://www.treasury.gov.

U.S. Department of Veteran Affairs. *About VA*. http://www.va.gov.

U.S. Securities and Exchange Commission. *About the SEC*. http://www.sec.gov.

Uyemura, Dennis G., and Donald R. Van Deventer. *Risk Management in Banking: The Theory and Application of Asset and Liability Management*. Chicago: Bankers Publishing Company, 1993.

Van Dun, Frank. "National Sovereignty and International Monetary Regimes." In *Money and the Nation State*, edited by Kevin Dowd and Richard H. Timberlake Jr., pp. 47–76. New Brunswick, NJ: Transaction, 1998.

"Wal-Mart Savings and Loan?" *CFO*, June 2006, p. 24.

Wasendorf, Russell R., Sr., and Russell R. Wasendorf Jr. *Foreign Currency Trading: From the Fundamentals to the Fine Points*. New York: McGraw-Hill, 1998.

Weatherford, Jack. *The History of Money*. New York: Crown, 1994.

WM Financial Strategies. *Bond Insurance*. http://www.munibondadvisor.com/BondInsurance.htm.

World Bank. *About Us*. http://www.worldbank.org.

World Bank and International Monetary Fund. *Developing Government Bond Markets: A Handbook*. Washington, DC: International Monetary Fund, 2001.

World Federation of Exchanges. *The Handbook of the World's Stock, Derivatives, and Commodities Exchanges*. Datchworth, UK: Mondo Visione, 2003.

World Trade Organization. *The WTO*. http://www.wto.org.

Wray, L. Randall. *Understanding Modern Money*. Cheltenham, UK: Edmund Elgar, 1998.

Yergin, Daniel, and Joseph Stanislaw. *The Commanding Heights*. New York: Simon and Schuster, 1998.

Zipf, Robert. *How the Bond Market Works* (3rd edition). New York: New York Institute of Finance, 2002.

Index

ABOUT THE AUTHORS

MARK F. DOBECK is the Chief Financial Officer for the National Association of Schools of Public Affairs and Administration (NASPAA) in Washington, DC. Previously, he taught courses in business administration, finance, international investments, financial risk management, organizational behavior, and public policy at Collin County Community College and the University of Texas at Dallas. He has over twenty years of management experience in banking, securities, and information technology, and worked on major financial and banking projects throughout the world, including the development of the Moscow Interbank Currency Exchange. He is certified as a Project Management Professional (PMP) by the Project Management Institute.

EUEL ELLIOTT is Professor of Government, Politics and Political Economy and Associate Dean for Graduate Education, School of Social Sciences, University of Texas at Dallas. He previously served as Director of the Master of Public Affairs program and Director of Graduate Studies at the university. He has published in a wide range of public policy, political science and economics journals, including *Social Science Quarterly, Policy Studies Review,* and *Journal of Policy Modeling,* and has coedited two books, *Chaos Theory in the Social Sciences* and *Non-linear Dynamics, Complexity and Public Policy.*